THE
WORLD
ORNAMENT
SOURCEBOOK

THE WORLD ORNAMENT
SOURCEBOOK

VIVAYS PUBLISHING

Published by Vivays Publishing
www.vivays-publishing.com

English language © 2011 Vivays Publishing Ltd.

Original Russian edition published by Art-Rodnik Publishing House, Moscow
© Art-Rodnik Publishing House, 2011

A catalogue record for this book is available from the British Library

ISBN 978-908126-26-9

Publishing Director: Lee Ripley
Design: Ian Hunt
English translations by Dr. John Sowerby in association with First Edition
Translations Ltd, Cambridge, UK and Antony Wood

Printed in China

CONTENTS

LIST OF PLATES

GENERAL INTRODUCTION

THIS BOOK HAS above all a practical purpose. It is an album of illustrations rather than a treatise, and gives examples rather than precepts. In it we wished to avoid the underwater hazards of theory, which, however correct they might appear, are always too imprecise and generalized as presented in abstract form. Masterpieces always speak for themselves, and the surest way to draw lessons from them is to analyze them, and not to try to make them exemplify a conclusion already reached, which often turns out to be too abstract to cover exceptions or special cases. The latter seems to us too dangerous a procedure to apply to those branches of art which would appear least amenable to fixed rules and in which the most important place is occupied by the artist's instinct, imagination and even caprice.

We do not wish to say that such art forms may not be subject to rules and principles that should be applied to any artistic project. Thus an ornamental composition can be truly beautiful only if it gives the viewer a feeling of peace and satisfaction springing from a balance and harmony of all the elements of which it is composed. The laws of proportion, of balance and symmetry, subordination of detail to the ensemble, variety in unity, all these, urged by instinct and proclaimed by science, have a firm place in the art of the master of ornament just as they do in other branches of art.

Whilst painting and sculpture have broad similarities in their approach to the meaning and logic of their subject or in their imitation or recreation of natural objects, while architecture must take account of a large number of requirements concerning durability, the purpose of a building and the relationship between exterior and interior, ornamentation, on the other hand, especially polychromy, the predominant subject of this book, seems to belong to a more modest sphere in which a considerable degree of freedom reigns.

Open to the art of ornament are many ways of achieving the proportion and harmony that produce the feeling of beauty. If it can make use of the various approaches of each of the fine arts – the concern with general forms and repeated patterns in architecture, the power of plastic relief in sculpture, the appeal of subjects and natural forms in painting – it will have the capacity to tap inexhaustible resources without forsaking its own sphere.

From the simplest figures such as square, rhombus and triangle, which in repetition and in combination are often sufficient to form an interesting design by themselves, to the most complex and exquisite interweaving patterns, the most capricious arabesques, the most weird combinations of lines, colours, animal and even human forms – how vast is the field that stretches before the master of ornament, the master of a fantastical and beautiful realm which deals not in the natural order of things but entirely in the creations of his or her own imagination! What a seductive, even treacherous freedom this would be were these deliberate caprices not to be governed by taste and did not achieve the end result which irrespective of the means employed must be expressed in harmony of form and harmony of colour!

Consequently, ornament holds an important secondary place in the spectrum of art. If it is not as ambitious as other art forms, if it does not seek to elevate our souls or arouse our most intimate feelings, it still fulfils the most unconscious demand of human nature, the desire to make the objects that surround us beautiful. Sometimes combined with and supplementing the highest works of art, sometimes present in the humblest articles, elevating and ennobling them, ornament provides a link between industry and art, and represents one of the most familiar, most practical and most varied forms of the latter.

Thus the principal characteristics of ornamentation are the enormous quantity and variety of ways in which it is used and an almost unlimited freedom in the choice of media. But as we stated at the outset, for these very reasons it is extremely hard to establish rules in any other way than by experience, which might have meant *a priori* compilation of a *codex of types of ornament.*

However, our intentions were otherwise. On the basis of a historical analysis of the different styles exemplified in our illustrations we attempt to explain what gave rise to these styles, so that anyone interested in a given example might be enabled to imitate it or, better still, make creative use of it with informed judgement. With this as our underlying aim, at the beginning of our historical survey we have presented only brief introductory observations in order to illuminate broad trends and offer markers for the reader to make his or her own decisions.

There are three components in the making of an ornament: a *drawn design, choice of colour,* and the *creation of relief.* By means of these, the first two of which will concern us most of all, artists are able to achieve the most diverse displays of their mastery, which fall naturally, in turn, into three categories:

1. *Invention* of motifs which are the product of pure imagination and bear no relation to natural objects.

2. *Conventionalized representation* of real-life objects depicting only typical basic features in generalized form.

3. *Imitative representation* of objects with the appearance of reality by means of drawn line and colour.

The first of these categories borrows nothing from imitative art forms and is present in palpable degree in ornament of all styles and periods. Line and geometric combinations (interweaving patterns, meanders and rosettes), the primal forms of expression, demonstrate the propensities of the human brain for order and measure; they are the direct product of pure imagination, creating something that did not exist before. This genre of ornament is prominent among specific peoples, for example the Arab and English-speaking populations, but is found throughout the world. In direct or indirect form, it is the basis for the majority of ornamental compositions throughout history.

The second category, *conventionalized representation*, has links with the two others and is often confused with the first, which it approaches in the idealizing capacities of its invention, in its abstract generalization in the forms of models and prototypes appropriated from natural forms. It is thanks to this idealized representation that the artist, in Charles Blanc's happy phrase, 'enters the greatness of human life', and it is from this genre that ornaments of the highest style are to be expected, since, in the words of Henry Balth (*Grammaire du Dessein*), 'style is the imprint of human thought on nature.'

With purely *imitative representation* we enter the modern period, where the painting style of verisimilitude is more frequently employed for the full, detailed depiction of objects with all their typical characteristics, distinctive properties, fortuitous and exceptional features. Arising out of the enhanced role of painting by comparison with the other traditional art forms, and the increased technical mastery of painters, this genre, producing less austere and more graceful results than the other two methods, has splendidly met the refined and elegant tastes of the developed world. Skilful masters of ornament have found inspiration in imitative painting to create superb designs bringing renown to art of the modern period, and especially French art of the 17th and 18th centuries. However, all this has not come about without some detriment to certain forms of industrial art, for example, ceramics, mural painting and carpet-weaving, which have found success only by recourse to more simplified and more decorative methods.

In sum, the use of colour in ornament, which is the main theme of this book, is closely connected with one or other of the categories of ornament set out above. Where the representation of an object is idealized or conventionalized, colour is likewise conventionalized; the artist is master of his palette. In this case the austerity of the design is counterbalanced by the artist's freedom of colour range, that is, the artist commands choice of colour and its employment to suit his own intentions, without the restraints imposed by imitation or verisimilitude, and following only the laws of harmony and correlation. This approach is always a fertile one for creativity and originality; Eastern artists have never forsaken it and have achieved an incomparable mastery with it.

Through the prism of different historical epochs we shall now trace the use of colour in the different genres of ornament we have distinguished.

THE PRIMITIVE STYLE

PLATE 1

Among the examples shown in Plate 1, the term primitive, that is, a style preceding any conception of fully developed art, strictly speaking applies solely to nos 1–17, which represent the spontaneous conceptions of Oceanic and Central African peoples applied to the adornment of everyday articles.

To this general overview of spontaneous ornamentation we should add some separate monochrome fragments of carving or fretting which embellish its naïve appearance.

With the exceptions of examples 4, 8 and 12 in Plate 1, where some floral outlines are seen, all these spontaneous designs are entirely invented. Their extreme austerity in the use of colour, which may so easily be abused, is as striking as the line compositions. This style, thought of and referred to as 'primitive', nevertheless possesses distinctly high quality in that from the very beginning it displays, without benefit of any collective organization or knowledge of general principles, the requirements of order, symmetry and harmony, in compositions, it must be said, on a small scale but already highly distinctive and with a consistent palette. Nowhere shall we find a more active use of the colour black than in examples 2 and 10 and especially 4, where the isolating principle of a white outline gives strong support to a background of bright red, an effect for which the most subtle Eastern masters strove.

We have placed these designs displaying the typical features of the primitive style alongside examples from a more developed culture (Peruvian and Mexican) partly because space has not allowed the lesser-known art to be allotted a place of its own in this book and partly because in order to show stylistic differences it seemed useful to compare the products of individual endeavour from less developed cultures with those in which the influence of architecture is felt to produce a unity of typical features.

The examples of Mexican art (nos 22–47) undoubtedly have a palette of scant appeal; however, despite this these designs possess a worth of their own springing from the sophisticated principles underlying them, which could only have been derived from architecture. The

Detail of fretwork (Louvre)

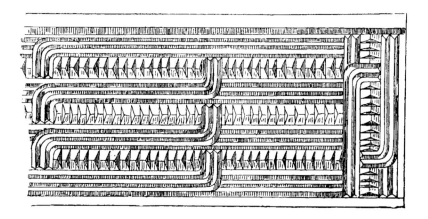

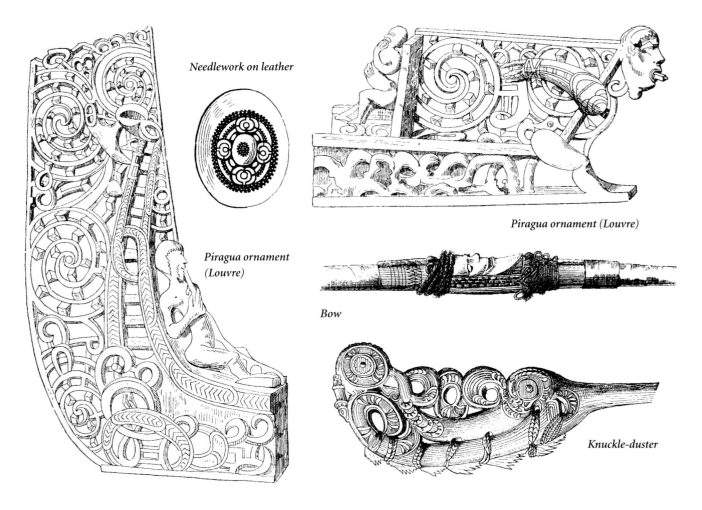

Needlework on leather

Piragua ornament (Louvre)

Piragua ornament (Louvre)

Bow

Knuckle-duster

prototypes of these designs come from the relatively young cultures of Yucatan and Mexico, and are reminiscent of architectural monuments in Egypt, India and Japan and especially those of the Assyrians.

Some time after the first appearance of the primitive style, the product of isolated individual initiative, came the establishment of architectural principles; the period between, which saw the maturing of the primitive style, we cannot measure or investigate.

Modern Mexican decoration: leather sewn with soutache (Louvre)

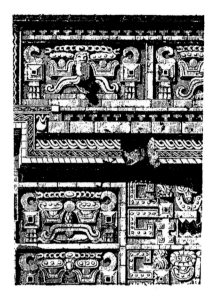

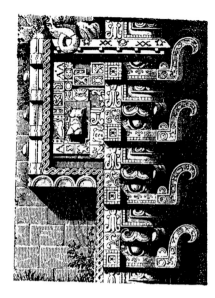

Detail of tombs: Uxmal, Yucatan

History that we regard as reliable does not begin even with the most ancient architectural monuments; we know nothing of the civilizations that built them, or of the civilizations that preceded those. 'In the mixed situation in which the broad human races are today distributed over the surface of the globe,' wrote Viollet-le-Duc ('American Towns and Ruins' in *Habitations of Man in All Ages*, 1876), 'it is difficult to distinguish the original elements of each.' This is unfortunately true; we can, however, with the help of Ziegler, without studying prehistory, examine pottery to seek out those of its elements that inspired the creation of forms of architectural drawing. The principle is the same; people learned how to handle clay in order to make domestic vessels before using wood or stone to make architectural structures. Consequently, the productive principles of idealization and generalization of natural forms, on which architecture and the art of ornament have so extensively drawn, apply above all to ceramics.

ANTIQUITY

PLATES 2–7

Applying the term 'Antiquity' to Egyptian, Assyrian, Greek, Etruscan, Roman and Greco-Roman art, we seek to avoid according priority to any one of these (and it should be remembered that the history of Asian art is contemporaneous with all these, and that some of its forms may lay claim to even greater age). We seek to employ this wide-reaching term to denote those civilizations whose history comes down to us through the medium of Greek and Latin literature, the study of which became widespread with the Renaissance and has remained the basis of our Classical education.

This group of cultures has a very clear-cut profile, which facilitates their study separately, each tradition being relatively easy to trace through distinct historical phases.

EGYPT AND ASSYRIA

Ancient Egypt. Our survey of the art of Antiquity will begin with Egypt. Whether we consider the art of Ancient Egypt, serving as a point of contact with the Semitic, Ethiopian and Berber cultures, as a general summary of the projects of preceding civilizations and so remaining virtually unfamiliar, or whether we consider it as a point of departure for Greek, Etruscan and Greco-Roman art, that is, as the chief source of the great Classical tradition, it appears to us equally valuable for its age and its high achievements.

The art of the Egyptians possesses overall an elevated spiritual and symbolic character, expressed most strikingly in ornamental compositions.

Elements of the real world in generalized forms compose the background to their décor. Enclosed in bold outlines of varying breadth, these images express the generality, not the individual case; in an idealized form they represent a limited number of types in very diverse depictions. The palette consists of flat colours without gradations, employed, like the images themselves, in a conventionalized manner (see the explanation to the colours of the Egyptian palette accompanying Plate 4).

Almost all objects decorated in this way have a symbolic purpose. In his book *The Wonders of Ceramics*, Albert Jacquemart gives his explanation of most of the images shown in our first plates:

'It is easy to show the role of the plant as it appears throughout Eastern theory. The deified lotus is a gift offered in homage for the beneficial effects of water and the sun on the sleeping earth; it symbolizes the progress of the seasons of the year, which lead one generation to give way to the next and take life to where, it would seem, the immobility of death reigns. Even the sun belongs to a single generation, the form of which the priests have the pleasure to vary so as the more effectively to penetrate to the masses. Everyone knows the winged disc beneath which are depicted the two serpents of Ureus, which are royal symbols of Upper and Lower Egypt; this is the sun in its material form, as depicted at the threshold of temples, in sepulchres and cult buildings, and even on the clothing of priests and kings; the sun to which fervent and poetic prayers are offered, such as the following: 'All praise to thee, Ra, for thy light in the morning, and to thee, Tmon, in thy setting … Thou givest light and shine, thou art the ruler of the gods.' There is, however, another image of the sun which demands explanation.

In our villages there is an insect that everyone regards with disgust – the dung-beetle … And so, if the Egyptians chose such a worthless and repulsive creature to deify, they must have discovered something remarkable in its behaviour. And indeed, if you observe the behaviour of this insect on a sandy shore, you will see that it will penetrate the faeces of an animal, select a suitable-looking portion, lay an egg in it, mould that portion into a ball, and then drag it with its hind legs until its surface hardens under the effect of heat; then it buries the ball in the ground, where incubation and the transformation of the larva take place so that in due course a complete new insect appears, which in its turn will perform the various actions resulting in reproduction. It seemed to the Egyptians that the dung-beetle repeated the labours of the Creator, the ball of faeces containing the egg symbolizing the earth, the germ of life which grows, and the process of evolution it undergoes under the effect of heat. This parallel was sufficient to elevate the modest dung-beetle to the level of the most mighty of the gods.'

Balustrade

In Plate 4 no. 12 a black dung-beetle is depicted, holding the disc of the sun in its upper legs and a faecal ball in its lower legs: the complete symbol.

The Egyptians often appended hieroglyphs to these symbolic images. Consequently, for them written language was a means of ornamentation, neglected, it would appear, by the Greeks, but perfected by the Persians, the Arabs and the Moors.

The following description by Jacques Joseph Champollion-Figeac gives us an idea of the universality of the Egyptian use of ornament:

'Egyptian houses were furnished in common or rare and exotic types of wood or engraved or gilded metal, with plain or embroidered cotton upholstery…

Egyptian feather ornament

There were meticulously made footstools, beds with backs and heads, divans and day beds, double cupboards, sideboards, writing tablets, chests and caskets, and all such essentials of family life. A footstool was upholstered and ornamented similarly to an easy chair and was a supplement to it. There were folding wooden chairs with feet in the shape of swans' necks or heads, chairs of cedar inlaid with ivory and ebony. Small pedestal tables, large round tables, game tables, boxes of all sizes matched the splendour of the rest of the furnishings in the high quality of their materials and workmanship. Variegated mats and carpets, sometimes decorated with human and animal figures, covered the floors of living rooms or most-used areas. The astonishing elegance and diversity of the vases of gold or gilded materials, with their decoration in enamels or precious stones, can be conveyed to us only through preserved images.'

In boldness, precision and scale, the graphic achievements of the Egyptians have never been surpassed. Certain depictions of animals and hieroglyphic profiles drawn rapidly on papyri and stelae are well beyond anything even the Greeks did in this genre. Confining the dynamics of their depictions within strict forms, which might seem to us exaggerated, these skilled graphic artists demonstrate a strength of will that can only be ascribed to the strength of their religious tenets. The artistic principles that they followed in restraining their nimble, virtuosic fingers have retained their value to this day and continue to demand our serious attention. The study of the products of Egyptian craftsmanship reveals qualities that are not only inherent in them but have an impact undreamt of by their makers. The incisive lines of their draughtsmanship, whether in simple sketch or metal casing, remain timeless models such as to inspire all masters of ornament who seek to attain the level of the ideal and to understand and observe the requirements of high style.

PLATE 7   **Assyria.** Assyrian ornamental art, some examples of which are shown in Plate 7, belongs to a minor period and might be termed 'Scytho-Assyrian'. Its beginnings occur after the fall of the original city of Babylon, whose arts are thought to have had an Indo-Bactrian source and which were represented in Iran in the form of monuments the details of which are unknown to us.

Egyptian influence would seem to be recognizable in some architectural features found in Persepolis: the winged sphere, the headdress of the Egyptian god Sosharis, and images of Ureus and balustrades with a sphere rising up above prove that these structures with deified borrowed elements appeared after the Achaemenid conquest of Egypt. No rules or prescriptions of any particular schools appear to have inhibited the diversity of these architectural forms exhibiting more fantasy than proportion. It is as if the Egyptian craftsmen summoned by the successors of King Kambiz were losing their mastery in proportion to their distance from the localities where they had received their training, the traditions of which were already undergoing relative decline, and as if they were only partial exporters of Egyptian craftsmanship. When employed for the ornamentation of palaces, though not temples, in the new lands, Egyptian symbolism did not have its previous sacred meanings, and only spasmodically survived in the new culture. Plate 7 includes a painted bas-relief depicting a sacred tree (no. 1), one of the most frequently found Assyrian symbolic motifs. The winged human figures on either side of the sun (no. 7) symbolize the soul.

Assyrian ornamentation, including bas-reliefs, was entirely painted or gilded or silver-covered. 'I am certain', Charles Texier tells us, writing of Persepolis, 'that no corner of the palace would have been without the most exquisite and refined wall-painting; paintings such as may be seen at Khorsabad, Nemrud, and also Ekbatan, capital of Midia, where according to Polybius, who gives a description of the palace of the Persian kings, porticoes, peristyles and ornamental mouldings were covered with plates of silver and gold which had been seized by Alexander's soldiers' (Description de *l'Arménie et de la Perse, de la Mésopotamie*, 1842–45).

Judging by details of their manufacture, the superb examples of ornamental glazed bricks with regular pattern shown in Plate 7 would appear to have been exported from China (Charles Texier, *Asie mineure*, 1862); in any case, they are the direct precursors of the facing bricks of which present-day Iranians have made such skilful use.

GREEK, ETRUSCAN AND GRECO-ROMAN ART

PLATES 8–14 **Greece.** Classical Greek art is considered to have originated in the traditions of Egyptian art, as modified by Assyrian and Phoenician influences. The impact of these separate traditions on the heterogeneous Greek people, endowed with the highest artistic capabilities in human history, is well known. After a comparatively prolonged incubatory period, a new style was born in the region, which had only a distant relationship with the styles of the preceding civilizations, and an ideal was created which was to find its apogee in sculpture.

Under the influence of the latter, ornament, at the other end of the artistic spectrum, also underwent a profound evolution. Less sacral than its Egyptian counterpart, less contained in its own specific symbolism, less spiritual and closer to real life, Greek ornament possessed greater freedom, versatility and grace and did not abuse these attributes, maintaining a feeling of restraint which the refined Greek taste never lost.

Always retaining its purity, nobility and sublimity alongside its inventiveness and variety, never becoming florid or overblown, Greek ornament was to become a benchmark of the highest qualities in architecture, sculpture and the rest of the fine arts. At the same time, however, the primacy of other art forms left the art of Greek ornament in a secondary place, almost always subordinated to the depiction of the human figure and animals […] on vases and friezes.

If we now seek to identify the fundamental feature of Classical Greek ornament in accordance with the leading principle laid down at the beginning of our investigation, we find that it bears a markedly conventionalized character (when not idealized), inspired by the general forms found in the natural world but free of literal imitation of detail. A brief summary of its most popular subjects will help us to identify this dominant feature.

The graceful *palmette*, from which the antefix arose, seen in so many forms in friezes in temples, mouths and bases of vases, is taken from the carob pod, incorporated and framed in various ways in the forms of ligatures, bowls, plumes and the like; the divergence from natural forms here, however, is so great that this motif may be considered the product of original creation, to the same extent as meanders, spiral patterns and so on. Other palmette forms, taken from various plants – such as aloe, convolvulus, generalized depictions of ivy leaves, laurel branches or bunches of grapes, and most familiar of all, the acanthus leaf – complete the customary floral components of Greek ornament. Of the last, which ornaments the capital of the Corinthian order, Vasari gloriously writes: 'This acanthus stalk, O Callimachus of Tarentum! This acanthus stalk, which you find growing profusely in the burial place and with which you adorn the capital glorifying the name of Corinth – this ancient acanthus has lasted twenty-two centuries adorning the world of memorials without losing a single one of its leaves.'

Symmetry and balance are the dominant organizing principles of Greek ornament: 'Everything, including the waves of the sea,' writes Jacquemart of *scrolls and volutes*, 'whose foaming, wind-lashed crests seem so unstable and capricious, everything is subordinated to the demands of ornamental balance: artists will make a subtle point of these waves, placing them, from common sense, at the base of a bowl, while we, ignorant of their significance, place them where it makes no sense at all.' (See Plate 8, nos 11–14; Plate 10, no. 19.)

Further elements of Greek ornament, some of them especially present in architecture, are the following:

Meander, or ornament in the form of a broken line. Inter-weaving of a continuous line, curved or turned at a right angle, many examples of which can be seen in Plates 8 and 10 and which occurs so frequently in Ancient Greek decorative art that it often goes by the name of *Greek meander.*

Twisted or spiral pattern. Combination of curved or winding lines in series (Plate 10, nos 16, 25, 26, 27, 29); they may be either single or double in form (nos 16, 25).

Plaited pattern. Pattern imitating a braid of hair.

Pearl beads, or *astragals,* consisting of a series of round and oval-shaped pearls resembling beads strung together as a necklace.

Ornament in the form of heart-shaped scallops alternating with spears, also rosettes and leaves of water plants (Plate 8, nos 13–15; Plate 10, no. 3).

Flutes. Short grooves with bases filled with pointed leaves (Plate 10, no. 17).

Ovae. Carved ornamentation with egg shapes, often taking the form of open-shelled nuts.

Sculpted ornamentation in the form of bulls' heads, almost always with straps or hide strips, or horns decorated with flowers, rosettes or wreaths. Attached to the horns of the bull being sacrificed, these straps and wreaths were placed on the animal's forehead and were afterwards hung with the head on the wall of the temple, burial-chamber or altar. Reproductions of these

Stele from Asia Minor, with palmette and acanthus ornamentation

Interweaving patterns   *Greco-Roman frieze with ornaments of acanthus, ovae and pearl beads*

sacrificial offerings formed the basis of magnificent ornamental friezes in temples, executed, like everything that the Greeks did, with consummate mastery.

The arts of our time have lost sight of none of these enchanting and fertile inventions, some of which belong to other cultures as well as the Ancient Greek (as, for example, *meanders*, found amongst all peoples, and the taste for which is innate) and some of which are peculiar to the Hellenic style. Not only architecture but the decorative applied arts too draw freely upon them.

In Greek ornament, colour as well as form is always symbolic, and is widely used in ornament; the Greeks were fond of polychromy. This is to be seen, in the first place, in architecture. No doubt remains today that Greek architecture was polychrome. Skilled restoration work performed by French architects and especially Rome scholars has played a major part in establishing this as a fact, which furthermore receives almost daily corroboration through the excavations and new discoveries of scholars and artists. Some striking examples of architectural polychromy are shown in Plate 10.

Mosaic, which employs materials of different colours, is essentially also a polychrome medium.

Sculptural ornaments in the form of animals' heads, Ionic capitals and astragals

The general effect of *metal inlay* is obtained through juxtaposition and sequencing of nuances of colour, and this form of ornamentation was much loved by the Greeks.

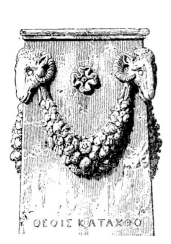

And finally, colour serves as the chief decorative means in ceramics, the importance of this form of polychromy, in our view, being such as to justify its being allotted one whole plate of the three devoted to the basic types of purely Greek ornament.

This type of pottery seems to have spread from Corinth to other regions of Greece and as far as Italy; most vases found in Apulia and Etruria were of Greek manufacture. They existed in Homeric times. The oldest known of these, stylistically similar to Egyptian pieces, date from the 10th or 12th century BCE; most are decorated, in black on a light-coloured ground, with patterns that are reminiscent of embroidery. Nos 1, 7, 8, 9, 10 and 26 of Plate 8 are of this type and period. A black background appears in later decoration, at the moment when Greek art reached the high-point of its development. These patterns (nos 17–20 of Plate 8), from Apulian vases, with their diversity and decorative freedom, demonstrate all the possibilities of the genre.

PLATE 11 **Etruria.** Before tracing the development of what became of Greek art on Italian soil, Greco-Roman art, we should say something of another contemporaneous tradition which to some extent merged with it.

The Etruscans, who populated central Italy, possessed an art of some antiquity. The Etruscans are thought to have been an ethic mix of the Pelasgians and the Phoenicians, from which, Winckelmann concluded, came the population of Tuscany, which provided the Romans with craftsmen, including builders. Besides their long celebrated pottery, which is today linked to the Egyptian or Greek style reproduced or introduced, the Etruscans significantly developed the crafts of gold and silver ware. Plate 11 illustrates this side of their national production.

The work of Etruscan gold- and silversmiths was celebrated in Antiquity, and there was a demand for their stamped and engraved goldware even in Athens. They made full use of all the potential of the art that they brought to perfection, their gifted hands working upon a huge range of subjects and forms – plants and flowers, fruits, real and fantastic animals, legendary and deified human figures, acorns, nimbi, cornucopias, rosettes, half-moons, flat or lentil-shaped medallions, vases of diverse forms, chains of different forms and sizes. The emeralds that they employed were said to possess curative powers, and their particular hue of green blended perfectly with gold, pearls and precious stones, solid glass, enamels, cameos and intaglios. This diverse and complex work was executed with such precision and taste that many of their ornaments have remained models of their kind.

The Etruscan repertoire included diadems and coronets, hair-grips, earrings, necklaces, clasps, bracelets, rings, cult objects and large-scale burial adornments. A popular ornamental motif in necklaces, bracelets and rings was the scarab, commonly linking intaglios and stones. A hieroglyph or a figure would be incised on the flat underside, while on the upper side, always in relief, would be a more or less complete representation of an Egyptian scarab, a motif whose use not only on Etruscan ornaments but also on clothing, necklaces, domestic utensils and sword-hilts was probably connected with cults similar to the Egyptians', or at any rate with superstitions of various kinds.

Intaglios, much favoured at the high-point of Greek art, and to which the Etruscans too were much drawn, were as a rule translucent and monochrome. Among the most frequently used precious stones were amethyst

Etruscan grave ornaments

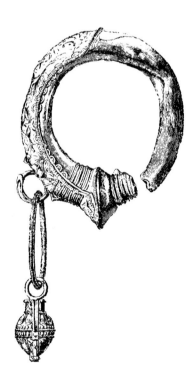

and hyacinth, and sometimes the opaque emerald; other stones often used included carnelians and chalcedony, and less frequently, jasper and lapis lazuli.

During the hegemony of Rome, and still more the supremacy of Greek culture, Etruscan ornamental art lost its special character and local ware exclusively followed the new trend. And so we arrive naturally at the beginnings of Greco-Roman art, which will complete the cycle of Antique art as we have defined it.

PLATE 8 **Greco-Roman art.** During its earliest period Rome had no art as such. During the period immediately following that in which building in the Etruscan style took place, that is, the period chiefly characterized in architecture by the arch and the arcade and by the changes that this brought to the uses of ornament, Etruscan craftsmen, as noted above, lost their originality on their arrival among Greek populations and gradually took over all of the Greek traditions. Only Grecian art existed in Italy after Claudius Marcellus returned from Syracuse, the consul Mummius from Corinth, and after them all the other Roman generals. Thanks to its art, the conquest of Greece left it the victor. The works of art that made Rome one vast museum determined the direction in which its tastes were to develop.

In the opinion of leading archaeologists and artists, wall paintings in Pompeii and Herculaneum were in the same style as those in Athenian houses (see Hittorf, *Architecture polychrome chez les Grecs*, ch. IX: 'Lettres d'un antiquaire à un artiste par Letronne').

> 'As for decorative painting in domestic interiors, archaeological scholarship confirms that the Romans took everything from the Greeks, their taste and the means of its satisfaction; that Greek artists painted in the same way in Rome as they had in their own country; that the Romans finally accepted the Greek heritage; and that consequently the decoration of dwellings in Ancient Rome such as the houses in Pompeii and Herculaneum, with their wall-paintings whose subjects and style were exclusively Greek, must give an exact idea of the decoration of houses in Greece not only of the same period but also of preceding times.'

Not all these paintings have equal quality. Some are manifestly by second-class artists; however, the beauty of many of them suggests that they are copies or imitations of originals of great renown.

Alongside this decorative painting, work in a further medium of polychrome ornamentation is found in Pompeii – mosaic, which without doubt attains the level of perfection. This branch of decorative art, however, underwent a number of modifications at the hands of Roman craftsmen in the period of the Empire, of which a just account is given by M. Janron in his book *The Origin and Progress of Art*. We consider that this passage deserves to be cited in full despite its length because within the confines of this particular art it enables us to trace the history of the decline of Greek art in general during the final period of the Roman Empire.

Roman spiral acanthus motif

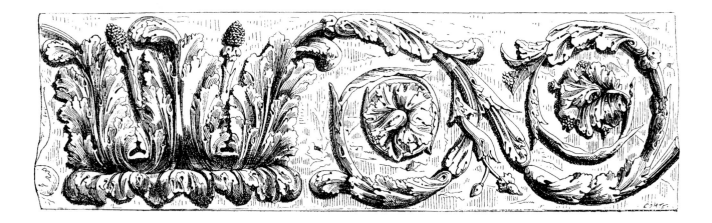

'The Romans, whose skills in mosaic were rudimentary, had taken the technique, as all others, from the Greeks in a highly developed state. Their passion for luxury and lack of concern with expense soon produced work on a large scale and real achievement, as finds have revealed … But it was not long before the Romans perverted what they had received from their predecessors. The fine taste of the Greeks, their precise understanding of composition and ornament, their sophisticated talent for imitation enabled them to create superb mosaics.

Of course, Greek common sense was never going to have their mosaics compete with painting, with its very exclusive principles. It would appear that the Greeks gradually began to decorate pavement areas with mosaic depictions – twisted and spiral ornaments, scallops and interweaving patterns – and, developing the fantastic forms derived from arabesques, proceeded to more significant symbols and attributes, such as griffons, chimeras, tragic and comic masks, the signs of the zodiac, vines, birds pecking at fruit, and all the rest of their well-known ornamental subjects. It may even be supposed that they would not infrequently place, at the centre of selected areas of pavement, scenes such as they had executed in previous times with such exquisite simplicity: nymphs sleeping or giving a fantastic animal water to drink, dancers, actors, flute- or castanet-players. Superb Greco-Roman decorative mosaics of this kind are familiar, such as that excavated in the 18th century at Otricoli, the finest ornamental exhibit in the round hall of the Museo-Clementino; the Italichi mosaic, and the famous mosaic which served as flooring in the magnificent temple of Fortune in Prenestina in the time of Sulla.

As is well known, however, the Romans were not inhibited in their enthusiasms. Caesar left a trail of marble statues after him through Gaul, and on his campaigns he had variegated mosaic flooring speedily laid in his tent (*opus tesselatum* and *sectile*). And in later times did not the Emperor Elagabalus lay his palace with a paving of precious stones, on which he once beat his head when wearied by Rome or her Praetors?

Long before Elagabalus, the Romans, who loved mosaic and wished to see it everywhere, were no longer content to limit it to decoration of the space in front of their houses and the floors of ground-floor rooms, and began to employ it to decorate walls, vaults and ceilings. Pliny tells us that this last seemed the most prevalent use of mosaic, when it was considered too beautiful to be thrown away underfoot and came to be in demand as pictorial decoration.'

Black and white marble mosaic from Pompei

Here Janron shows that because shingle, decorative stones, natural or decorative marble, paste and terracotta, earthenware pieces and shells could no longer compete with decorative painting at a time when painters, carried away by the headlong passion for brilliance and splendour, were using red lead, purple, cobalt, gold and silver for their meretricious enchantments and strident contrasts, mosaic craftsmen were obliged to turn to various precious stones – agate, jasper, carnelian, emerald, turquoise, lapis lazuli, and finally the rich effects of enamels – in order to keep up with the impact being so energetically achieved in the medium of painting, with its command of all the primary colours.

Mosaic from Herculaneum

Janron continues:

'Just when mosaic commanded more shades of colour, fewer primary colours became available to the craftsman; the match remained unequal. And the time had passed since the days when the claims and triumphs of the mosaic medium were related to the quantity and quality of its achievements. During the final stages of the Roman Empire, the demand for luxury each day brought new limitations to the scope of decorative art, but the fever of false allure continued to infect artist-craftsmen. Painting was nothing more than a pretentious piling up of objects, and the weakest forms were treated in the strongest colours. Mosaic, more costly, more pleasing to the eye, more attractive to the touch than the medium of painting, was inevitably expected to supplant its rival, and no more elevated idea prompted this gloomy revolution. Soon mosaic, trapped in the forms of its manufacture but subject to the most thankless transformation of the process as a whole, prevented from direct control of its design, and languishing in the long-drawn-out processes of manufacture and constant engraving problems, forgot everything it had been able to learn from painting, and became purely a trade. It was not long before mosaic craftsmen ceased to paint their enamels themselves; they passed round drawings and templates among themselves as needed in the manner of industrial collaboration. And so, when you think that despite the deplorable degeneration of the truly artistic sides of the mosaic craft, it nevertheless deprived painting of its most beautiful and basic functions, then you will have a good idea of the rapidity of the decline of all forms of Roman decorative design at the end of the imperial period.'

And finally, in the period of the rule of the Syrian princes and the incursion of Eastern religions, when all culture was engulfed in a tidal wave of magic and sensuality, science and experimentation vanished, swept away by the obsession with unnatural and boundless

Greco-Roman frieze

splendour. Cameos were turned into amulets, medals into talismans, and in these conditions, on foreign soil and penetrated by the ideas of an alien people, the pure and measured art of the Greeks was to disappear completely. The last lingering expression of this art is to be found in the symbolic hieroglyphic ornamental painting of the Roman catacombs, serving new cultural ends.

APPENDIX ON COLOUR RELATIONSHIPS

We shall not discuss colour in terms of the system of 'colour space' and numerical identification of colour by coordinates which has been devised by ingenious scientific minds having no direct contact with colour. Fortunately, we have the opportunity to present a number of examples in colour which, despite sometimes less than ideal juxtaposition, will provide the reader with clearer and, it is hoped, more useful demonstrations than could be achieved by physiological explanations.

However, paintings found in Pompeii have revealed to us a system of such importance, by virtue of both the simplicity of its method and the effects achieved, that we decided to include the present theoretical appendix in order to show that in Antiquity people possessed a perfect knowledge of the sources of colour and their relationships. First of all, we shall note that in the wall painting *Casa delle suonatrici* (Plate 13) a relief effect is given to an architectural structure which is designedly placed in a space, and this double effect is achieved through the use of tones with their full colour value without intermediary shades. As we shall see, there could be no better demonstration of the precision and depth of the Ancient Greek mastery of decorative painting.

The sky-blue background colour has the same saturation throughout: the effect of this colour becoming fainter, that is, greater saturation in the upper area with a gradation to a paler tone in the lower, giving a quality of airiness, is a well-considered result of experience, and is in complete accord with the conclusions of present-day theory of advancing and retiring colours.

Here we shall cite Professor Ernst Brücke[1].In his chapter on the theory of advancing and retiring colours, he says: 'The eye functions on the principle of a camera. When a light ray emitted by a clearly visible object enters this organ, it meets a point on the retina.'

In the accompanying diagram, AB denotes the object; CC the transparent cornea; DD the iris and the pupil; EE the lens of the eye; O the optical centre of the lens; CAC and CBE the diverging light rays emitted by the object at AB entering the eye; CBC and CAE light rays diverging due to the slight refraction in the watery liquid in the lens and vitreous body; *ab* the inverted image of the object.

---

1 *Colours, from the Physical, Physiological, Artistic and Industrial Points of View* by Ernst Brücke, Professor of Physiology, University of Vienna (J.-B. Baier, Paris, 1866 ([translation from German]).

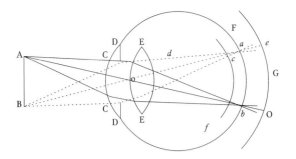

*Projection of light rays entering
the eye*

Depending on whether the retina is at points F or G, the image received may be either clear or blurred. Thus an inverted image of the object is formed.

Just as it is necessary to alter a camera setting in accordance with the distance of the object if we wish to keep the sharpness of the image, the eye needs special adjustment for each distance of the object. The eye performs this action by contracting a muscle, which causes certain changes in its internal disposition. The reader will find further detailed explanation in any physiological textbook. We have as yet only unconscious knowledge, as it were, of this process of the eye's adjustment.

When all means by which we normally ascertain distance from an object of unknown size have been used, when neither a proximate object nor aerial perspective gives us any reference point, a dim feeling down inside us intimates that the object in front of us is either near or far away. This feeling is connected with the nature of advancing and retiring colours in the following way. Light rays of short frequency (see below) deviate from their direction, when passing on an inclined plane from one sphere to another, to a greater extent than light rays of long frequency coming from the same point of light, and meet our retina more rapidly than the latter.

It follows from this that if two points of light, one red and the other blue, at different distances from the eye, emit rays that meet at the same distance from the lens, it can be assumed that the red point of light will be further away.

In the diagram below, R is the red point of light, B the blue, which is less distant from the eye; each places its image on the retina at the same distance from the lens, and if this distance coincides with the distance from the retina, we shall see both points of light with equal clarity in a single accommodation of the eye. Our eye has no means of informing us that points R and B are at different distances. Now let us look at point D, and suppose that it is blue. So that a clear image of this point of light can be received on the retina, the right eye will require a slight adjustment to allow for its greater distance. If it seems to us that the blue point B is the same distance away as the red point R, then the blue point D will appear further away.

*Two points of light at different
distances from the eye meet
at the same distance from the
lens of the eye*

To quote Professor Brücke:

'If we look at a stained glass window composed of red and blue squares in a black frame from some distance away, the red squares will seem nearer to us than the blue and appear to stand out; the black parts formed by the frame will create the effect of an inclined plane on the rear side of the blue glass. The reverse case has never been observed.

Advancing colours comprise red, orange and yellow. Retiring colours comprise different shades of blue including light blue and violet. Green is an advancing colour in relation to light blue and to some extent to ultramarine, but in relation to red, orange and yellow is retiring.

… If a painter uses an advancing colour to depict relief and a retiring colour to depict background, the illusory effect is heightened; in the reverse case this effect is diminished …

Certain artists can create a relief effect which is obscure, as if seen in a dream; and therein lies the fascination that such work possesses for us. It is easy to see that the advancing and retiring properties of colour must exercise a considerable influence on the production of such effects, and that a thorough knowledge of these properties can play an important part in the choice of an artist's palette.'

We can apply this theory, without wishing to be too strict, to the painting shown in Plate 13. Bright red, orange and yellow are used in the area where retiring blue is to recede and green move to the background. Furthermore, so as to bring out the background blue somewhat more in the uppermost part of the picture, orange and red are avoided here, and their advancing properties are lost as they turn to pink. The achievement of this wall-painting is enhanced by the fact that it gives further demonstration of the colour theory that has been described: in artificial light, in candle-light or oil-light, the intended effect is increased, not diminished. And finally, this theoretical refinement emerges: adding to the saturation of red, orange and yellow makes yellow brighter, and as long as the yellow is not affected by blue, which will subdue it, then blue will appear darker.

Mosaic

THE EAST

PLATES 15–32

UNDER THIS HEADING we include all forms of decorative and applied art of the East and Far East, two of the most fertile sources from which present-day art takes its models. This grouping comprises a diversity of periods, the earliest of which would appear to have preceded even the Ancient Egyptian culture and the latest turns out to be almost contemporaneous with our own. This vast terrain, however, considered from the point of view of its general features, is in fact less complex than might at first be supposed.

The tradition of the arts in the East, with many successive generations handing down their experience and knowledge of the processes of craftsmanship and production to the next, often makes dating difficult, and has not on the whole made its arts of great interest to art historians outside the sphere of valuation of precious individual pieces and study of the general properties of their ornament, which today's imitators take from Antiquity with greater or lesser degree of authenticity.

Our brief survey, then, freed from scrupulous chronology, will keep to the main contours corresponding to primary and original classifications, which take in all subdivisions and modifications. We shall eschew ethnographical questions, fascinating in their own right, as being beyond our competence and outside the field of our investigation. We shall instead follow our own inclinations and distinguish three broad groupings, or families of ornamental art: the Chinese, the Indian and the Arabian.

The first grouping, comprising the arts of China and Japan, will be treated on its own, as appropriate to its particular character and history.

Next, we shall turn to two great cultures, that of the Indian subcontinent and the Arab region, the Near East, and examine their distinguishing features and points of contact, the chief of which, originating in India, is Persian art – which however was transformed by the coming of Islam.

China. With Chinese civilization we are face to face with a nation whose history goes back to earliest times. In the course of its long existence this people, this world, has always been self-sufficient, and in conditions of static isolation, which formed its originality, it developed its own manner and cultural constructs, quite unlike those of any other civilizations, not counting some geometric concepts of which all known peoples have some instinctive grasp.

The exceptional degree of fantasy in Chinese ornamental compositions, the absence in them, as a rule, of order and plan are wholly explicable if one takes into account that the Chinese have always been without architecture as an art according to Western understanding and definitions – that is, an archetype of coordinated idealization giving rise to stylistic ornamentation thanks to which the most insignificant themes are filled with grandeur, as for example in Egyptian ornament. 'This absence of architecture,' Chavanne de la Girodière has observed, 'is explained by the very soul of the Chinese nation. It seems as if this people is doomed to concern itself exclusively with the particular, and this applies to everything. The idea of a monument is beyond their imagining. We must add to this observation that the light and shapely houses of the Chinese always have the cast of the tent, the mobility and proportions of which exclude any significant features belonging to architecture.[2]

In the circumstances of Chinese history it is understandable why the graphic arts remained in a primitive and rudimentary state in China, and why stylistic ornamentation so rarely entered their conceptions of scale and simplicity.

---

2 'Pagodas and triumphal arches, occurring throughout China, form the only exception to this rule. Pagodas, almost all of a single type, differ from each other only in their height, ornamental richness and beauty of materials. They alone have a truly monumental character' (Chavanne de la Girodière, *The Chinese*). Despite the size and splendour of some Chinese palaces, this type of structure has no other distinctive features.

On the other hand, for the Chinese, variety is the first sign of beauty. The leaves depicted on their decorative screens alternate without repetition; next to an area of landscape another area of bright colour will be found, covered with metallic arabesques. Chinese artists seek to avoid straight lines and right angles, or if they do occur they are modified; they follow their unbridled imagination in finding whimsical forms for their furniture or seeking to conceal its actual purpose by making its external form seem to serve a quite different purpose.

To these principles, so alien to Western ideas, to this graphic art in which the marks of real grandeur are so absent that any alteration of proportion seems stylistically unacceptable and which attracts little interest except on screens and curtains, it should be added that Chinese art does not adhere to the rules of perspective and has no acquaintance with the play of shade and chiaroscuro.

Nevertheless, despite such a number of points of fundamental inferiority, in certain fields, notably ceramics, inlay and weaving, Chinese ornamental art displayed such wealth of imagination and inventiveness in the use of colour, and found such diverse and enchanting

applications, as to become a touchstone of harmony and execution in these genres, surpassing the achievements of other nations in a number of respects.

Deficiencies become sources of qualities which are inherently Chinese. The whimsical mobility of the Chinese genius can put almost anything to ornamental purpose – clouds and waves, shells and rocks, objects and creatures from the real world and the realm of fantasy, florae in all manifestations, wooden articles and crystal ware, fireballs and flashing insects, vases, scrolls, inscriptions, and much else of all shapes and sizes.

In addition to all this is a quantity of sacred figures having mostly symbolic significance, including monstrous dragons armed with mighty claws and terrifying heads with numerous teeth, often seen in Chinese decorative compositions; armoured winged dragons, some with horns and some without, coiled before taking off for the empyrean; the dog Fo, with claws, sharp teeth and curly mane, transformed by fantasy into a lion; a sacred horse; the rare bird Fong-Hoang, with silky neck and peacock-tail, the sight of which is a good omen; a white deer, a second neck vertebra, crane, mandarin duck, and many other figures and creatures that have special symbolic meaning.

It seems odd that an art which seems to us so fanciful and chimerical in conception should be so immutable in the processes of its execution, its style of communication and depiction of the concrete that only after the passage of several centuries does it become possible to notice any significant changes in these things.

It is probable that the above-mentioned characteristics are simply manifestations of the basically imitative and traditional instinct of a civilization which has become highly developed in some ways but remained primitive in others, while always being itself. It is also possible that Chinese punctiliousness in continuing to employ the same traditions of forms and colours is connected with centuries-old secret rules and rituals.

This finds support in certain Chinese symbols of basic forms and colour, and Jacquemart, in his book *Wonders of Ceramics*, analyses these:

'Records of customary usage dating from the year 2205 BC refer to five established colours. These are found in the *Cheu-li* (12th to 8th century BC).

The work of embroiderers using coloured thread comprises a combination of five colours.

East – blue. South – red. West – white. North – black. Sky – dark blue. Land – yellow. Light blue combines with white. Red combines with black. Dark blue combines with yellow.

Land is represented by yellow; its special form by a square. The sky will change according to the seasons.

Fire is represented in the form of a circle. Water is represented in the form of a dragon.

Mountains are represented in the form of deer.

Birds, quadrupeds and reptiles are represented in their natural forms.'

The Fong-Hoang bird

Dragon

The dog Fo

Sacred horse

Changes were made to the imperial book with each new dynasty: having previously been white and green, it became yellow during the Tai Chin dynasty which has lasted into modern times.

If we now consider Chinese ornamental art from the point of view of the basic categories listed at the beginning of this book, we shall see both an *ideal* and an *imitative* element, the latter being used in a *conventionalized* way.

Colour also has a conventionalized significance here, and it in no way serves the purpose of reproduction of natural colours; from this point of view the palette (which may be subject to rules of a different order) can be used with complete freedom.

In Chinese art, ornament is used in the most diverse ways.

Chinese cartouches

All lightweight articles of furniture, curtains, screens, caskets and fans are excellently suited to the Chinese ornamental manner.

The subject of weaving also provides a variety of ornamental motifs.

Meanders are used with consummate mastery on inlaid bronzeware and cloisonné enamels, which would be sufficient to place Chinese ornamental art on the highest level if Chinese *ceramic work* were to be on the same level.

Chinese craftsmen reached their summit in the decoration of kaolin ware, on which they would put reserves of cartouches of uniform or irregular dimensions and a variety of shapes – round, oval, polygonal, or having the outline of a fruit or leaf, or a fan, and as if by chance, making each of these the basis of some geometric design. These reserves were decorated with landscapes featuring mills, mountains, rocks, groups of flowers, real animals or fantastic beasts; in the opinion of many, this kind of ware attained its high-point between 1465 and 1487, the period of its most fascinating designs.

At the present time Chinese decorative art is in decline. The reasons for this are complex but chief among them is the excessive division of labour practised in China.

Prof. d'Antrecole tells us that in a Chinese porcelain factory 'one painter first paints the coloured edges of the ware; then another paints the outlines of individual blocks of colour, which yet another paints in; one painter draws water and mountains, one does birds, one does animals, and so on.'

With such methods, all individuality disappears. As for bronze work, enamels and vases, the Chinese themselves consider the old superior to the new, which is nothing more than imitation.

Japanese ornamental art, while having its origins in Chinese art, is distinguished by its greater individuality, and it has avoided the extreme division of labour which is customary in contemporary China. The Japanese have studied natural history, particularly ornithology, more seriously than their predecessors and rivals in art, because their *imitative* style is less conventionalized. It must be said, however, that if their exquisite output has added new enchantment to the ancient Chinese ceramic achievement, they have not infrequently diminished the characteristically masculine principles that were present in it in its earlier periods. The art of ornament sometimes requires not only deliberate boldness but also restraint, the importance of which has not always been felt by the Japanese. They added their own palette to the Chinese, and this is what mainly distinguishes the work of each nation. At the present time Japanese ornamental art is on the threshold of new development; it is in the hands of gifted graphic artists who study nature, seek new forms and are conversant with the rules of perspective. One of the chief stimuli for the general progress being made by this art in Japan is the incredible scale on which models of all kinds created by real artists are reaching a wide public.

From our Western point of view, there are elements of progress here, although bringing a certain loss of originality for both Chinese and Japanese ware now being produced.

APPENDIX ON COLOUR RELATIONSHIPS

The passage from *Wonders of Ceramics* cited above would have been merely an archaeological curiosity, as we noted, had not this symbolism concealed the true principles of the most rational palette.

The chromatic symbolism prescribed by Chinese custom turns out to be nothing other than a confirmation of the only primary colours recognized by artists, which Siegler, in his *History of Ceramics*, picked out of the colour spectrum, discarding their combination as an erroneous practice.

These primary colours are: 1) yellow; 2) red; 3) blue (undifferentiated); 4) black, which, being absolutely negative, that is, obtained in the absence of light, is recognized as the maximal saturation of each primary colour (inasfar as different shades of black are recognized) and consequently the most powerful oscillator; 5) white, a colour unit without light, which all colours approach out of maximum brightness.

We can learn a lot by studying the formation of colours and how they differ from each other in different contexts, as understood by the masters of chromatic harmony. Such study should be accompanied by observation of how these masters separate and combine different colours to serve sometimes a rigorous order and sometimes the requirements of a particular palette, utilizing all available resources to exploit the effects of colour in contrast or combination in an overall ensemble.

In the cloisonné enamels in Plates 22–26, gold contouring is a means of picking out the design from the background, and especially of gathering the different parts of the design into a unified whole.

In Plate 21 and the lower part of Plate 28, the outlining in white, as the strongest colour, has a separating effect and is the essential element; only the saturated blue in one of these illustrations and the dark-green in another can do without it.

In the upper part of Plate 28 the contours of dark-brown and black are diminished where they are present at all; it was essential for them to be used in quantity so that the lightness of the background in moderate saturation was maintained, without impairment of the exquisite design. It can be seen that this use of outlining is worth special analysis, for it can be assumed that without it, or if it had been done in an inappropriate way, the motifs would have been completely spoilt and the combination of colours used entirely wrong.

INDIA, ARABIA AND THE MOORISH STYLE

PLATES 33–68 **India.** Less isolated than the Chinese and having more contact with the rest of the world, Indian culture, for all its antiquity, has not undergone the changes that have left their mark on the history of other nations. Social and religious structure, priesthood, temples, castes, sacred texts, poetry, morals, education, preconceptions – even repeated invasions have been unable to eliminate any of this from the Indian sense of identity and innermost feeling.

Art must account for a considerable proportion of this cultural load. Apart from some insignificant modifications that are best explained by comparison with Arabian and Persian art, the essentials of Indian ornament may today be defined by features that have resisted fundamental change.

The most striking of these features is probably *decorative consistency and fullness*, which most frequently covers the entire surface with an abundance of similar or single-plan motifs, achieved by the simple means of repetition of one element and its links with the background, the colour of which is sometimes light though more often dark, but always warm and harmonious, and is the basic element behind the overall effect. This manner, with its enchanting feeling for colour, lends Indian ornament an unbounded richness and an ineffable aura of tranquillity about which the only reservation that might be made is that sometimes one might wish for greater variety.

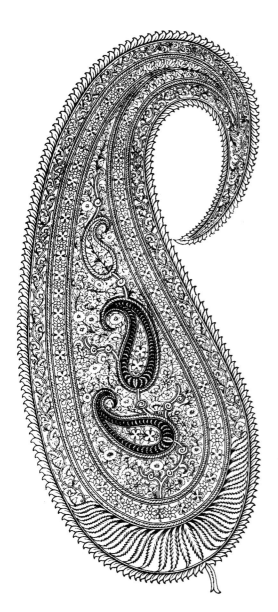

Almost without exception, the content of Indian decoration consists of floral motifs treated in a conventionalized manner. And although a generalized type stands out amongst a variety of other forms, imitation of floral forms is closer to actuality than it is in the majority of genres considered in this book up to now. The real-life floral motifs are as a rule made fairly easily recognizable without literal imitation, and if they are sometimes represented in the ennobling and lapidary Egyptian style, most frequently they are handled in a gentle manner, with a painterly freedom which appeals to modern taste.[3]

This treatment, however, never reaches representation of relief, which is alien to Eastern decoration of surfaces, but is restricted to a drawn silhouette with its outlines usually hidden beneath colours darker than those of the rest of the motif when the latter is executed against a light-coloured background and beneath lighter colours when the motif is against a dark background.

It would not seem misguided to suggest that these characteristics are typical of the earliest original Indian decorative art, which have remained predominant despite the incursions of a structural element borrowed from the Arabs and modified by the Persians, a style which, as we shall see, may be considered a meeting-point and fusion between the great Arab and Indian traditions.

We shall have something to add about the use of colour in Indian ornamental art when addressing the factors that link the three traditions.

Arabia. Alongside the Indian genius we shall consider the Arabian, attaining the summit of its achievements in apparent fulfilment of that natural law by which the human mind is led from simplicity to complexity.

The supremely gifted Arabs, obliged to avoid direct representation of natural forms by the Koran's prohibition of image-making, replaced the floral ornament predominantly used by the Indians with a *structural* principle which opened the way to the play of geometric patterns based

Indian palm leaf ornament

on the hexagonal *Solomon's seal*, of which they made striking use, enriching it with secondary patterns.

Arabian decoration, like that of the Indians, tends to cover entire surfaces without including any inappropriate element. The method of each, however, is different: where the

Indian sandal

---

3 As the above drawing shows, the palm leaf lends itself to conventionalized treatment more readily than other floral motifs employed in Indian decorative art. Frequently in decorative use today, either doubled to form a symmetrical frame ornament or itself forming a frame set in the centre of a flower arrangement, it would seem very much to belong to the Indo-Arabian style.

Ornamental patterns of Arabian design; on the central ornament is Solomon's seal

Indian style often involves repetition of similar motifs, Arabian decoration is built on all its elements; everything is interlinked – if the decorative element is, for example, a rosette, all volutes and flourishes from the perimeter to the centre will have common roots.

Often a pattern will be double, that is, formed by two complete systems, accompanying each other throughout without merging, but their meeting and overlapping producing intermediate or alternating figures at points of intersection in branching patterns, picked off from their immediate area by a colour change.

Despite these intellectual intricacies, Arab decoration is direct and intelligible, thanks to its purity and delicacy of line, its general regularity which excludes all excess, and its strict adherence to the principle of construction by which broad branches are placed at the perimeter and linked by diverging lines to their points of origin at the centre of the pattern, where exquisite design defines and fixes the centre of the circle and locks the whole composition together.

Arabian rosette patterns

We must add that it was probably the Arabs who invented the ingenious design having a double effect, a two-edged silhouette producing with a single line two figures placed opposite each other, as can be seen in Plate 33 no. 14, Indian in execution but in the Arabian or Persian style, in Plate 47 nos 7 and 11 (Persian work), and in the marquetry motifs shown in Plate 68.

In this most intricate of designs, what has become of that most precious decorative element the floral motif?

In the earliest Arabian style, before it had merged with the Persian, flower-like forms are found which appear to have direct affinities with the natural world. It is not by chance that these forms, intermediate motifs between invented and floral forms, appear in the branch-like designs that they complete; they are an inseparable part of these, as Owen Jones correctly points out in his book *The Grammar of Ornament* (1856); they do not disrupt the linear system of the designs but continue it, extending it at a stroke.

Arabian ornamentation in its original state, conceived and employed before the admixture of the Persian style, was conventionalized to an even greater extent than Greek, and entirely decorative in character, beyond and as it were above the bounds of the natural world. Since the Islamic religious canon expressly forbade symbolism, Arabian artists substituted a realistic style for the previous symbolic/conventionalized manner, which came to be widely used, most often with inscriptions in Kufic lettering or handwritten script which were skilfully incorporated into ornamental designs, one monument being known that is decorated in glazed ingots on which the whole of the Koran is inscribed on a background of floral ornament.

Arabian feather pattern

Such were the basic features of a rigorous and enchanting art so strongly stamped with the Arabian genius that the term arabesque came to be applied to the entire ornamental genre and used by other nations who knew nothing of its origins.

When we come to describe Persian and Byzantine ornamental art, we shall have occasion to say something of Arabian contacts with Asian, Greek and Greco-Roman cultures. The peoples of Asia Minor often mingled with the invaders of Persia and India, Egypt and Syria, and provided them with numerous models which gave inspiration to their arts. Even without knowing the precise results of such interchanges, what the Arab peoples received and what they transmitted, we should see their ornamental system as entirely original to them, and as having created prototypes that preceded the encounters and merging with other cultures that modified their creation or gave rise to intermediary genres.

The Moorish style. The Moors, the mixed Arab and Berber people dominant in North Africa and regions of the Iberian peninsula from the beginning of the 8th to the end of the 15th century, left a strong mark in architecture and ornamental art. The Moorish style, with some special features of its own, belongs to the Arabian family. Certain methods of structuring and forms of ornament (especially the elegant *Arabian plume*) and ubiquitous use of inscriptions are points of contact between the Moorish genre and the pure Arabian style, which are seen in their full splendour in the monuments of Cairo.

The chief hallmark of the Moorish style is the construction of a third dimension superimposed on the other two, serving a framing or linking function. Slightly protruding from the rest of the surface, this is a tangible constructional element which without any further modification serves as tracery work, a favourite genre of the Moors.

Moorish ornament as a rule has a consistent polychromous system using three basic colours: blue, red and yellow-gold. In the decoration of buildings and pavements, which helped them with their discoveries in geometry, the Moors enhanced their palette, in which green, the colour of the Prophet, often played a crucial role.

Space does not allow further comment here on Moorish ornamental art, which is a keenly pursued subject of research by architects and anyone concerned with the decorative arts.

Persia. Latter-day linguistic scholarship has given grounds for supposing that the population of Iran originates with the people of the Indian subcontinent (in earlier times the name of Persia was that of one of the provinces of Iran, and it was during a period of hegemony enjoyed by the Persians that they gave their name to the whole country), and the origins of Iranian culture are traceable only through Indian cultural history and the dynasties of the invaders of India (see J.J. Champollion-Figeac, *A History of Persia*). 'Persia,' wrote Louis Batissier furthermore, 'was for a long time a province of extensive empires founded by various conquerors of Asia. Consequently, its history has merged with the histories of other nations.'

What is historically true of the Arab, Seljuk, Ottoman and Mongol conquerors of Persia must have a bearing also on earlier conquerors. Outside the bounds of history as such, however, one glance at artefacts from Indian and Iranian civilizations will be a sure pointer to the link between Persian ornamentation and its Indian roots, the result coming in time to find a home in Indian national culture and subsequently to merge with Arabian art.

Through the prolonged period of relative peace preceding the conquests, the Persians were well known for their love of luxury and the perfection of their decorative arts. When, following the defeat of the Chosroes dynasty, the victorious Arabs seized the ancient Persian capital Madain, these inhabitants of temporary dwellings were amazed by the magnificence of the public buildings and the variety of the opulently decorated private houses that fell into their hands.[4] In the 7th century AD the Persians lived on a level of luxury and splendour that can only be compared to the descriptions of extraordinary riches in the Sanskrit epic *Ramayana* (c. 300 BC) and accounts it contains which are independently confirmed by Strabo and Megasthenes.

During the period from which Persian art is best known to us, in the course of which it reached its apogee, its compositions as a rule borrowed their general style from the inventions of Arab architecture as modified by Indian culture, with its characteristic avoidance of harshness and severity, its freedom and elegance, and drew a number of different elements from the merging of these two sources.

Floriate forms in particular are used in these sources in two ways: sometimes they are freely scattered about the decorated surface, sometimes incorporated into a linear structure, usually at points of intersection; in the latter case they hover between an elevated Arabian conventionalized style and Indian quasi-naturalism. The followers of Umar, Persian schismatics, lovers of wine and adherents of Ali, adopted the symbolic language of flowers which they gathered into bouquets called *Salam*,[5] and took every opportunity to depict them in their ornamental designs, in which they also incorporated real or fantastic animals and sometimes, though much more rarely, human figures.

If these characteristics as a rule make it possible to distinguish Arabian decorative work (though not without difficulty, as can be seen in Plates 61–64, showing designs from the Koran by way of examples of the extent to which Arabian and Persian decorative art merge), it is sometimes considerably harder to identify the Persian origins of woven fabrics and manuscripts. Many miniatures, in particular, were executed in India by early adherents of Zoroaster (Zarathustra) who emigrated from Persia under Islamic persecution, keeping their Persian or Farsi names.

The selection of decorative cloth of Persian manufacture and Indian style illustrated in Plate 46 shows almost the whole gamut of Indo-Persian floriate design in semi-free style: inflorescences of large flowers in full bloom on curling stems; pineapples, hazel-nuts, pomegranates, honeysuckle, camomile, carnations, poppies and other flowers, and this world of flora also contains birds of various sizes and quadrupeds. In the opinion of Jacquemart, the depictions of peacocks and young fern shoots bring out the specifically Indian origin of this work, which is supported by the aquiline nose, eye shape and arched brows of the winged spirits which bear the stamp of the Indian race.

To the resources acquired as a result of this merging of traditions the Persians added their own mastery of needlework and their remarkable and productive craftsmanship in other fields. Artists in gold and silver inlay on steel, bookbinders, faience craftsmen, embroiderers and miniaturists vied with each other in taste and virtuosity. Persian carpets remained the finest in the world, and dishes, vases and glazed bricks from Persia the authentic models to which European taste aspired and European craftsmen sought to be compared with their imitations. Persian gold and silver inlay on steel defined this type of ornament in the 16th and 17th centuries AD, the reign of Shah Abbas the Great (1587–1629) seeing the apogee of Persian art.

---

4 'When the Arabs advanced on Madain after the battle of Kadesia (636 or 638 BCE), gold crowns, bracelets and necklaces … fell into the hands of the commanding general, who divided everything among his soldiers, as prescribed in the Koran. Amongst these articles was a magnificent woven carpet 60 ells in length, with a depiction of a garden in which flowers were represented by precious stones sewn into the cloth. Not knowing what price this booty might fetch, the commanding general sent it to Umar, expressing his desire that the carpet should be sold for the highest price and the money received would be shared according to law. Umar took no notice of this request and ordered that the carpet should be cut into pieces. Ali sold the piece allotted to him for 20,000 drachmas.' – **Kosta**, *Arabian Architecture*.

5 The Persians were so fond of flowers that the flowering of the tulip-tree, which was a favourite subject for decorative depiction on porcelain and glazed bricks, was an occasion of universal rejoicing for them.

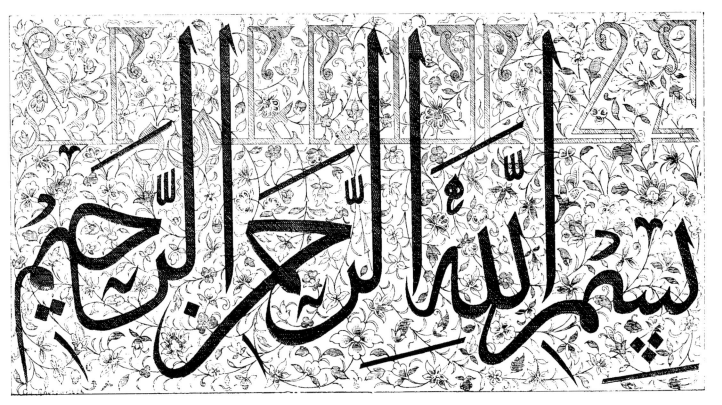

Inscription in Farsi

Indian, Arab and Persian decorative arts, already having much in common overall in composition and most favoured forms, were especially close in their use of polychromy. In this connection, the comment already made about the absence of any inclination towards representation of relief in Indian decorative art may be applied to the East in general.

The fundamental design principle here is that forms are drawn in silhouette in a chosen colour on an overall background colour. This is the principle of brightness and rest, when a design is first thoroughly worked out, and then colour is added to best effect. Different palettes can be built up out of black, off-white, blue, red and yellow body colour with a scattering of linking or separating elements any of which may be dispensed with according to the nature of the technique; however, this variety is always produced by means of homogeneous tones and firm outlines, from black to white through an intermediate stage depending on the artist's conception.

The Persians are masters of every kind of ornamental resource, and the best lessons in choice of palette in decorative art can always be expected from their work (see the two carpets shown in Plates 57 and 58 and the faience work in Plates 49–54, in which green, favourite colour of the Prophet, predominates). The use of gold is a leading feature of Moorish bas-reliefs, with their three basic colours and delicate lighter specks (see Plate 67).

The use of gold on illustrated manuscripts can produce pages beautiful to behold, an especially enchanting effect being attained by massed small stars in the work of Indian craftsmen of our time (Plate 37 no. 12). On a background of two differently coloured areas of equivalent size, alternating black with white, red with green, an effect characteristic of Indian taste and here coinciding with subtle changes in the design, which undergoes an analogous colour change, the Indian artists succeed in neutralizing the full colour values within a framework of overall harmony. It is the gold placed on top of the strong colours, linking them together rather like a transparent veil of woven gold, that gives rise to this harmony.

THE BYZANTINE STYLE

PLATES 69–77

THIS IMPORTANT STYLE, not naturally belonging to any of the three broad classifications adopted in this book, Antiquity, the East or the West, will be considered separately. It may be thought of as a link between the first two categories, from the merging of which it took its origin, and the last, for which it was an inspiration over a long period of time.

Byzantine art may be regarded, in fact, as the product of Greek art in degeneration and fusion with the culture of Eastern peoples. The starting point of the latter process will be, then, the part-conquest of the Near East by the Romans who, ever more interested in grandeur in ornamental art, found new elements there meeting their demand for luxury. What exactly were these elements, their nature and significance? This moment in history remains unclear.

In the pre-Islamic period, which saw the simultaneous unfolding of Arab genius and power, these people had already created their own original art. The only trace of it today, however, is found in certain legends telling of grand monuments dating back to earliest times. As a result of some catastrophe, perhaps a flood, the Arabs moved from Africa to what we today call the Near East or West Asia and founded a number of caliphates in Syria, including that of Khir, of legendary architectural and material splendour (see Costa, *Arabian Architecture*). We know that nomadic and settled tribes called each other *felt people* and *clay people*, which would indicate that the latter made pottery – although we know nothing of its decoration – and also weapons, cloth and permanent dwellings. These lines of thought lead to the conjectures that Arabian arts of African origin were brought to West Asia in the course of migrations that took place in unstable times, that these arts, coming into contact with the Greek, Indian and Persian populations, absorbed a number of modifications which are unknown to us, but that in large part they formed a variant tradition which became known as Byzantine art.

At a later time, following the period of Byzantine hegemony, Arabian art, under the impact of Islam, assumed the form which so enthrals us today. In some of its manifestations and in some territories Byzantine art exerted a certain influence on Arabian techniques; however, it would be an exaggeration to trace, as was once done, the emergence and development of the Arabian style itself to the Byzantine tradition, for this style possesses too many distinctive features, too much integrity of its own, to be said to lack overall originality.

Byzantine-style church window

In our opinion, the truth is that influence may be two-sided, and that this is inevitably what happens in encounters such as the present case. If, however, Arabian art took something from Byzantine art, it should be said that it must have lain among aspects borrowed from Eastern sources, during either its formative period or that of its highest development.[6]

Be that as it may, Byzantine art occupies an important place in the history of ornament, uniting two great traditions, the Greco-Roman and the Asian. As it was disseminated in a north-easterly direction, it has been definitive of the Russian style of ornament up to our day; and spreading west, in combination with certain tendencies of the Celts, Latins and Lombards it introduced the fundamentals of the *Roman style*, and eventually, on its new encounter with the East at the time of the Crusades, made its contribution to the formation of the *Gothic style*.

---

6 When he built Constantinople (consecrated in 330 CE), Constantine invited Eastern building craftsmen who later, during the reign of Justinian, worked in large numbers under the Greek masters Anthemius of Tralles and Isidore of Miletus on the building of Hagia Sophia and other monuments of the Justinian era on which traces of their hand are visible.

Byzantine ornamentation from the church of Theotokos, Constantinople

Byzantine ornament was much simpler in structure than the Arabian. Its logic was the same, but its nature was less sequential; in inscriptions, for example, carried-over words were far less common, according with Greek practice.

The forms of palm-shaped blooms on stems, taken directly from Classical Greek vases, have close Arabian analogues; but their serrated outlines, with fewer resources available to the artists, are on a lesser scale than Arabian depictions. Although the rendering of detail is less fine, the ornamental execution is of high quality, good use clearly being made of the Greek style. Byzantine polychromatic ornament with simple silhouettes, rational structure and a background providing greater free space than in the work of Eastern artists, always gives rest to the eye; ornamental interweaving is superior; bold, broadened floral depictions, fully obeying the laws of nature, often play a major role. See Plate 69 nos 31 and 32, Plate 74 nos 9, 14, 18, 19, 23 and 24, and Plate 86 no. 4.

However, there is great variety in this ornamental art, and as a result of the merging of two original artistic traditions the presence of individual resources and an awareness of all styles is evident. It contains background ornaments and borders in the Indian manner consisting exclusively of floral motifs used by Indian artists, and here again we see that unique style in which bold juxtapositions can produce an effect of great richness (Plate 75 nos 1, 3, 4, 6, 7, 8). Alongside the principle of regular repetition, Byzantine artists employed that of symmetry as conceived by the Greeks, that is, a balance of forces rather than exact repetition, in direct or inverted form (see Plate 69 nos 30 and 32 and Plate 76 no. 6).

Border from an evangeliary, 8th century

Mosaics from an episcopal throne in the church of San Lorenzo Outside the Walls, Rome

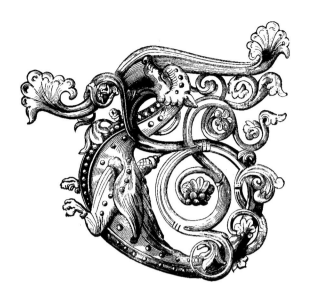

Among the most distinguished examples of Byzantine decorative art are geometric compositions, especially those in mosaic, where monotony is avoided by subtly planned interweaving of usually straight lines and angles (Plate 74 nos 1, 5 and 6; Plate 77 nos 13–16 and so on; and Plate79 nos 7 and 23). Byzantine mosaics in geometric style may be distinguished from Latin mosaics by this particular design, which lies at the core of every detail. The Latin geometric design as a rule has an external character, constructed by means of architectural lines transferred to mosaic, which fulfils the function of the stone transom of a Gothic window, formed by a simple square or triangle of marquetry.

We show some examples here which will make these differences clear. They come from the Church of San Lorenzo Outside the Walls in Rome. This is what A. Lenoir says of them:

'These wonderful mosaics, which can be found only in Italy, are very difficult to make because marble inlay is a problematic technique in general, and because the geometric designs they contain, with their small dimensions, demand the highest precision in all adjacent details. Mosaics of this kind were very popular in the 12th, 13th and 14th centuries, especially in the Roman provinces; in some churches, for example in Orvieto, they were used to decorate parts of façades; the great galleries of the monasteries of St Paul Outside the Walls and St John Lateran in Rome are decorated with the most sumptuous work in this style … Eastern pavements designed in the same style are found which writers of Antiquity would call *opus Alexandrinum*. This style was used in churches of the East and the West from the first centuries AD up to the High Middle Ages.'

Byzantine design and consequently its palette have a completely *conventionalized* character. Very slight representation of relief is found in illuminations of so-called 'Greek' manuscripts and Sicilian mosaics which are direct imitations of Byzantine designs. On the other hand, colours are everywhere used in full saturation by Byzantine artists and stand in stark contrast to each other on a common background, as indeed everywhere in the East.

Byzantine ornament lacks symbolism, except in representations of the cross, which take many different forms, all more or less removed from historical type. However, it frequently incorporates apocalyptic beasts and human or celestial figures having religious significance.

THE WEST

F OR THE REST OF THIS BOOK, chronological rather than ethnological sequence is adopted for the three broad periods: the Middle Ages, the Renaissance, and the 17th–18th centuries in France.

THE MIDDLE AGES
CELTIC, ROMAN AND GOTHIC

PLATES 79–112 **Celtic.** As Byzantine culture spread westwards among the Celts, it came into contact with local cultures with their individual customs and characteristics. Ornamental art was among the most striking aspects of Celtic culture, and its range is displayed in Plates 81 and 82 (see also the accompanying notes there). The most remarkable examples of Celtic ornamental art

Celtic interweaving patterns

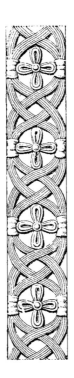

are illustrated in J. O. Westwood's *Facsimiles of the miniatures and ornaments of Anglo-Saxon and Irish Manuscripts* (1868). Westwood refutes two assumptions: first, that Celtic ornament had Roman origins, which is disproved by the consistent historical pattern in which the interweaving designs of Roman mosaics have been found to be used in alternation with the knot-form junctions of Celtic spiral patterns; and secondly, that it had Byzantine origins, disproved by the absence of any analogue between the earliest form of this Celtic design and ornamentation in Hagia Sophia. From these refutations he drew a conclusion regarding the spontaneous nature of Celtic national art, although leaving aside the problematic question as to whether its point of origin was Scandinavian or whether it originated in Ireland and subsequently spread to England, Scandinavia and northern France.

The present editor is inclined to share both these opinions, considering the earlier period more likely and ascribing an Eastern origin to Celtic ornamental art, as also to the Celtic people in general, related as they are to the Scythians of Aryan descent, who gradually penetrated to the main land masses and islands of the North, the clearest case of which ethnographic science recognizes in the Irish. Thus common Eastern roots and early mutual propinquity could explain a certain kinship between the Celtic and Arabian cultures, in geometrical discoveries, for example, irrespective of the differences between the two cultures in the application of these, which is a topic to be touched on later.

Celtic-Byzantine motifs

Celtic carved initials

Not insisting further on this hypothetical line of thought, which, supporting the independence of local Celtic art from Byzantine and Gallo-Roman, could explain original features in different Northern peoples and at the same time a common origin, we shall extend a little further the general description of the Celtic ornamental style given in the notes to Plate 81.

The interweaving pattern is the hallmark of the earliest Celtic ornament, and this alone would be sufficient to establish the antiquity of the genre, for this kind of pattern is earlier than any other. Its special quality lies in the placing of ornamental elements to maximal effect, so that they always develop the central idea. There can be no doubt that real lengths of cord were originally used as templates for this pattern before a quasi-geometric idea was decided upon. The flexibility of this element provided a range of different ways of forming spirals and curving right angles, and this is the chief difference between Celtic ornament and the geometric Arabian principle. The diversity of Celtic articles made up of such a humble element is striking, and it is fascinating to trace their progression in complexity and depth and the skilful command of transparent links and inventiveness in curves and intersections that marks truly coordinated ornamental design.

Nevertheless, the resources of Celtic ornamental art were in danger of exhaustion, even with the use of all possible combinations provided by natural objects, because the living element was lacking, and so Celtic ornamental art took this from Byzantine culture, with which it came to be in close contact.

A mixed period. The Romanesque style. This transformation, or compromise, it would be better to say, during the 9th and 10th centuries, the epoch of Charlemagne and his successors, saw the emergence of two distinct styles, and the beginnings of the superiority of West European applied art.

While absorbing the floriated nature of the Byzantine ornamental style, Celtic artists progressed in their own way, sometimes keeping the original 'cord' element as such and sometimes turning it into a stem with efflorescences and flowers. As it attains ornamental richness, the Celtic style is raised to the level of fine art. At the same time, the difference from the purely geometrically conceived Arabian designs already noted increases, with more and more frequent use of heads of quadrupeds and birds as ending points of lines. These are used in combination with extended and exaggerated body forms around perimeters, out of which feet and paws associated with the heads emerge. These fantastic and grotesque forms constitute an original ornamental style that would not have been possible by means of interweaving designs alone (see Plate 85 nos 13, 15 and 16). Similar figures have been found on carved stones in Britain and Scandinavia, relating to ancient monastery regulations and forms of prayer, and our examples of polychromy are taken from such sources; they help towards giving an inclusive representation of this original style in its maturity.

Examples of the second successful Celtic style are also shown in Plate 85 (nos 18 and 22); in these, rosettes and plastic ornamental shapes are

(far left) Border from the bible of St Martin of Limoges, 10th century;
(left) Border of an evangeliary, 11th century (Munich Library)

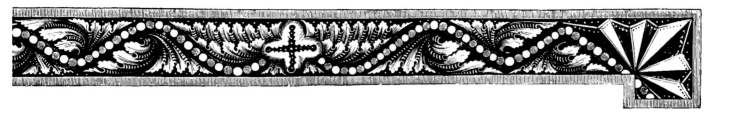

Border from a book belonging to a junior deacon of the Cathedral of Metz, 9th century

employed with great expressiveness. The initials in a free space (nos 19–21) are comparable with the finest ironwork, and those on a coloured background (nos 34–37), with rich and well-planned saturation, in which Celtic and Byzantine styles are on equal terms, are an even fuller expression of 10th-century ornamentation. To be noted in these compositions are their energy of design, unerring juxtaposition, consistent logic, with paring and unfolding governed by common principles, and the overall clarity achieved by a soft palette which heightens the decorative effect.

In Byzantine practice as throughout the East, representation and palette are wholly conventionalized; in these designs there is only a slight effect of relief, its aim being to denote the roundness of stems or calyxes out of which heads or new vegetal ornamentation issue (nos 19–21). Celtic ornament would appear to contain no symbolism, with the exception, perhaps, of recurring images without beginning or end, which maysymbolize eternity (see Plate 81 nos 8, 18, 23, 24 and 31).

The mixed Celtic-Byzantine style in ornament did not wholly give way to Gothic, but coexisted with it for a considerable period of time. It was this style that determined the most beautiful types of ornamentation of stained-glass windows and manuscripts. From the 11th to the 14th centuries, the most brilliant period of the Middle Ages, the margins of the latter were treated as windows in miniature form. Even in 15th -century Italy there were still direct traces of the Celtic style in the marginal vignettes that were fashionable at the time (see Plate 102), competing with marginal illuminations in the Latin style of the Renaissance.

Through the large number of illustrations in this book devoted to the Middle Ages, two elements of the mixed Celtic-Byzantine style are discernible, either in combination or separately. Illustration no. 1 in Plate 90 shows two styles: the two corners on a purple background are in the Celtic style, as are parts of the initials on a purple background shown in nos 13–16; the rest of the ornamentation in no. 1 is in the Byzantine style. The Scandinavian frescoes and designs on enamels and silk shown in Plate 94 have a strong flavour of the Byzantine style.

In the examples of stained-glass window designs shown in Plates 98 and 100, the combined or separate use of the two styles is easily recognizable. Plate 98 nos 1, 19 and 28 and Plate 100 nos 28–30 show combinations of the two styles.

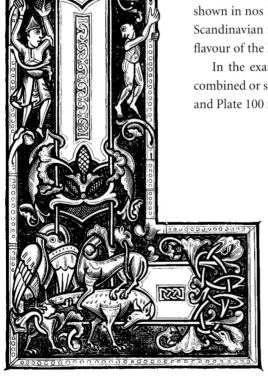

Capital, 11th century

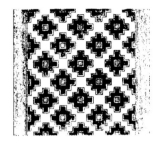

Enamels from the front of a church altar, Komburg, Germany, 12th century

Plates 97 and 102 show manuscript decorations found in Italy, where the Byzantine style lingered longer than in northern Europe, and illustrate how the pure Byzantine style underwent modifications on the eve of the Renaissance.

The Pointed style. The term 'Pointed' or 'Lancet' today refers to the architectural style long called 'Gothic', since it was the pointed arch that was its leading feature in all aspects including ornament. 'A "lancet" is an arch formed by two arcs of equal radius which meet at their upper end to create a curving angle' (Louis Batissier, *Histoire de l'Art Monumental*). Here it will be useful to call to mind the spread of the new style after the discovery of the lancet.

Pointed arch in the choir screen of Notre Dame Cathedral, Paris

Examples of the latter, along with other finds, have come to light in the Crusaders' Vault at Mycenae and at Pelasgian burial sites, at some Roman tombs, and in an aqueduct in Tuscany; also at the Ibn Tulun mosque in Cairo built in the 10th century under Byzantine and Persian influence, and at further 10th-century Arabian and Sicilian sites, from where it was brought to Neustria with the Norman conquests.

Taking hold in northern Europe from the second half of the 12th century, building in the Pointed style was the norm in the region until the end of the 13th century. The new style was restricted to exclusively architectural use during this first period, when the pointed arch coexisted with the round Romanesque,

Details of left image

just as in Arab regions it was employed alongside the horseshoe arch in one and the same building. Nor was it used in its pure form; during the Romanesque period its ornamental features were borrowed from the preceding styles.

It was not long, however, before northern European masters developed this transitional stage into a new style and a new world of ornamental forms emerged which fixed the contours and detail of the celebrated style that was employed almost exclusively for three centuries and furnished the Western world with so many architectural masterpieces.

Plates 90 and 98 illustrate the period of transition from the First Pointed phase to the Second. The ornamental style shown in Plate 90 still belongs consistently to the Romanesque, while Plate 98 shows a later stage at which key differences are emerging in ornamental design.

Detail from a Celtic cathedral

The illustrations of Plate 90 show designs from a precious 12th-century manuscript from the Abbey of Luxeuil-les-Bains, Haute-Saône, which display almost all these new ornamental features and make up a detailed all-round selection of Romanesque ornament. Forms in the Celtic style are juxtaposed with elements in the Latin style, just as in architecture of the time the round arch was placed side by side with the pointed. Nos 26, 33 and 54–58 show the Celtic style.

The novelty here lies in the treatment of columns, the shaft being embellished to its full height with vegetal, foliate and spiral ornaments (nos 15, 16, 37 and 38) and the capitals (nos 47–50) also being ornamented with leaf forms, some turned towards the top of the column, some downwards, some beside a human figure. One of the last (no. 51) was originally employed as a support for the whole column.

On the other hand, on friezes and borders the Greek key ornament is found (Plate 90 no. 17) and a variant with a broken line (no. 18), as well as counter-posed zigzags (no. 41), hollow pyramid shapes (no. 42), and serrated images enhanced with alternating foliate ornamentation (nos 30 and 31). The rest of the patterns shown in Plate 90 are more or less reminiscent of Antiquity: a heart-shaped scallop ornament alternating with spears, misty leaves and succulent plant growths, fully covering the background. Alongside nos 45 and 46 and numbers 1–16, in Byzantine or Celtic-Byzantine style, imaginary or exotic types of conventionalized antique flora from a contemporaneous manuscript are represented, which the new taste of the Gothic period was quick to substitute with local flora.

Although the silhouetted stained-glass window motifs shown in Plate 98 retain the character of the Byzantine style, a departure from Antique principles is evident in the detail. What the isolated Celtic style looked forward to in the 10th century, still restricted within the bounds of its own development, was attained in its full form in this later period. In a freer space the familiar conventionalized floral forms are developed, but petals, elegantly separated and spreading widely, are gracefully linked by a structural element which is often employed to delimit alternating backgrounds. Sometimes this structural element is a simple winding stem-like ornament (nos 16 and 38), which sometimes becomes double, with the individual ornaments crossing over (nos 6, 14 and 36); there are interweaving designs (no. 35), sometimes in chequered pattern (nos 4, 8–10), combinations consisting entirely of a floral element (nos 11, 24 and 26), borders covered with pearl-like ornaments or grooves (nos 22 and 35), sometimes turning round on themselves in the manner of Celtic junctions. Constructive elements are added to floral, which often issue from the former (nos 1, 15, 22 and 35) and complete it to govern the whole.

Key to Plate 90

Details from a Celtic cathedral

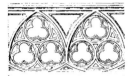

Strict organization, clarity and abundance of images, ingenuity and diversity in composition, logical strength, energy of invention, everything shows this work to be the creation of a vigorous people confident of the superiority of Western art.

From the end of the 13th century the old style, lingering on in certain details of ornamental art, had entirely vanished from the architecture of Europe, where the Pointed style, with a number of modifications which there is insufficient space to describe, held complete sway. We shall not enumerate here the pointed arches and arcades, soaring, elongated vaults with trefoil ornament, arcades with convex vaulting and a salient sometimes in the form of a guttered block and sometimes a basket handle, which were analyzed so minutely in the *Instructions* published by the Commission for the History of Art and Monuments in 1846 and figuring in all architectural treatises thereafter. All these we shall refer to insofar as their outlines generated ornaments associated with them. This fact is amply demonstrated by study of the illustrations of grisaille designs in Plate 100. Curvilinear forms constructed by means of an optical square are the basis of these 14th-century designs (nos 1–10, 12, 14 and 15). From these outlines quatrefoil, trefoil and rose ornaments emerge, built up in the manner of architecture itself; these constructions leave the imprint of their silhouettes on a richly coloured background which, with the exception of references to Antiquity, is borrowed from geometric patterns, interweaving Celtic designs and as yet tentatively essayed local flora.

Carved door in the Abbey of St Albans

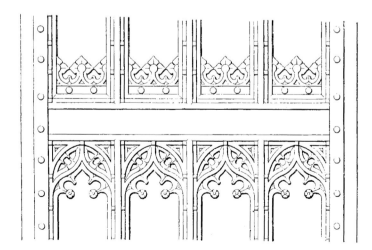

This ornamental style is completely original, not only in its forms but also in its principles. Ornamental detail had never before now been drawn directly from architectural contours. For these Western artist-craftsmen, ornament was not a matter of spontaneous invention, as it had been, for example, in the case of the Arabs; it implied real construction and the practical planning of all its outlines and forms. All its details flowed directly from the overall principles of its architectural setting, in such a way that a trefoil ornament on a balustrade or panel would exactly indicate the period and type of the whole construction. Ornamental detail, in the most primitive styles and in the most splendid caprices of *Flamboyant Gothic*, takes its due place in this construction, accommodated to its architectural profile without distortion.

This ornamental art, with its logical rigour and precision in the minutest detail, manifested throughout the Middle Ages in stained-glass decoration, exterior facing, enamelling and tile decoration, stone and wood carving, ironwork, and countless manuscripts which are precious historical artefacts to scholars today, was a flourishing genre based on observation of and contact with the real world and naïve imitation of natural forms.

Italy, the Netherlands and France most strikingly exemplify this new movement which, opening up wider and more varied opportunities for ornamental art, was a prelude to the great flowering of the 16th century.

After manuscript miniatures became stained-glass windows on parchment or, as Adolphe Napoléon Didron put it, 'windows in card', they wrote a new chapter in art history alongside that already written by cathedrals. Independence and naivety lent painterly ornamentation distinct charm. In the 15th century the main elements of ornament were rooted in floral design, where local varieties had a more prominent place than they had been accorded hitherto. Manuscript margins (see Plates 106–08) were filled with ivy, wild vine, cultivated vine, creeping cinquefoil, water lilies, buttercups, oak leaves, wild strawberry bushes, reeds, mallow, cabbages, thistles, holly, chicory, camomile, roses, carnations and pansies.

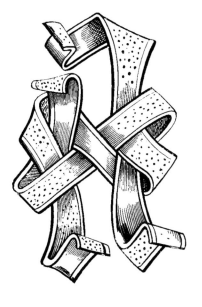

'Chopped, flat, winding and pinniped forms, alongside digitated, palmate or trefoil leaves' (*Instructions of the Commission for Art and Monuments*), revolve round and change places with branches or fruits which are at times easily recognizable and at times difficult to identify. Sometimes this floral world with its iridescent glow will illuminate a butterfly's or an insect's wing, or an ingenious combination of broad ribbons (reminiscent of the Celtic style) bearing inscriptions will unroll.

Border from a Latin evangeliary, 13th century

The Renaissance

PLATES 113, 124–75

Even by the end of the Middle Ages Italy still retained traces of the culture of Classical Antiquity from which it took its origins and its genius, although after many centuries it could see Antiquity only through the prism of Byzantine culture. Every time excavations took place in Italy, masterpieces of the nation's forebears came to light. While a new revolution in literature impelled all minds towards the study of Antiquity, Italy became the forge of that great movement, the Renaissance, which was to change the face of art and make its impact on many nations.

No attempt will be made here to analyse this all-embracing movement which belongs to the history of art on a global scale and has been described many times, but its influence on the topic of our investigation will be traced. As far as ornament is concerned, besides certain inventions of a new type, we shall discover the stamp of highest genius in the employment and coordination of genres of art borrowed from Antiquity, the East and national genres from Western Europe.

Leading Western sensibility towards a renewed ideal keener and more versatile than the ideal of Antiquity from which it sprang, the incomparable phalanx of Italian masters took the decorative arts to their apogee, contributing the breadth of ideas and universal knowledge which they owed to their artistic education. Each of them was at the same time an artist, architect, sculptor, frequently engineer, artisan, engraver, musician, but always an educated and cultured man who found within himself all the resources and means for his work.

In these hands, ornamental art was to find new qualities and broaden the scope of its use. It was to make greater endeavours to move away from the uniform types and formulas that had long held virtually undisputed sway in architecture or continued to support traditional craft methods, and to lead the decorative arts towards comparative freedom, for which that element of fantasy characteristic of late Gothic, especially in manuscript illumination, had already prepared the way.

At the same time, the art of drawing, perfected through contact with the best models of graphic art and freeing itself from medieval naivety and jejunity, moved towards wider compositional use of the human body, and its presence in works of art determined the relative proportions of the surrounding world. Henceforth, ornament was increasingly linked with and also subordinated to works of fine art, which had attained a summit of perfection and transmitted some of their qualities to the decorative arts. Thus, in their golden age the Italians transformed decorative art into an encyclopaedic fine art.

Branch ornament,
15th century

The full flowering and definitive development of the Renaissance style was preceded by the work of a number of Italian masters of ornament which may be considered as a transition from medieval art to the characteristic style of the 16th century.

Plate 124 shows this transitional style in work by the late 15th-century painter and manuscript illuminator and miniaturist Girolamo da Cremona. The precisely conceived ornament is redolent of the sumptuous forms of Roman sculpture. Definitive features are its theme of luxuriant plant growth and its palette and line, which have a certain pagan feel. The objects depicted are outside the normal boundaries of ornamental art in 15th-century manuscripts. It must be said that the volumes that contained these illuminations had a format resembling fresco ornamentation. They were church manuscript collections, some containing antiphons and some masses and canticles, of the sort to be found in the cathedrals of Siena and Florence and the Chertoza-Paviyskaya monastery outside Milan, and they would measure at least 1.25 metres in height.

The work shown in Plates 127 and 128, by the well-known Florentine artists Gerardo de Simone and Attavante degli Attavanti, is also manuscript illumination, less austere in style than the work shown in Plate 124. Refined and sumptuous in moderation, it consists of branch ornaments in elegant tones, somewhat mannered but executed with taste. The familiar

Hanging ornament made by Benvenuto Cellini (Cabinet of Antiquities, Bibliothèque Nationale, Paris)

acanthus is used, and crowning full-blown roses in approximate botanical form. These designs are frequently decorated with putti, pearls or cameos, attributed to Giulio Clovio (Plate 37 nos 3–5), the hallmarks of this style.

The highest expression of Renaissance ornamental art comes from Raphael. He was preceded by a number of other masters; in the judgement of Alfred Dumesnil, however (*Italian Art*, 1854), 'he develops, harmonizes and transforms everything that was known before him.' With the help of the decorative artists Polidoro da Caravaggio, celebrated for his grisailles, and Giovanni da Udine, who excelled in painting fruits, flowers and animals, Raphael painted the walls of the Vatican with decorative frescoes. Their motifs (Plates 133 and 134 and Plate 135 nos 1–5) were taken from the same designs as those of the engraved work in ivory shown in Plate 135 (nos 1–5) and likewise recast. This decorative work was imitative of Antiquity, models from which had recently been unearthed during excavations of the Emperor Titus's baths, later to be backed up by finds at Pompeii and Herculaneum, and which the genius of Raphael to some degree anticipated. The hand of the master is clearly evident in the panels *The Seasons* and *The Three Parcae*; everywhere the strict and sure taste of the divine young man is felt.

Work such as this gives a very good idea of the role that ornament can play and of the enormous range of knowledge that must be possessed by anyone who aspires to the ideal in this art.

Along with the remarkable resurrection of the Antique style by Raphael and his school, another striking development took place at this time. Having resuscitated Antique ornament, artists in the 16th century felt a need to enhance its detail with all kinds of new elements to produce more decorative effects. The crowning glory of Renaissance decorative art was surely the introduction of this rich enhancement. The *branch ornament with volutes*, replacing or combined with the branch ornament with leaves, was the novelty of the era; the cartouche, creating a more imposing effect of centralization than the preceding style, quickly brought in its wake the intersecting *thick double volute*. Enriched with this enchanting new element, the ornamental genre pursued a wholly original development which possessed such logical strength that, taken up by the foremost masters of architecture and surviving all changes in taste thenceforth, it continued to play a major role in Renaissance design, its popularity extending to the embellishment of even the most insignificant detail.

Branch ornament with volutes, reign of Francis I

Branch ornament with volutes, reign of Henri II

It is time to take a glance at the evolution of the *cartouche*. In order to facilitate study of this important decorative element, a study which is essential for all students and practitioners of decorative art, we have placed illustrations of it by period, showing its many successive varieties, leaving aside a large number of supplementary images within ensembles (see the List of Plates).

The earliest cartouches of the 16th century patently belong to the age of wood; they not only look like planed lengths of wood, but very likely originally were. The next type of cartouche, dating from the end of the century, is of more complex construction, consisting of identical elements – a volute with two interweaving and protruding planes.

Branch ornament with volutes and some thick flourishes, reign of Charles IX

The branch ornament with volutes served as the element of ornamental construction, similar in function to those elements for which Arab craftsmen felt a need. This ornament, like the plant stems with which it would be combined, had a curving line and the grace of Classical form. Its bareness of line pleasingly contrasted with the serrated edges of the ornament from the acanthus family which returned to fashion in the

Branch ornaments with volutes, reign of Henri II

Renaissance. In this stylistic merging, the width of the ornament is balanced by the light profile of the leaves, and also by the exposed delicacy of the elements that give it relief. Borders made up of the branch ornament with volutes varying in length according to perimeters increase the verisimilitude of the various kinds of figures they contain, some at rest, others in movement and intersecting the ornamentation, the harshness these might otherwise have had being softened by the effect of mascarons, ribbons, flowers or fruits giving areas of repose in the ensemble. Alone or in combination with other features, these elements of ornamental construction, which in all their characteristics accord with the age-old Western aesthetic traditions that have been noted, may be the main factors inherent in the finest manifestations of European art of our own time.

The advent of these elements ended the domination on friezes and panels of the broad bear's paw and acanthus leaf of Roman tradition and the ornamental vase with double flourishes rising from it. A whole world of real or imitation cartouches was the foundation for the new direction in ornamentation. Coinciding with the arrival of the new genre, the art of carving reached a high-point in the hands of the finest masters and its potential was quickly recognized and its images disseminated throughout Europe, from the Netherlands to the German lands, from France to Italy, from Britain to Spain, so that everywhere analogous conceptions sprang up and local originality increased its scope with every day that passed.

Branch ornaments with volutes, reign of Henri II

Cartouche with thick volutes, 1556 (printed date)

The more we investigate the 16th century, the more we find that the impulse towards Antiquity, revival of which was the aim of the earliest Renaissance masters, but which slackened as a result of the break-up of the Roman School after the death of Raphael, began to take in ideas gathered from various other sources in the contemporary spirit of assimilation. The term *arabesque*, as given to the ornamentation of the loggias of the Vatican, was testimony of a certain interest in Eastern styles which could be studied and used through the channel of the commercial activities of the Italian republics. Arabian models certainly influenced the design of the new type of branch ornament, and the faithfulness with which the Venetians employed the Persian style (see Plate 167) in the 16th century leaves no doubt as to their thorough knowledge of Eastern styles and the uses to which they could be put.

It was noted earlier that the Renaissance movement was not slow to move beyond the region of its origin. From Italy it quickly spread among other nations, where all indigenous arts underwent modification in some degree under the impact of Italian art, with prolonged and lasting consequences. After the death of Albrecht Dürer, however, the style of which he was the leading representative did not spread beyond his circle of pupils in the north, and in the 16th century too the Netherlands, which in the previous century had been a leading artistic centre rivalling even Italy, lost some of its forceful originality.

In France the impact of Italian art was just as large-scale, and French artists were carried along on the irresistible current with the rest. However, the results of this revolution, which without doubt raised the level of art in France, have been assessed in more than one way. On the one hand, in the sphere of the decorative arts France had its own original primitive tradition in course of independent development. On the other hand, at a time when large numbers of surplus Italian artists were pouring into the countries of

Europe, especially France, where they were invited by enchanted royalty, they brought with them a simplified taste and tradition which had already moved away from the brilliant era of the Raphaelian Renaissance and so, their personal achievements notwithstanding, they represented merely varieties of decline. It could be that French critical opinion today, more impartial than that of earlier ages with regard to the culture of the periods preceding the reign of Leo X, reflected a certain regret that the national genius was checked in the full flow of its development.

Was this inevitable? Could French art of the time have continued on its course unaffected by the influence of such a neighbour and not taken advantage of Italian artistic achievements and search for the highest ideals? Would it not have lost that naivety and naturalness which gave it a special charm, in part because of its very lack of experience? Would it not have become more conscious and more freely? In art little real progress is achieved without the cost of a loss of originality and native strength, and it is impossible not to regret this. However, the human mind cannot go backwards, but must take the path of change, which has a right to its existence whenever it occurs.

Model ornamental motifs from Jean Cousin the Elder's Livre de perspective, *1560*

Renaissance motifs from a monastery, Pavia

Ornamental motifs attributed to Jean Cousin the Elder

Renaissance motifs from a monastery, Pavia

Among the numerous illustrations of designs having French origins among the Plates to this book, some belong to the high-point of the Italian Renaissance or to its eve, and some to a later epoch. They all bear pronounced traces of an Italian style and of the particular uses found for it by the 16th-century French masters Jean Goujon, Jean Cousin and Baptiste du Cerceau.

Branch ornament with volutes, reign of Henri III

THE 17TH AND 18TH CENTURIES

PLATES 176–220

THESE TWO CENTURIES achieved their greatest distinction as a result of French influence. The period falls into four distinct phases.

The first of these, characterized by the merging of Flemish and Italian forms, comprises the reigns of Henri IV and Louis XIII; the second completes the 17th century with the full splendour of the reign of Louis XIV; the third embraces the end of Louis XIV's reign and all Louis XV's, in the course of which French decorative art pursued a direction of excessive mannerism up to the awakening of the taste for Antiquity aroused by the discovery of bronzes and decorative wall-paintings at Pompeii and Herculaneum, which provided the basis for the last style of Louis XVI's reign.

If French schools in particular were prominent during these two centuries after making use of the discoveries of the Italian Renaissance, the influence exerted by French art actually relates in greater degree to an earlier period which has left a series of monuments universally admired by modern opinion. Thanks to its geographical situation on a cultural crossroads between north and south, and to the faculty of assimilation characteristic of its balanced and keen-eyed genius, from the beginning of the Middle Ages France produced art whose hallmarks came to be recognized as typically French – rigour, a sense of measure, truth of graphic depiction, and clarity of ideas.

A brief survey of the first stages in the development of French art would now be timely; it could not be given in its chronological place earlier because of the necessity of maintaining continuity in our account of the Italian Renaissance and its influence.

Priority in Gothic belongs to France, possessing the oldest and most numerous monuments in this style, and throughout the Gothic period, especially from the beginning of the 13th century, French sculpture and stained-glass windows were celebrated. French masters travelled Europe and brought their style to the German-speaking lands and England, where it flourished most of all. Giving the world an idea of architecture which, in the words of the great architect Émérique David, was 'great, daring, and profoundly thought out', the French 13th, 14th and 15th centuries also produced a large number of painters, sculptors, goldsmiths and glaziers having their schools in provincial towns all over France, each with its own local

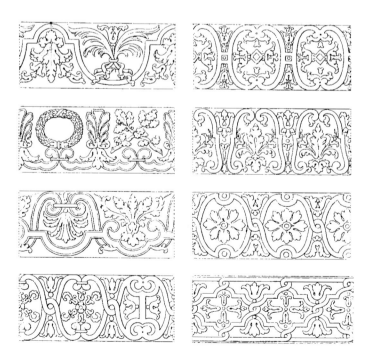

Ornamentation from the church of Saint-Étienne-du-Mont, Paris, 17th century

character. Here was a heaven-sent preparation for a revival of Antique traditions as prescribed by the Italians.

It has today come to be recognized that in all these active schools known by Parisian, Picard, Lotharingian, Tourangeau, Norman, Breton, Burgundian, Gaston and Southern names, in which leading masters worked, the new Italian art was quickly grasped, employed and transformed by French sensibility with results that could not be equalled by the schools of Bruges or Cologne, which earlier in the Gothic period had been successful rivals of the French schools.

While in Italy the brilliance of the first decades of the 16th century was already fading, French artists, already familiar with the new refinement, turned their experience and innate abilities to making full use of it, and regained their former supremacy. Jean Goujon, with his elongated figures of nymphs, came nearer to Ancient Greek art than any of his contemporaries, and Jean Cousin, skilled in all branches of art, graced glass and canvas, manuscripts and book pages, goldwork and faience with the deep knowledge and true taste which singled him out as the real leader of the French school of his time.

The old schools of northern Europe, now transformed (Flanders, the Rhineland provinces and France led these, ranked above the Italian schools), preserved the traditions they had acquired from Fra Giocondo, Leonardo da Vinci, Rosso, Primaticcio, Andrea del Sarto, Benvenuto Cellini, Serlio and Paolo Ponzio Trebati. They included architects such as Jean Bullant, Philibert de L'Orme, Pierre Lescot, and later Baptiste du Cerceau, and with their exquisitely designed ornaments fully belong to our story, as do minor masters of engraved work like Étienne Delon, Theodor de Bry, Virgil Solis, Heinrich Aldegrever, and their 17th-century successors Jacques Maistre, Etienne de la Belle, Michel Blondus, et al.

The engraved work of these masters lies outside the scope of this book, but their ornamental jewellery, little of which has survived, affords too many examples of inventive genius not to be mentioned. The articles made by these master engravers, goldsmiths, carpenters, and ceramic and metal workers (one at the height of the 16th century, the rest towards the end of the century and at the beginning of the 17th) are proof that ornamental work in northern Europe during this period was at a level no longer to be found in Italy, now devoted to Mannerism, popularized by the pale imitators of Michelangelo's lofty but restless style – a style, it was said at the time, in process of being consigned to history. This kind of ornamentation was forging a fanciful style whose cosy and careless principles were to lead to the emergence of the so-called Louis Quinze style a century later. All the same, glorious memories of a golden age of ornamentation gave it a prestige and vaunted superiority that were confirmed only by the past.

Hanging ornament by Gilles Égaret, 18th century

Incised gold incense bowl, 17th century

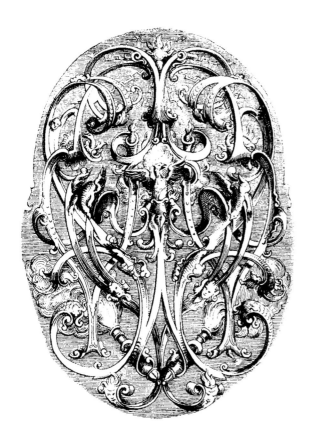

Ornament by Jansen

This was made quite clear when Louis XIV invited Bernini, at the height of his Europe-wide fame, to Paris to complete the building of the Louvre. The master arrived with much pomp, but his plans were found unsatisfactory because his ideas were in conflict with the grand but solid conceptions of the French architects, and he was quickly showered with gifts and honours and sent back home.

Around the turn of the 16th and 17th centuries, the free employment of principles that had become the norm with the Renaissance and that had hitherto been maintained by artists and architects of vigour and originality gave way to a more literal and timid direct imitation of models from Antiquity, which were becoming increasingly plentiful and arousing universal rapture. Following the disasters of that time, a period of relative sterility set in. As a critic of our time puts it: 'at that time Antiquity was inadequately understood; there was probably more desire than ability to imitate it, but enthusiasts were far from understanding its real power and splendid purity' (F.H. Guillemard, *A History of Ornament*).

It should be added that after the Italian digressions during the last period of Valois rule, one reaction of a constructive kind was an impulse to return to common sources. Among these attempts, the first of them so primly elegant, albeit not totally devoid of true grace, the elevated sincerity of Nicolas Poussin's love for Antiquity along with his strongly contemporary character shine out. Plate 176 nos 2–7 and Plate 178 nos 1 (panel at Fontainebleau) and 2 (ceiling in the Louvre) show products of the return to the principles of Roman Antiquity, this being the sole concern of the time. By contrast, the arabesque decoration of Maria Medici's room in the Luxembourg Palace (Plate 178 no. 3) breathes a Renaissance freedom of style, a last reflection of the influence of the Italian school through Louis XIII's first minister Concino Concini.

Contemporaneous with this came a relatively direct return to the Antique style in the detail of decorative and applied art, which was at first furthered by the military victories and style of rule of Henry IV and to which an important part is attributable in the formation of the dominant style of the reign of Louis XIII and the beginning of that of Louis XIV. Flemish ware became fashionable. The modifications that occurred in this style are traced in the anthologies of incised ornaments published between 1607 and 1625, and their special character may be seen in the relevant illustrations to the present volume.

Preserving a reflection of the Italian Renaissance, the new style of ligature in manuscript illuminations and enamels (Plate 178), cartouches, piers and coats of arms (Plate 180) supplements, together with the patterns shown in Plate 177, this multi-faceted model of the new style, which was not long in becoming ponderous and excessive. The style of the first half of the 17th century finds its fullest and most successful expression in the compromise version shown in Plate 180 (nos 1–4). We shall not be detained by the strange forms of the cartouches which make up the rest of this Plate.

Chinese ware, found from this time in the Netherlands, exercised a substantial influence on the emergence of or at least the encouragement of the taste for such designs, the main asset of which was their adaptability, for they could suit all needs and all combinations. The Italians, keen producers of ware of this kind, were content to seek no further.

This success was achieved largely by the joiners, who, like Briez and Christoph Fenlin from Flanders and Friedrich Untentsch from Frankfurt, made a large quantity of heavy and elaborate furniture, imitations of which are still produced to this day. These sumptuous Renaissance

Detail of a fresco by Annibale Carracci, Palazzo Farnese

pieces, surviving examples of which are ample demonstration that the Germans, French and Italians were equally skilled and inventive in this work, represented the meeting-ground for a transformation and merging of the above-mentioned genres. Not even jewellers or painters went to such care in minutiae as the joiners, who at this time were highly educated men.

As a result of Richelieu's appeal following 'the disappointment with the celebrated and unique Mr Poussin, the pride of the French in his profession and the Raphael of our time,' in the words of one of his contemporaries, Jean Le Pautre was placed in a position of virtual leadership of French taste of the era. His emergence from the workshop of Adam Philippon – who called himself 'Joiner and General Engineer to the King [Louis XIII at the end of his reign]' – where he had been an apprentice from an early age, was cause for no little surprise. Philippon was obliged to send his apprentice to Italy in search of 'the most distinguished men in the arts of painting, sculpture and other skills required for the decoration of the royal palaces, and a number of craftsmen and a large quantity of bas-reliefs and sculptures were thus brought to France.' The modest term 'joiner' conceals the huge range of knowledge and expertise that was necessary to this pivotal trade.

When he returned from Italy, Le Pautre was ready to create the numerous and richly detailed compositions which were to usher in the most brilliant splendid era of the Louis XIV style. The lessons he had learned in Italy were not those of the pellucid and graceful school of Raphael. Much time had elapsed since Giulio Romano in Mantua and pupils of Raphael in other parts of Italy had largely exhausted the arabesque genre, which had declined with its increasing tendencies towards garishness.

When Le Pautre was in Italy, he sent back many craftsmen from there. Bernini reigned in Rome; best of all was the fact that this moment was the eve of a great resurgence which the school of Carracci, formed in Bologna at the end of the 16th century, brought to Italian art. At a time when all other Italian schools were in a state of decline, the Bologna school was resuming the finest traditions of the decorative arts, the source from which the fertile mind and lavish tastes of Le Pautre were to draw inspiration. Nothing could have suited his predilections better match than the pomp and grandeur of this Italian decorative school, which on occasion could be marred by bombast and excess.

The decorative work of the Le Pautre school is not of a kind that could be represented in our colour plates. Conceived to be seen in wide perspective and with sharp distinctness, giving an almost trompe l'oeil effect, this decorative style is too remote from today's culture for it to be of practical use outside the architectural context for which it was designed.

Despite its passionate enthusiasm for Antiquity, the culture of the period could not lay hands on it without distorting it, uncomfortable with its starkness. Greater splendour was desired, and so to perfect its image, relative proportions were changed and exaggerated with the abandon shown in the friezes illustrated above.

Frieze with motifs after Jean Le Pautre

The impulse to create greatness was the stumbling-block of the era. Its best outcome was the grand unity which it owed to the great artistic organizers and managers, the architect François Mansart and the painter and aesthetic codifier Charles Lebrun, men who possessed the essential qualifications to direct the course of art in all its manifestations. Each of these artists headed a collective of great Italians, presiding with absolute authority over all domains: 'sculptural work, ornaments of domestic interiors, tapestries, jewellery and metalwork, mosaics, tables, vases, chandeliers and candelabra – everything passed through his hands, and nothing was done at court that had not been conceived by him and executed under his direction' (L. and R. Menard, *A Historical Picture of the Fine Arts*).

The Louis Quatorze style. The prodigious quantity of public and private buildings created more or less spontaneously under Louis XIV gave France an appearance radically different from previous times. From north to south, east to west, everywhere that this style of architecture was to be seen which, by no means devoid of greatness, by placing external splendour before all else often found itself in disharmony with the main objective. The urgent task of simultaneously decorating a huge quantity of new buildings throughout the country

Details of cartouches with motifs after Le Pautre

*Frieze with motifs after Jean
Le Pautre*

*Everyday ornamentation,
17th century*

necessitated a massive construction effort from French industry and the employment of a multitude of craftsmen and artisans. Inevitably this led to a large-scale slackening of attention to the planning and execution of detail.

The individuality of the provincial schools vanished in this mighty flow, in which only models approved by the central authorities could be proceeded with. Unfortunately, the forms employed were oversimplified and sometimes faded and strange, mannered and heavy, and would not infrequently spoil the look of an ensemble in which an excess of detail wearied the eye, but overall, thanks to its unprecedented splendour, the style won through.

At this time when most Italian craftsmen were busy at their worst work and all the rest of Europe was following them, the French were exceptional in employing these excessive forms while at the same time maintaining their innate sense of correctness and measure. The national level of education rested on outstanding institutions initiated by Richelieu and developed by Mazarin and Colbert. The direction of highly trained master craftsmen developing the Louvre Palace produced high-quality work in all specialties which gave the whole ensemble a special distinction, notwithstanding some defects of principle.

The shortcoming already mentioned in relation to architectural style was everywhere apparent. As a rule, there was a lack of feeling that could inspire the decorative arts to special adaptation to specific objectives. There was one model, and one model only, for all the construction planned, and little attention was given to the special purposes of different types of building.

On the other hand, the accumulated expertise was very great, and although it was sometimes abused, every master was well able to make use of his knowledge. Eastern techniques were among those employed in the decorative field. Rational use was made of these in fashionable forms; faience was given an Oriental look with a decoration comprising lambrequins and a conventionalized geometric pattern in optional colours with light branch ornamentation on a plain background (see Plate 196). The tapestry decorations shown in Plate 194 follow the same principles. Of these, in which garish colours and doubtful taste create much confusion, it must be said that the design itself (nos 1 and 2) is surprisingly instructive. These decorations display practically the whole gamut of elements that can be combined in endless variations without changing their essential character. Thick rose forms at intersections, canopies, cartouches, urns and bouquets, freely designed volutes from which acanthus leaves sprout, concealing them or being revealed from them, plastic embellishments placed upon branch ornaments, and finally, the firmly drawn curving lines of a branch ornament with a figure chancing to appear on its end – all this is included in these decorations, typical of their period.

Lower parts of an ornamental chalice, style of Berain

The Boulle style overlays shown in Plate 190 also follow the sound decorative principles to be seen on Eastern ware, as do the motifs illustrated in Plate 195. The branch ornaments with

slender volutes and the leatherware shown in Plates 186 (no. 4) and 197 respectively belong in this series. Comparison of the separated and richly decorated palmettes which feature prominently in Plate 197 with their Classical Greek originals will be sufficient to give an exact idea of the decorative technique being employed at this time. These palmettes, together with the elements enumerated above, run through the entire Louis Quatorze ornamental programme.

The leading representatives of this period of French decorative art are Jean Berain and Daniel Marot. The former was in much demand; if some reservation is to be made regarding the taste which dominates his work, with its abundance of grotesques, it certainly springs from a powerful imagination. As for the frescos in the Apollo Gallery in the Louvre (Plate 191), which he was inspired to paint by Raphael's pyramidal compositions and erudition, they undeniably display a genuine and versatile talent.

Daniel Marot, whose graceful designs and fertile imagination in due course brought him to work in his homeland, was not, like Berain, a graphic artist at the French court from the beginning of his career. This Protestant master was obliged by the Revocation of the Edict of Nantes to emigrate to the Netherlands and then followed Prince William of Orange to England, where he became architect to King William III. His 260-plate album published in 1712 testifies to his remarkable talent and inventiveness. He could turn his hand to anything: beds, dining chairs, fauteuils, tables, mirrors, torchères, wall clocks, tapestry and horse-cloth designs, fabric patterns – and 'thousands of everyday articles, from kettles to clock hands'. At the same time he was director of festivals and organizer of state funerals, which he portrayed in engravings.

Robert de Cotte and Claude Gillot are among the representatives of the last phase of the Louis Quatorze style. De Cotte's carpet and tapestry designs shown in Plates 201 and 202 achieve a new refinement, and Gillot's work in the tapestry border images seen in Plate 203 (nos 1–3) even more so. Increased highlighting of decorative detail and rigorous use of basic elements are the hallmarks of a refined style the effect of which is somewhat spoiled by the cartouches of barbarous figures intended to convey a state of peace.

Emblematic cartouche, 17th century

This style is also seen in the same transitional forms in the rich decorative painting on a gold background shown in Plate 204 and in the exquisite ceiling decoration in half-grisaille in Plate 199. There is an increasingly marked tendency, in this stylistic progression, towards a more distinct palette for the background of decorative work, and this will soon become the norm.

The Louis Quinze style has become the inter-national term for the next stage in the evolution of ornament, which took place in the 1720s. Its leading initiators were the architects Gilles-Marie Oppenord and Juste-Aurèle Meissonnier, and it receives its full portrayal in the decorative engravings of P.E. Babel and J.J. Balechou.

This development came about in the first place because of the vast amount of ornament that had become part of the stock of French craftsmen in the time of Louis XIV, and secondly because of the impact of Francesco Borromini. This great Baroque architect and sculptor worked at the basilica of St Paul Outside the Walls under Bernini and died in 1667, having caused lively excitement with his airy broken lines and great inventiveness.

In spite of this brilliant precedent and the revived energy of Italy, it fell to France to give the new style the name of its king, which was universally accepted, even in Italy.

Typical moulded ornaments, 18th century

After mastering the means of overthrowing all hitherto accepted principles of the orders, the French school succeeded in setting a seal of lightness, grace and its own spirit on free use of the forms that it favoured, something that the Italian and the German craftsmen of the period were unable to do.

The new principles, or rather the overthrow of all hitherto established principles, and the invasion of the new forms did not prevail in France without an intense struggle, in which the adherents of the old principles had some success in their defence. Never before had such inventiveness, such knowledge and such art been brought to bear on such controversial doctrines.

'We rejected all the forms for which,' wrote Charles Cochin ironically, 'we felt a superstitious respect, our guide was simply our personal taste, and each of us had to show it.' And if, despite the dangers of such freedom, victory went to the side of the innovators, this happened because the artists who protested on behalf of more rational principles did not have the rank enjoyed by those who were the protagonists of the mannered style that was to seize the upper hand.

The deviations that took place when less able hands took control brought such excesses and such artistic decline that no more appropriate moment could have been imagined for Greek Antiquity to come back to life, in all the glory of its immortal youth, when it cast aside the cover of lava that had preserved it.

However dubious from the point of view of general principles the independent and audacious ventures may have been of the brilliant school from which the glory of French 18th-century decorative art emerged, it is impossible not to concede that it gave the nation an enchanting style from which, beneath its apparent frivolity and through the prism of a thousand of its caprices, we gain a remarkable understanding of the requirements of domestic furnishing which play such an important role in modern manners – and that this style sets, in sum, an example which has not been lost for the decorative and applied arts of our own time.

On the other hand, it should be remembered that this style replaced that of the first years of the 18th century, when Gillot, and his pupils after him, especially Watteau, produced lightly whimsical, unnaturalistic decorative designs acceptably enough for their clients. From this point of view, the advantage of the models for the new school, whatever their origins, was at least their form – more rational, more in accord with the traditional logic of the nation. It seems quite understandable to us today, therefore, that the new style, despite its limitations, possesses these qualities and has won the day despite opposition from numerous critics, given most powerful utterance by the engraver Cochin in the *Mercure de France*, whose fiery tirades now seem excessive.

Moulded ornament, 18th century

In fact, time, giving its due to certain errors, did not uphold all the partial opinions that had been so forcefully expressed, the prejudices of all those who maintained, for example, that *a candlestick should always stand up straight and completely perpendicular to give the best light, and not be bent, as if someone had forced it into that shape*. With such a store of gifted artists during this exceptional period, the real connoisseurs had long since settled questions which were now superfluous in the prescriptions of the ornamental genre.

Overall, this period, with its audacity and high levels of skill, may be said to be one of the most fascinating in the whole history of ornament. It met, however, with an incommensurate fate.

The higher forms of art descended to the humble level of ornamentation and performed an active service to it. Following in the wake of the magic world of Watteau, so finely drawn and so warmly painted, came the pearl-grey empyreans and bucolic scenes and hazy blue landscapes of the erotic Boucher. Here were developments of special significance for ornament, such as, in particular, the frames of cheval glass.

The work of ornamentalists rose in status, and they began to lay down prescriptions with an authority that had been denied them when they had been artists on a secondary level.

Following Oppenord, Meissonnier, a trained architect who had worked on the church of Saint-Sulpice, Paris, took up the new style with some reservation. Calling himself 'Painter, Sculptor, Architect and Designer and Decorator of the Royal State and Private Rooms', he aimed to encourage the impulse that Le Pautre and Marot had given the decorative and applied arts – what Cochin unjustly dismissed as 'jolly architecture freed of all the rules that used to be called good taste'.

The Paris jeweller and decorative engraver P.E. Babel, who understood Rococo better than anyone else, set up as a provider of architectural models. Such an appropriation of the rights of others may seem surprising until it is realized that the all-round knowledge and training of the leading decorative artists of the time to some extent explains their claims without justifying them. The famous jeweller Thomas Germain provided architectural drawings and at the same time made silverware; it was he who executed the drawings for the new church of St Louis in the Louvre, built in 1738 on the site of the old collegiate church of St Thomas.

An analysis of the ornamentation of this period, when every artist wrote his signature on his work with his witty pen, which today's specialists seek to identify, need not keep within the strict bounds of our story. Every ornament of this era, whether from the hand of Meissonnier, Babel or Balechou, Jean-Daniel de Preisler or Jacques de la Joue, Jean-André Telot or Jeremy Wachsmuth, Jean-Léonard de Vuyst or Jean-Léonard Eisler, Charles Potier or A. Masson, is executed with a painterly truth that is very often at odds with the actual requirements of surface decoration.

Cartouche with motifs after P. E. Babel

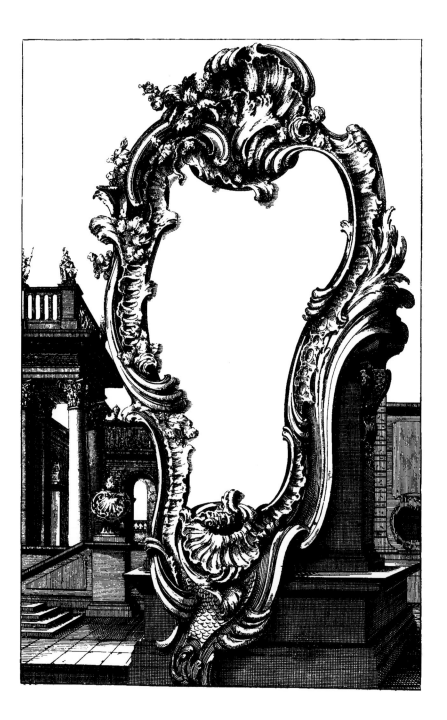

Thus the main consequence of the dominant role of painting was its impulse to replace the *conventionalized* image with the *imitative* one which we noted at the beginning of this survey as belonging to an essentially modern approach.

The main formal feature of the Louis Quinze style is the almost complete avoidance of straight lines in favour of every possible permutation of S-shaped lines, and the absence of all square, round and oval shapes, all in a grand manner. Its most successful exponent was Meissonnier.

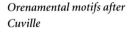

Orenamental motifs after Cuville

The *rocaille* style, which was to take possession of all the decorative and applied arts in the 18th century, would seem to have originated in garden design, already fashionable in the 16th century; its exact source is unknown. The Chinese frequently made use of rocaille, central in the formation of the Rococo movement, in garden design and in decorative design in general, and it is likely that the 18th century took this element of the Louis Quinze style from these opponents of symmetry. Be that as it may, the French were the main creators of the models for the Rococo style.

Cartouche in rocaille style

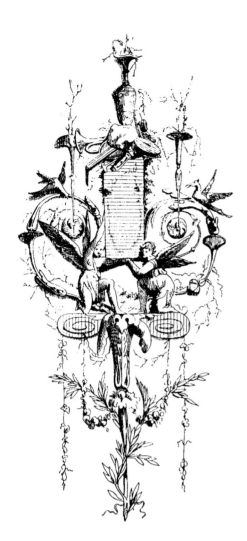

Ornament with motifs after Salambier

Plate 209 shows a series of cartouches contrasting late examples of the Louis XIV style by artists persisting in their 'errors' with creations of extreme fantasy by artists of the fashionable new school of the time. Nos 2, 3, 12 and 13 are by Bernard Picart, who worked in Amsterdam from 1720 to 1730. No. 1 was painted in Paris in 1740. Nos 4 and 5, in symmetrical style but without straight lines, employ branch ornaments and belong to the transitional period between Louis Quatorze and Louis Quinze. No. 9 by Isaiah Nielson (1752) and nos 10 and 11 by de la Joue belong to the high-point of Rococo. These last examples and no. 8 and the frame behind the fan shown in Plate 213 include shell forms and chicory motifs which had come into fashion, replacing the acanthus leaf which almost completely disappeared.

The danger of over-fanciful ideas, which were pursued for some time by unquestionably skilled artists who could handle all materials with exemplary versatility, was soon seen when their conceptions fell into less skilled hands. Having produced a whole world of enchantment from such illustrators as Hubert-François Gravelot, G.-F. Lebas and Augustin de St Aubin, to name three of many, the Louis Quinze style was to fade with the awakening of the passion for Antiquity. While representatives of Louis Quinze style continued to work up to 1789, this last phase was marred by the above-mentioned excesses of bad taste.

The Louis Seize style. Even at the beginning of Louis XVI's reign there were many advocates for a return to a simpler ornamental style. The discovery of Herculaneum early in the 18th century focused minds on the site long before excavators achieved tangible results in the 1750s. The architectural response led by Giovanni Servandoni and his pupil Charles de Wailly soon had its effect on other forms of decorative and applied art, but did not find its ultimate expression until the reign of Louis XVI.

The works of Reisner, Gouthière and Demontière, the compositions of Lalonde and the superb branch ornaments of Salambier represent *par excellence*, in their different genres, the Louis Seize ornamental style, which has come into fashion in our day (see Plates 213–18 and accompanying text). The style was thoroughly demonstrated in a number of reference works published during the period, with titles such as *Ornaments for Domestic Interiors: Paintings and Sculptures; Sculptures, Furniture, Jewellery and Ironwork; Decorative Paintings of Flowers and Ornaments; Jewellery Pieces*; and *Candlesticks and Chandeliers*.

If we end this brief survey on the threshold of the Revolution of 1789, it is not for want of appreciation of the significant developments that have taken place in our own century in the various fields of decorative and applied art or of the prospect of a fruitful outcome of those developments in the future. The moment has not yet come, however, for dispassionate appraisal of the achievements of the 19th century, and especially not for any final determination of their character as seen either through the prism of the successive partialities with which they were first viewed or from the broad eclectic viewpoint that has replaced them in our own time.

For France, the finding of an enduring new direction in the decorative arts has been particularly problematic and beset with obstacles. Our political upheavals and long-drawn-out wars scattered and disrupted both our aristocratic and enlightened connoisseurs and, worse still, the craftsmen and artisans educated in the spirit of the strong and long-standing traditions of French working life, cast by fanaticism and unemployment into the cauldron of 1792 from which few were recovered. Consequently, the task for the century following those events has been twofold and long-term: the reform of public taste and the creation of new educational centres.

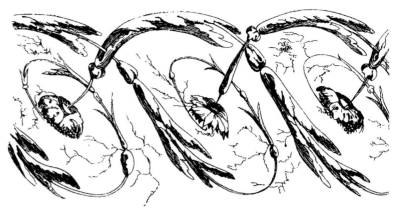

It is no surprise, therefore, that the stylistic quest required time: first, during the Empire, turning to Antiquity once more, and then, during the Restoration and the literary movement of the 1830s, to Gothic, before a wholesale return to the decorative styles of the 17th and 18th centuries and eventually to a fruitful study of Far Eastern ornamental art. Out of these experiments and the vigorous controversy that they aroused, a more enlightened, liberal and rational view of earlier periods has been reached today. Art history has been rewritten for our time by many writers and archaeology has contributed new knowledge that enables us to restore missing links to the broken chain of tradition. Thus freed from exclusive and preconceived ideas, we can now conduct knowledgeable investigations of the past and make rational choices from the riches amassed for us by our predecessors.

The resources and diversity of art of the present time have been bequeathed to us by the 16th, 17th and 18th centuries in countless magnificent models of decorative ensembles, excellently attuned to our own way of life. And in the arts of Antiquity too, in the ware of Asia and the Near East, 13th- and 14th-century stained-glass windows, Limoges enamels, Renaissance faience, art of our time can find, or already has found, strong and original elements, simple and direct methods, lofty ornamental conventions; it can find that power of affect latent in colour, that opportunity for creation or idealization which elevates the work of the ornamentalist and inspires a modern master to give this definition of his art:

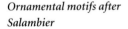

Ornamental motifs after Salambier

'Ornament,' writes Mr Guillaume, Director of the École des Beaux-Arts, should not deform the surfaces that it embellishes; it settles on these surfaces, it forms an entity with them or attaches itself to them; it should not proclaim itself, either by penetrating them or in any way separating itself from them … *This is a very ideal form of art.* To a greater degree than the painter or the sculptor, the ornamentalist imagines that his art must not serve the representation of the real world, but some organism which is at the same time elevated and dependent.

Reared on such principles, we can be confident that our school of today will take new steps along the path that our recent exhibitions have pointed out to us, discovering in the study of the best styles not the easy path of slavish imitation or commercial copying but the inspiration to produce original work which will in its turn come to be taken as exemplary and one day help to write the history of decorative and applied art of the 19th century.

PLATES

1   PRIMITIVE ART

Fabrics, wood carving and painting

Although the examples of motifs shown are taken from various sources, their civilisations have a distinct similarity.

1 Fabric (Oceania);

2 Fabric (Central Africa);

3 Woven matting made from coloured plant fibres (Central Africa);

4 Fabric trimmed with woven braid (Oceania);

5 Fabric trimmed with woven braid (Central Africa);

6–11 Painted deep carving on wooden utensils (Central Africa);

12 Circular fan made of coloured feathers (Central Africa);

13 Edge of a painted wooden vessel (Central Africa);

14–17 Painted decoration on a canoe and utensils (Oceania);

18–21 Painted decoration on Peruvian utensils;

22–47 Pictorial miniatures from Mexican manuscripts.

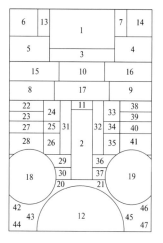

PLATE 1

2 EGYPTIAN ART

High reliefs and bas-reliefs
Small decorative objects

This plate displays objects that vary greatly in
size, from monumental statues to miniature
bottles (18) or a pot of eye ointment (13),
as well as examples of murals and bas-reliefs.
This has been done so as to stress their
individual features and to draw our attention
to the multiplicity of artistic means that were
used by Ancient Egyptian craftsmen, despite the
stylistic unity of the ornamentation. A lack of
space obliges us to give merely an indication of
individual groups of ornaments and individual
allusions to religious symbolism, and also to
give a generalised indication of the rules for the
plastic arts of the time.

The lower part of the plate contains frontal
and side depictions of the high relief figure
of a caryatid (14, 15) that decorates one of
the columns of the sun god, Ra, in Ipsambul
(called Abu Simbel, 'Father of the Ear of Corn',
by the Arabs);

Depiction in profile of the goddess (21)
from the Temple of Isis on the island of Philae
(2nd century BC);

So-called 'standard' from the tomb of Ramses
the Great (Sesostris) (20).

Vase paintings also include exotic human
figures (4, 12). A vase (4) with a characteristic
stopper was intended for keeping balsam:
the aromatic was brought to Egypt as a
tribute that the pharaohs of the 19th dynasty
(the dynasty started by Ramses I) demanded
from a conquered Syria.

The animal kingdom is represented by a
hedgehog-shaped vessel for holding eye drops,
and fitted with a small spoon or spade, and
the magnificent depiction in profile of a heron;
as active helpers of mankind these insectivores
were especially revered by the Egyptians.

The sacred scarab (8) is part of the bas-relief
surround to the entrance to the tomb of Ramses
V in Thebes. According to ancient authors,
only a few varieties of these Coleoptera were
the 'sacred scarabs' that were venerated by the
Ancient Egyptians.

The lotus flower, the symbol of rebirth, was
a very widespread decorative motif (1, 3, 9,
16, 19, 22); it could be moulded or painted, as
a bud or an open flower and by itself or in a
magnificent bouquet.

Crowned by a solar disc, a lotus flower on its
stem (5) decorated the bow of a ship;

The same motif, in a more schematic form,
became the handle of an ordinary metal
mirror (11).

A slip-glazed ceramic bowl is strikingly
decorated with lanceolate leaves that emphasise
its shape.

Necklace (23) made of lapis lazuli beads and
gold pendants.

Plate 2

3 EGYPTIAN ART

Sculptural decoration

1, 2 Columns from the palace of Tuthmosis III in Karnak (18th dynasty). The ornamentation consists of lotus and papyrus stems with open flowers (left) and stylised leafless plants (right). Bas-relief;

3 Pillar from a pavilion. Its pattern goes back to the 4th dynasty, in the period when buildings were made of wood. The pillar is in the form of a stem surmounted by a bud; a cord is wound five times around the young shoots at the base of the flower's calyx, representing the birth of the concept of the bouquet. It has a very low socle;

4, 5 The tops of similar pillars, made of wood with polychrome decoration;

6 Pillar from a pavilion, surmounted by a half-open flower. Great attention has been paid to the ornamentation whose magnificence is emphasised by the magnificence of the bouquet formed of young shoots with buds that are more open;

7, 8 Columns from stone buildings (18th dynasty). The carved capital is in the shape of a closed bud; the upper part is smooth so that its diameter coincides with the width of the square socle. This is the earliest and most widespread form of capital in Egyptian stone architecture. On the left is a column that is typical for the buildings of the temple ensembles of Amenhotep III in Thebes and Tuthmosis III in Karnak. On the right is a column from the palace of Gurnah, which is known as the Menephteum, from Menephta I who reigned after Amenhotep III (called Memnon by the Greeks);

9 Capital of a column from the hall of columns in the Ramesseum (Temple of Ramses II) in Thebes (19th dynasty) The Egyptian 'plant' capital here achieves its peak, and is a magnificent combination of grace and strength. The shape of the open flower recalls an upturned bell, and decorative elements in the form of the stalks of stylised bouquets of flowers are located around it;

10 Capital with carved 'digitate' decoration from the Great Temple on the island of Philae. The pointed leaves of the capital, which is also shaped like an upturned bell, form the pattern of a basket made from woven plants. Bunches of figs and even the scaly bark of a tree appear in the ornamentation. As the flora changes, so does the plant decor.

4   EGYPTIAN ART

Decorative painting

As a rule, the significance of the main elements that make up Egyptian ornamentation is linked to the hieroglyphic writing system. Thus a pink sphere with hawk's wings (6) symbolises the rising sun. The tall water plants alternating with the stems of reeds (4, 5) grow up out of the waters of a river. The scarab, whose black body stands out against the background, is a symbol of immortality. The Egyptian palette consisted of red, blue and yellow, as well as black and white (for outlining); green was normally used for plant forms, and was often replaced by blue.

1–3 Stylised plant motifs;

4, 5 Backgrounds, friezes and stylobates from Theban columns;

6 Painted stone carving from the Memnonium (the Mortuary Temple of Amenhotep II) in Thebes;

7 Continuous frieze;

8, 9 Painted wood carving from pillars;

10, 11 Continuous friezes;

12 Painted vaults.

5   EGYPTIAN ART

Murals
Repeating backgrounds and friezes
Decorative curtains

Apart from the friezes (4, 5), the fragments consist of ceiling paintings from the necropolis in Thebes and funerary monuments of various periods. The compositions spring totally from the artist's imagination.

We can still make out the lotus flower, but the stem (if there is one) has lost its plant nature and turned into a decorative loop (6): in reality there is no stem and the flower is depicted freely.

The artist is interested only in the play of the lines formed by his outlines in order to create repeating patterns on horizontal friezes (4, 5), or else, using alternately upturned elements, to fill out the horizontal bands of the background (1, 3).

The picture is made more prominent through the combinations of colours, and the examples given here speak louder than words of the mastery that the Ancient Egyptian artists had achieved in this field.

It should be remembered that the ornamentation of the paintings has a very specific nature: this is in reality the typical décor of the woven curtains that were popular in the East in antiquity.

Curtains complemented Egyptian architecture beautifully: they were hung on walls and between columns so as to separate the main hall from adjacent rooms; they were laid on floors, closed off doorways and, in the case of most of our examples, covered the ceilings of rooms.

6 EGYPTIAN ART

Jewellery

The examples of Egyptian jewellery found in tombs are of great interest to the ornamentalist. The rigid nature of Egyptian decoration that was typical of metal-working proved to be an excellent means of expression in the hands of a stonecutter.

1 Pectoral ornament using cloisonné enamel, with the name of Ramses II in the cartouche (19th dynasty, Middle Kingdom);

2 Ornament made of gold with cloisonné enamel. From the Temple of the god Apis in Memphis;

3 Scarab with lapis lazuli body and wings made of rows of variegated beads. Egyptians considered the scarab to be a symbol of immortality;

4 Necklace with a pendant shaped like the head of Apis;

5–7 Cloisonné enamel bracelets (details);

8, 9 Rings;

10–26 Ear-rings, necklace and amulets;

27 Sphinx: a lion with a human head (detail from the decoration of a stele). In Egypt the sphinx personified physical and mental strength;

28–34 Jewellery copied from Theban murals.

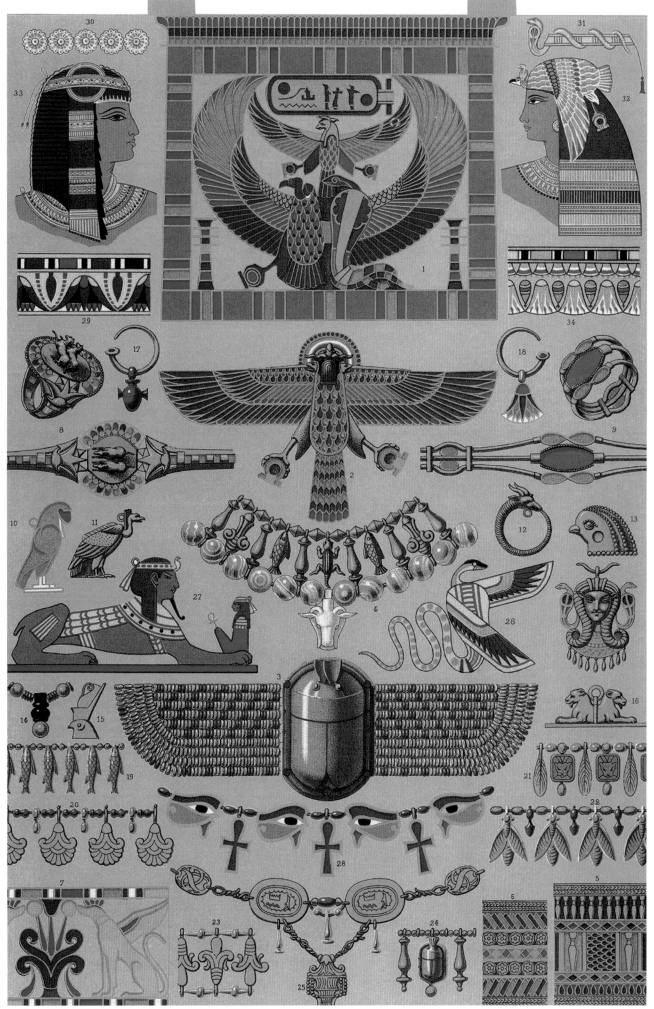

7 ASSYRIAN ART

Polychrome ornamental motifs

Assyrian art divides into two distinct periods. The first period dates from the founding of Babylon by the nomadic tribes of the Nabateans (or Nabutheans) in a marshy valley in the Kingdom of Chaldea. Reeds, wood and adobe were used for building, due to the lack of stone, and this unavoidably limited the possibilities for Babylonian architecture. The second period is marked by the founding of Nineveh, the Assyrian capital, by Scythian conquerors of Babylonia, where an abundance of stone and basalt gave an impetus to the appearance of monumental architecture on a scale previously unknown to the Babylonians. Many of the Assyrian architectural monuments in the museums of Paris and London, like the motifs shown in this plate, belong to the period of Nineveh, or Scytho-Babylonian period. *Palace of King Nimrod in Khorsabad, Nineveh.*

  1–4 Painted stone carving;

    5 Brick with an inlaid coloured pattern;

 6–10 Slip-glazed tiles;

11–18 Stylised ornamental motifs;

19, 20 Murals;

21–23 Restored decorations. *Persepolis.*

24–33 Restored decorations.

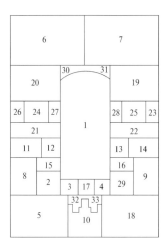

Plate 7

Stylised plant motifs

The stylised flora of Greek ornamentation is a long way from an accurate representation of specific types of plant. The types of ornamentation and the structure of plants, which are all based on free lines, are quite monotonous, and Greek vase painting echoes the decoration on architecture. Individual plant forms are, however, treated naturalistically, and as a rule laurel, ivy, vines and aloe are easily identifiable.

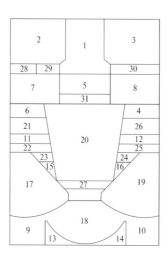

The plate shows plant features that decorate Greek architecture, and the same flora expressed with much more naturalness on vases from Apulia.

1 Painted antefix from the Temple of Zeus Hellanios. Aegina:

2–4 Terracotta articles from Athens;

5, 6 Vase painting;

7 Vase painting. Campania;

8–12 Vase painting;

13–16 Rows of egg and dart ornamentation in conjunction with a meandering wavy frieze;

17–20 Vase painting. Apulia;

21–30 Meandering ornamentation. For the Greeks this ornamentation symbolised the separation of water from dry land.

PLATE 8

9 ANCIENT GREEK ART

Standard polychrome and monochrome ornamentation of the finest periods.

Motifs 2 and 12–14 are capitals of Ionic columns (12 and 13 are front and side views of a capital with moulded volutes). Both motifs go back to the decoration of the Temple of Nike Apteros and the Erechtheion in the Acropolis in Athens. In this type of architectural decoration only the flat surface between the elevated sections was painted, or the actual low relief pattern in the Egyptian style.

Details of painted ceramics (1, 3–8, 10, 11) illustrate two different principles in ornamentation. Monochrome vases with yellow figures against a black background or black figures against yellow are shown, as well as small vessels with a polychrome colouring consisting of yellow, red, blue and green tones on a white background.

Motif 11 decorates an amphora (found on the island of Chios in 1851) made in the Etruscan style.

Motif 3 shows the decorative frieze of a vase: the inhabitants of the undersea world, including a squid, are swimming in their element, which is indicated by the wavy lines of the meander above and below.

Motif 4, the seizure of Ganymede by Zeus in the form of an eagle, reflects the combination of the worlds of earth and air; Mount Ida is represented by fern stems.

Motif 10 shows a detail of a Bacchic scene.

Motifs 1, 3, 4 and 10 decorate vases from Apulia. The Greeks established a large number of colonies in southern Italy, and the decoration of most Apulian vases is linked to the cult of Dionysus (the Roman Bacchus) that the Greeks brought with them to Etruria.

Motif 9 is a decorative plaque in the form of a mosaic bas-relief showing a personification of Hope, called 'Elpis' by the Greeks and 'Spes' by the Romans, and who was especially revered by both peoples.

PLATE 9

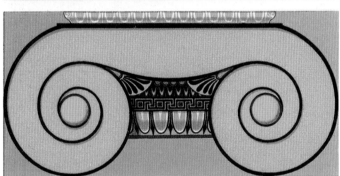

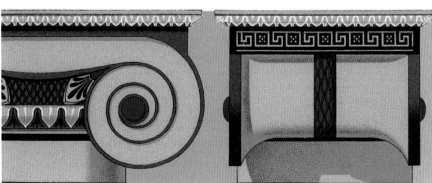

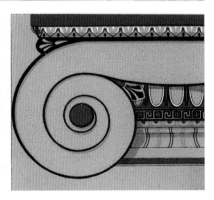

10 CLASSICAL ART

Polychrome ornamental motifs

Multi-coloured decorative motifs are typical for various periods in Ancient Greek art.

1–3 Decorations on friezes and a drainage trough after the restoration of the Parthenon. Athens;

4 Decoration on a frieze in the Temple of the goddess Nike Apteros. Athens;

5 Detail of classical architecture (cornice);

6 Antefix from the Temple of Nike Apteros. Athens;

7–9 Details of classical buildings. Athens;

10 Moulded decoration above a door in the Temple of Athena Polios. Athens;

11 Decoration on a frieze from a temple in Paestum;

12, 13 Decorations on friezes from the Temple of Zeus Hellanios. Aegina:

14 Star of the Propylaea. Athens;

15 Upper part of a cornice forming a drainage trough. Found in Metaponto;

16 Front and lower surface of a terracotta decoration from Metaponto (it formed the facing on beams);

17 Painted shaped decoration;

18, 19 Decoration: volutes;

20, 21 Decoration: meander;

22 Detail of a sarcophagus with painted coloured decoration from Agrigento (Italy);

23 Topmost part of a parapet slab from the Temple of Nemesis. Rhamnous;

24 Detail of a mosaic. Sicily;

25–27, 29 Decoration: interlacing (Greco-Roman style);

28 Meander (Greco-Roman style);

30–33 Decoration on terracotta artefacts found in Palazzolo Acreide;

34 Decorations;

35 Decoration: palmettes.

11 ETRUSCAN ART

Jewellery

The oldest ornaments shown in this plate belong to the late period of the Roman Republic. The choice of motifs clearly demonstrates the influence of Greek and Egyptian decorative art, and the popularity of the scarab is an indication of the latter influence.

The hand-shaped brooch, with a bracelet and a ring on its finger, which turns into a snake (top centre) is probably of Greek origin, as is the signet ring mounted with a precious stone (2). The pendant earrings are considered a masterpiece of Etruscan jewellery art. In the upper right of the plate is an earring shaped like the miniature body of a child supporting a cornucopia.

The necklace (1) is shown half its actual size.

The rings (2, 3) and earrings (6, 7) are reduced in size.

Intricate hairpins (4, 5); the head of the pin, which is shaped like the hand of the goddess Venus holding an apple (right), is probably of Greek origin.

The purpose of the remaining decorations is not so clear; some betray indications of late-Byzantine and even Gothic influence, and this leads to doubts about their Etruscan origins.

12 CLASSICAL ART

Murals
Painted bas-reliefs and their imitations
Features of architectural decoration
The palette of Pompeii

Motifs 1 and 2 go back to the decorations of a temple (possibly the Temple of Venus) near the forum in Pompeii. This temple, a kind of hybrid of architectural styles, was built in the severe Doric style and was subsequently decorated with architectural features from the Corinthian order. Colour was used to emphasise the dividing lines and the wide border, and also to make the features of the moulded bas-relief stand out.

3 An example of painted architectural ornamentation that imitates a relief. It decorated a temple in Pompeii that, according to legend, was dedicated to Jupiter.

4 A socle painted onto a flat wall, imitating black and brown masonry. A simple change in colour is sufficient to give the impression of different designs and moulding. This imitation was on the walls of the Comitium (a building in the forum where public assemblies took place), which formed part of the forum's portico.

The second example of this type of 'architectural' decoration (5) was located in the so-called Pantheon, which was intended for solemn ceremonies such as religious sacrifices, funerals of public figures or important political events.

The picture in the last fragment (6) is so elegant that it could be successfully transferred to decorative glass. Bands with this type of painted ornamentation often provide upper and lower borders to Pompeian decoration.

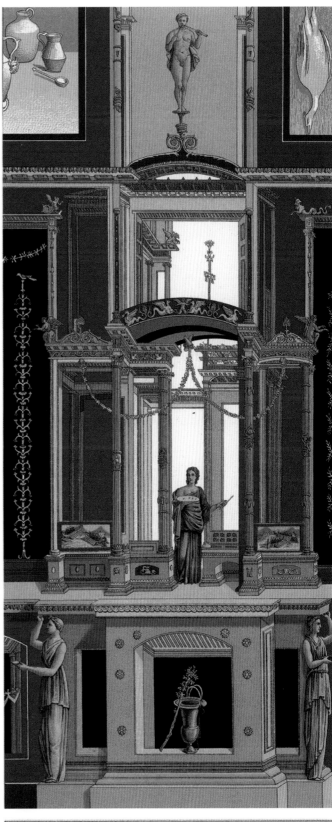

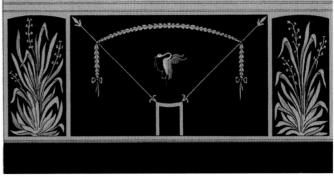

13 CLASSICAL ART

Architectural decoration
Pompeian style

These conventional and purely decorative architectural compositions, which originate from the frescoes of Herculaneum and Pompeii, belong more to the realm of the imagination than to reality. Tradition has it that Ludius, an artist of the time of Augustus, painted these graceful and improbable compositions which are often placed on a background of marine views or landscapes, and sometimes contain human figures. Compositions like these, which were produced by Greek or Etruscan masters working under Greek influence, delighted the Latins who looked not so much for the familiar forms of local architecture with its characteristic vaults and arcades, as for the elegance and poetry of the Greek art that they adored.

Neither figure is part of the original decorations. The central one, a sculpture of a woman dancing, was discovered during excavations at Torre Annunziata. It is the finest of the twelve figures found there, and belongs to the type that Pliny called *libidine* (lustful). The small figure of the winged genius with Bacchic features (in the upper medallion) was discovered during excavations at Civita Castellana.

Plate 13

14 CLASSICAL ART

Mosaics, painted bas-reliefs and frescoes

Even in remote antiquity decorative mosaics were very widespread. It is difficult to identify exactly when the Greeks, and then the Romans, took the step from the decorative mosaic floor to figural mosaics. The oanly certainty is that sumptuous mosaic floors came into use in Greece through Asian influence during the time of Alexander the Great. According to Pliny, mosaics imitating frescoes, and made from cubes of natural coloured stones or chemically coloured pieces of glass, did not appear in Rome until the time of Emperor Vespasian (69–79 AD). Multi-coloured geometric patterns that combined features of classical and eastern ornamentation, and often with inserts of figures, covered all the surfaces in Roman houses, villas and temples.

1–7 Mosaics from Herculaneum and Pompeii (imitating the marble reliefs of Greek craftsmen of the Classical and Hellenistic period);

6 From the House of the Fawn;

7 From the House of Polybius. Pompeii;

8, 9 Relief mosaics from the same place;

10–20 Ornamentation on panels, borders, friezes and frescoes.

15 CHINESE ART

Ornamentation: meanders and lambrequins

The motifs shown here decorate both ancient and modern Chinese bronze vases that are inlaid with copper, silver or gold. Many of them can be seen in the 42-volume engraved catalogue of the complete collection of Chinese vases in the Imperial Museum in Peking (French National Library, Paris). Many of them were unfortunately lost during the storming of the Summer Palace.

In this catalogue the ornamentalist will find a large amount of material to study, in addition to the meanders shown in this plate; their liveliness is quite unlike the linear severity of their Greek counterparts. The symmetrical yet varied decorative compositions give an excellent idea of ornamentation in Ancient China and could find a wide application in the field of modern manufacturing.

PLATE 15

Embroidery and imitation embroidery

The two motifs shown here decorated Chinese official dress. The upper one is the pectoral decoration of a Chinese mandarin and the lower is the edging to the hem of a ceremonial dress.

There were 18 ranks of civil and military mandarins (senior officials) in China, with different pectoral symbols, i.e. squares of cloth sewn or pinned to the dress and with an embroidered or drawn representation of a real or a mythical bird (for civil mandarins) or four-legged animals (for military mandarins). Our example, with the depiction of a phoenix, belonged to a civil mandarin of the first rank. The semi-naturalistic and semi-symbolic decoration that fills the small square represents a cosmogonical panorama of the world to which the presence of the mythical bird gives real meaning: the magical awakening of nature under the life-giving rays of the sun.

From *The Sun*, we move to *The Flood*. The part of the edging on the hem of the ceremonial dress is a segment of a circle: the clothing was cut in accordance with the globe (the Ancient Chinese had a clear idea that the Earth was round, and had even developed plans to flatten out its poles).

The motif of the continuous flood on the edging of the clothes of a senior state official, beginning with the emperor, was a direct expression of symbolism: the responsibility for establishing and maintaining order. In this way the pillars of society who wore the prescribed emblem of rank on their breasts rose above the initial chaos.

The decoration of both motifs is traditional. *The Flood* uses the technique of silk-thread embroidery and the pectoral decoration imitates embroidery.

PLATE 16

17 CHINESE ART

Painted and gilt ornamental motifs on
lacquered wood

In principle the nature of these decorations
bring to mind the bas-reliefs on the walls of
Egyptian buildings. An engraved outline isolates
the motif which lies in the plane of the surface.
Other engraved lines emphasise details; they
are sometimes left in place to act as links joining
up the depressions. The Chinese mastered
this technique to such an extent that the
objects appear to be in relief. The illusion was
strengthened by the addition of artificially worn
patches on the gilded parts of the decoration:
such worn patches appear on the convex sections
of old wood carvings.

With its liveliness and dynamism, this type of
decoration is fundamentally different from
the motionless and frozen décor of Ancient
Egypt. Chinese masters expressed life in motion
with unsurpassed force and scope, and were
unrivalled in this field. Both civilisations turned
to decoration as an artistic language, but in
different ways: the ability and observation of
the Chinese was more naive and simpler than the
complicated symbolism of the Egyptians.

When we look at the multiplicity of ornamental
motifs drawn from the plant and animal
kingdoms, we notice that some of them speak
of direct contact with creatures in their natural
surroundings; we are perhaps detecting the
first attempt to formulate a language of vision,
a language that has nothing in common with
hieroglyphs and does not need a Champollion
to decode it.

The motifs shown here were placed in the
same order on the wooden frame of a large and
magnificent 16th-century screen.

PLATE 17

Free or symmetrical designs

The upper part of the plate is filled by a décor in the Asiatic style that rejects a strict correlation of elements. The comparison and contrast of tones is extremely refined. The reddish-brown highlights and the chance inclusion of black put an end to any comments about lifelessness in the composition, and they give the green background an ethereal lightness and serenity. In the ornamental motif placed on a dull yellow background (it is a fragment of embroidered cloth) the colour gradations are expressed more openly and the reinforcing lines bend more smoothly. In this magnificent sample the effective use of white seems to separate the picture from the dense background, making it firmer and brighter.

PLATE 18

19 CHINESE ART

Embroidery and decorative painting

Depending upon the object being decorated, Chinese craftsmen used two types of décor. Most embroidery was done in a traditional manner combined with a traditional colouring that could be bright, glistening or dull. In their use of broad synthetic forms the Chinese attained an unparalleled richness and expressivity in their decorations.

The embroidery on a black background (a fragment of clothing) emphasises their skill. The lines and colouring are traditional, but if you look at the strange barrel-shaped creature flying straight at you, you cannot help thinking that a real insect is coming towards you. Is it large or small, is it dangerous or harmless? There's no time to think: a monster is attacking you! The second method — a naturalistic picture in the 'plants and birds' genre — is characterised by an illusion of naivety and refinement. The 50cm-high vertical panels shown in this plate reveal a restricted range of components: the branch of a tree, birds, flowers and leaves. Lightly drawn, they seem to be soaring in a rarefied space. There will never be an end to our enjoyment of the variety of chromatic combinations in these light-filled compositions. The vertical panels, which were the most common type of Chinese painting, imitate the narrow opening of a window through which we can look out at the surrounding world. Small watercolour compositions like these were intended for the interiors of houses, and were usually hung on walls in pairs or groups of four, six or even twelve.

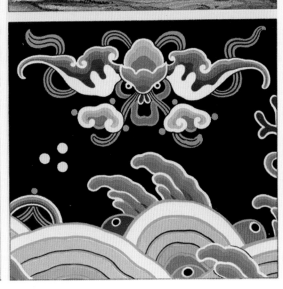

Painting. Embroidery. Printed cloth

This and the following plates show various aspects of the Chinese decorative style that almost all Japanese masters followed to a greater or lesser extent, whether it be painting in watercolours on silk or paper, embroidery or printed cloth.

We have added to the three narrow vertical panels in the upper part of the plate (their naturalistic subjects are amazingly fine) a horizontal composition showing a bird sitting on the branch of a tree in blossom. It is a typical example of the happy, airy and poetic manner that is characteristic of Chinese and Japanese artists.

The two vertical bands on a black background demonstrate a quite different type of naturalistic decoration. The plants, birds, flowers, insects and even ripples on the water stand out against the black background; their multi-coloured palette is notable for its brightness and even harshness, and the sheen of the silk gives it an added brilliance. Each of the complete motifs recalls a sumptuous bunch of flowers that is supplemented by birds and insects; the embroidery is done with a realism that is as good as the naturalistic subjects of painted panels.

The horizontal band with a raspberry-brown background demonstrates a higher class of décor. At that time the production of printed fabrics was very simple: as if divided up into separate sections by a grid (like cloisonné enamels), the basic drawing was printed together with the background, and the inclusion of soft colour tones gave variety and dynamism to the design. Following the rule of the optical merging of colours, in this type of ornamentation the specific harmony of the picture is subservient to the dominant background. Chinese artists brought this type of decoration to perfection, and this example demonstrates the experience of craftsmen who were able to produce the most refined enamels in the world. The bird depicted is the Chinese phoenix, which was an obligatory component of classical Chinese décor.

PLATE 20

21 CHINESE AND JAPANESE ART

Silk fabrics with regular patterns

The patterns on silk that make up the main motif of the plate (this cloth covered the binding of a Chinese manuscript book) are among the finest examples of decoration on silk.

The yellow of the background represents the colour of the Taiji princes of the Yuan dynasty (the rulers of the China of the time), and the dragons with four claws on their feet indicate the owner's title.

It should be noted that the cloth looks so striking due more to the direct chromatic contrasts than to the delicate colours used traditionally. The white outline that separates the coloured elements from the background leads the viewer's eye steadily on. This outline is thin enough not to interfere with the adjacent tones, apart from the white edges to the figures of the dragons where it is brighter and like a halo and creates a surrounding of light and air. By gradually altering the colour of the background from dark to light we have tried to reproduce the play of light on billowing silk. The large motif on a black background (lower centre) is of Chinese origin; the remainder are Japanese.

22 Chinese and Japanese Art

Cloisonné enamel articles

There are good reasons for placing cloisonné enamels from China and Japan under a general heading. Their ornamental motifs follow the same style, since Japanese ornamentation developed under the influence of Chinese ornamentation, and the high opinion that people have of both of them is justified by their craftsmanship and impeccable taste.

China: 1–7, 22, 23;

Japan: 18–21.

23 CHINESE AND JAPANESE ART

Continuous ornaments

It is difficult to imagine how such an effect
can be achieved by such laconic means: the
ornamentalist will not be wasting his or her time
and effort in studying these bold colouristic
contrasts.

Motifs 1–7 are of Chinese origin, and the
remainder are Japanese.

Metal working
Hilts, guards and sheaves of daggers and
swords

Japanese craftsmen decorated the small surfaces
of the hilts, handguards and other parts of side-
arms with gold, silver, steel, copper and bronze,
and also with a metal alloy called *Sawa* metal in
two forms, *shibuichi* and *shakudo*. The metallic
surfaces were covered with incisions, and the
decoration was finished off with engraving and
relief work.

The motifs shown here speak for themselves.
In actual fact some examples are miracles
of craftsmanship and impeccable taste. The
Japanese were famous throughout the world
as unsurpassed craftsmen who were capable
of turning anything (and sometimes nothing!)
into something unusual. The mythology of the
Empire of the Rising Sun occupies only a small
part of this plate. In general the décor presents
figures and objects that were as familiar to the
Japanese as they were to Europeans. Apple trees
in blossom, marine plants, vines, little birds
squabbling, ducks splashing about and birds
flying can also be found in European decorations
in conjunction with representations of horses,
fish, butterflies, insects and other creatures.

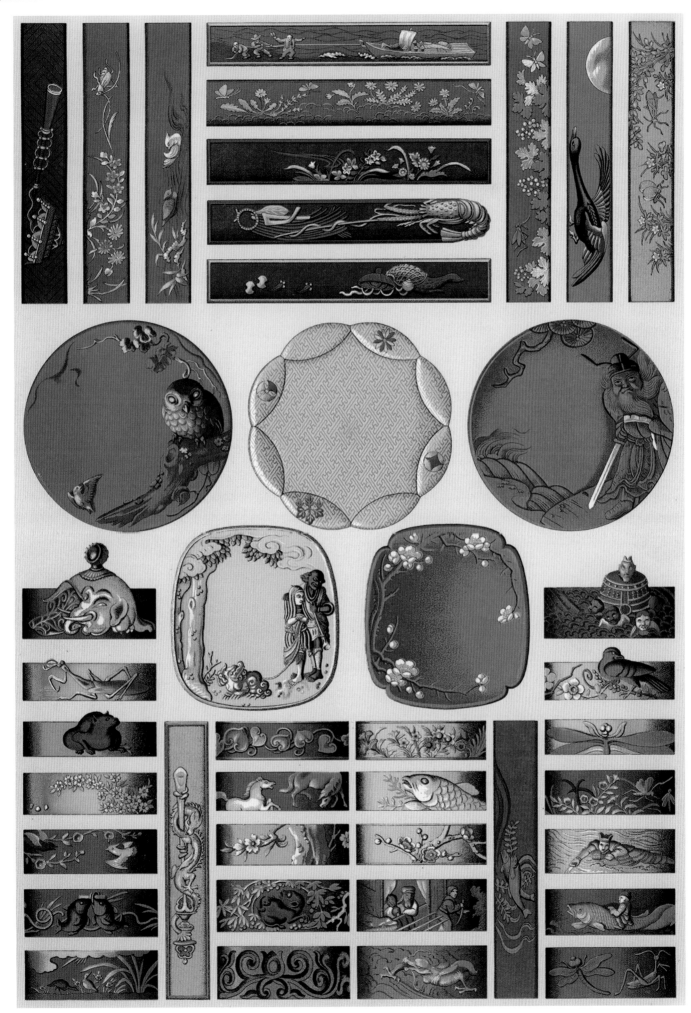

25 JAPANESE ART

Metal working
Weapons and fittings

Continuation of Plate 24.

This reproduction shows the decorated ends of sword hilts and some other items.

The Japanese did not wear jewellery as such and preferred to decorate everyday articles, including furniture, with gold and other noble metals. Medicine chests, silver teapots, netsuke, boxes for sweetmeats, little cabinets and the mouthpieces for pipes were covered with ornamentation using all shades of gold, silver and copper in countless combinations and infinite modifications. To achieve maximum variety in the decorative effect, sulphur, arsenic, iron or lead oxides were deliberately left in the copper artefact, or were sometimes added with other oxides. The appropriate addition of lead, for example, gives copper a purple, black or green hue (these alloys are known as *shido*, *udo* and *seido*); other additions were *sentokudo*, *shakudo* and *shibuichi* (the last contains 40% silver). The resulting colours stand out clearly against the others that form the background. The craftsmen used chisels to work the surface of the metal so as to achieve its roughness or smoothness and give it the softness and velvetiness of fabrics, the fluffiness of fur, the granularity of shagreen or the porosity of stone. The use of acids helped to achieve these effects.

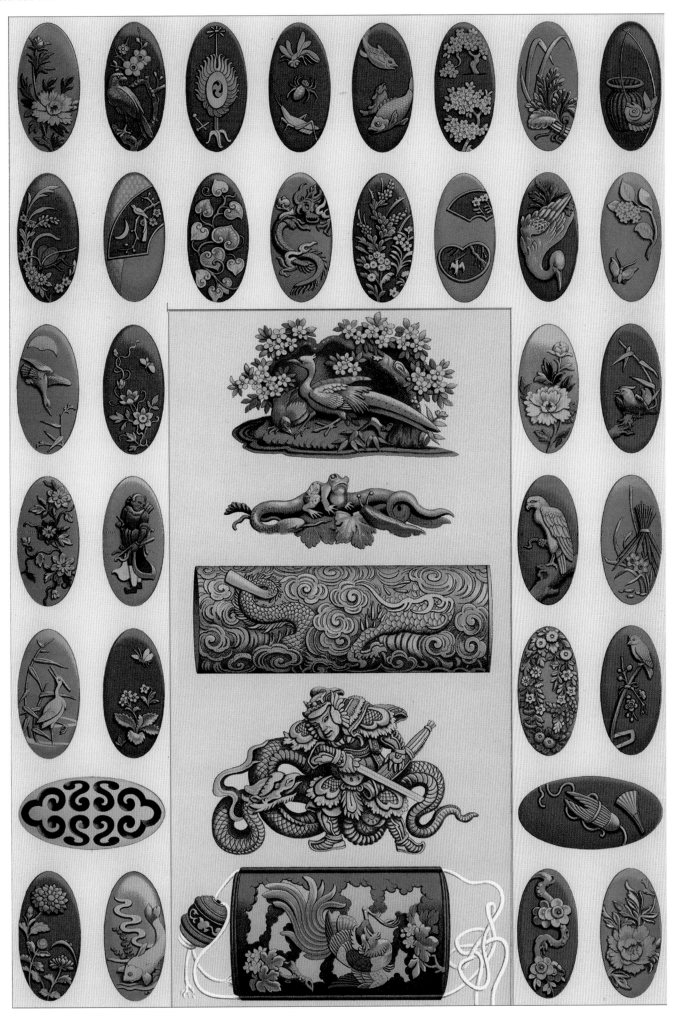

Cloisonné enamels

All the motifs shown here are part of the decoration of a copper tray with cloisonné enamel on both sides. A section of the whole tray is shown in the upper part of the plate, and individual motifs from the decoration are grouped together in the lower part.

Although it used combinations of geometric lines brilliantly, Japanese decorative art did not consist just of this. We also see both birds and flowers made with unusual precision, and it is simply amazing to what extent the technique of cloisonné enamelling facilitates the graphic nature of the composition. When it comes to relative values, the colour range of the ornamentation shown in the plate corresponds to the original, but the tones have been lightened slightly. It seems to us that a slight increase in the freshness and brightness will make the original decoration more expressive and will in any case turn it into a useful pattern for modern manufacture.

27 JAPANESE ART

Ancient fabric decoration

The motifs shown here are from the same sources as on the next plate (especially the screen 'with one hundred samples of cloth').

The subdued tones create a soft colour range, indicating impeccable taste. Primitive fabric decorations are used in some designs, and they remind us of the decorative work of artefacts from Oceania that were woven from plant fibres (mats, canoe paddles or domestic utensils). The samples of fabrics woven with gold thread form a very valuable collection and they are of special interest since they were produced in Japanese factories in the 17th–18th centuries.

Fabric decoration

To decorate screens the Japanese covered their leaves with pieces of the most varied brocades and woven materials, and in this way created priceless collections of fabrics. The pieces of cloth are positioned evenly and symmetrically, and each separate motif contains part of a continuous décor that becomes even more expressive through repetition.

The motifs reproduced here are part of the decoration of the screen 'with one hundred samples of cloth'. It would be difficult to find a better source of information about the Japanese textile industry: these samples were produced during the 17th–18th centuries.

Wallpaper
Chinese and Japanese manufacture

Printed wallpapers were popular in China and Japan a long time before the fashion gripped Europe. Japanese wallpapers differed from European ones not just in their type of decoration, but also in the way that they were produced. Instead of being wound into endless rolls and cut into sections when they were sold, as happened in Europe, they were printed from small-scale plates onto hand-made paper (even the cheapest!). Consequently the design was small-scale, and the limited dimensions of a piece of wallpaper made it impossible to create the flowing plant patterns that the Europeans preferred. Japanese wallpaper demonstrates a restraint in its composition that is often combined with entrancing flights of fantasy.

As a rule Japanese houses were repapered each year, and therefore wallpaper had to be cheap.

Apart from the wallpaper with the blue birds, the examples in the lower part of the plate only use two colours; the dull backgrounds and metallic tones are applied by brush. The design is printed from one plate and can be dull, coloured or with a metallic sheen. Each sheet is surrounded by perforations so that it is easier to adjust: they have to be carefully cut around before being glued.

In addition to cheap wallpapers there were also very expensive ones like the type shown in the upper part of the plate. The paper is of excellent quality and the priming is applied by brush, sometimes in many layers. This particular piece of wallpaper measures 62 x 50cm. Only one fragment of the three pieces that make up the complete design is shown in this plate. As a rule the Chinese and Japanese preferred continuous motifs and sometimes printed two or three pieces simultaneously, all brought together in one plate (cf. the three examples in the central section of the plate).

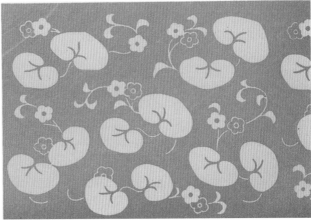

'Overflowing' decorations on flat surfaces

The Japanese skilfully used the simplest of means to create varied effects on flat surfaces such as fabrics or wallpaper. The plate shows examples with so-called 'overflowing' or 'pulsating' patterns. Japanese artists were entranced by the movement of life, and as they strove to embody it in their work they studied natural phenomena carefully; the proof of this is in the optical effects that give the illusion of movement (for example the twinkling of a star or the flash of fireworks).

This continuum of motion, which embodies life as it is, is reflected in individual motifs, in particular in motifs 1–3.

The black pattern (2) on a lighter background is formed of wavy lines that separate the surface into individual sections.

An undulating motif (3) is placed on a neutrally coloured background.

Example 4 is a depiction of birds outlined in white on a blue background that seems to shine through them as if they are incorporeal. Something noted subtly is that when the sun is at its highest the flight of birds above one's head can often seem to the dazzled eye to be no more than the constant movement of the air itself.

Motif 6 uses a flickering effect; this phenomenon is linked to stars and the way that the atmosphere seems to make them vibrate.

Motif 7 resembles the sun rotating on its axis and shooting out fire in every direction.

All these ornamentations go back to the decoration of clothing and the wallpaper that was glued onto partitions in houses.

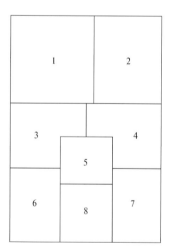

31 JAPANESE ART

Popular ornamentation and its symbolism

The majority of the motifs shown here spring simply from the imagination: they consist of meanders, interlacing, ribbon-like figures, etc, and it is not known whether they include any form of symbolism.

Even so, on the basis of traditional Japanese symbolism we can be certain that the beautiful motif of delicate butterflies against the background of a geometrical pattern (19) was likely to have decorated a bride's wedding dress.

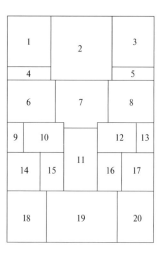

The portrayal of a stork (2, 7) is one of the symbols in Japanese ornamentation that has a large number of meanings. Among the depictions of gods and the protectors of both families at wedding ceremonies one can always find the figures of the 'first couple' surrounded by ancient attributes, a stork and a turtle, which symbolise the depth of knowledge and the loftiness of the human spirit. We can see a stork drawn in a circle on a norimono (the bride's palanquin) and two storks painted naturalistically on the walls of the marriage chamber.

The motif with storks (7) represents a pattern that was very suitable for mosaics: three birds enclosed in a hexagram.

Only wallpapers were printed in Japan, and other decorations were embroidered or painted by hand. From the printed wallpaper we can get an impression of the popular art of Japan, and the spirit that resurrected ancient artistic forms is truly national in nature.

Cartouches

Cartouches were widely used in decorative art in both Japan and China; they were positioned arbitrarily among ornamental motifs which they immediately pushed into the background. The variety in the form and colouring of cartouches enlivened the monotony of the background design. However, like European cartographers, the Japanese often used them to decorate maps.

As we can see from the examples shown in this plate, Japanese cartouches had a smooth surface and were outlined by a single line. However, their shapes were their most fantastic feature. Is it not indeed strange that, as a counterbalance to the logic of the humble scroll (the most primitive form of cartouche), the craftsman has given them the shape of a butterfly with open wings and even feelers, or the silhouette of a bird perched on a branch? More modest cartouches are in the shape of plants, a water-lily leaf or even a sword-guard. The most common design of cartouche is shaped like an open or closed fan, and simple geometrical forms are also popular.

As a rule the decoration of a cartouche, and it is usually a landscape, has not the slightest connection to its shape. If a human face is depicted it seems to be looking through a keyhole. Faces, both male and female, are usually caricatures.

In short, in the hands of Japanese craftsmen the defining characteristic of this eccentric genre was the integrity of the décor. Whether symmetrical or arbitrary in shape, the cartouches produce an impression of something that is light in weight and mobile, like a wood shaving, and this is their great virtue. In addition the variety of outline becomes essential if we remember the way that cartouches were used: they were often placed on the lacquered wooden surface of the item being decorated, so that they could break up the monotonous colour of the background.

PLATE 32

Niello and engraving

Many of the motifs shown are difficult to date, like those fruits of a civilisation in which an indisputable religious and political system is reflected, when it comes to art, there is a certain frozen perfection: it does not develop, nor does it fall into decay. It should be added that we are looking at an example of the characteristic Eastern gift for accurate imitation that allows modern products to look old (although collectors, naturally, prefer old ones). However, it is impossible not to be entranced by the impression that graceful decoration on metal produces.

Ornamental motifs decorating everyday objects:

1–6   Two narghiles (pipes for smoking);

7–9   Jug, basin for washing and open-work lid;

10   Jug for washing;

11   Plate;

12–15   Body of jug and of plate.

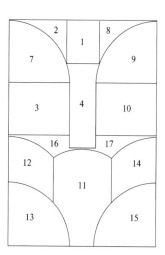

Enamel decoration on copper artefacts
Cloisonné enamel
Niello and chasing on steel

These fragments come from dishes, cups and vases made in Northern India, and principally in Kashmir, Tibet and Turkistan; the exception is the enamelled pendant (3), which is from Rajputana, the home of the most refined Indian enamels.

The nature of decoration on copper artefacts depends on whether it is applied to the body of the vessel or to the upper surface of a dish or cup. Spherical surfaces are as a rule divided radially, and if the body of the vessel is stretched vertically, the decoration is placed in vertical bands.

A continually repeated design can be seen in two types of ornamental combination (2, 4, 8, 10, 13, 14). The spherical effect is achieved by repeating a basic motif. The ingenuousness of the ornamentation on the other fragments in this series that are decorated with a niello design (apart from sample 2) is truly remarkable. As in Ancient Egypt, enamelling is one of the oldest techniques in India. Depressions were chiselled into the surface of the metal surrounding the design and were then filled with a glass paste; after being baked the surface was burnished and appeared unified, as in cloisonné enamel.

The richness of the decoration and the skilfully thought-out combinations (8, 10, 13) illustrate the ornamental merits of this technique.

14 – Copper with appliqué silver;

7,9 – Decoration on weapons: steel with gold inlay and chasing, gilding;

7 – Gilded ornamentation outlined by an engraved line filled with niello, giving it expressiveness;

3 – Fragment of a gold and enamel jewellery decoration. If we remember that each item in the plate is shown in its actual size, it is impossible not to appreciate the unprecedented grace of cloisonné enamels.

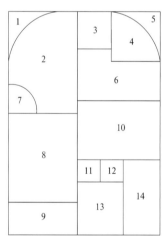

35 INDIAN ART

Painting and niello designs

A characteristic of most of these motifs is
splendour and harmony in the Eastern style.
The decoration of weapons is shown:

   1–4 Bow;

   5, 6 Dagger sheaf;

   7, 8 Sword scabbard;

      9 Ornamentation on a weapon;

 10–12 Ornamental motifs on the neck of
         a bottle;

     13 Ornamentation on a weapon;

     14 Edge of a water jug.

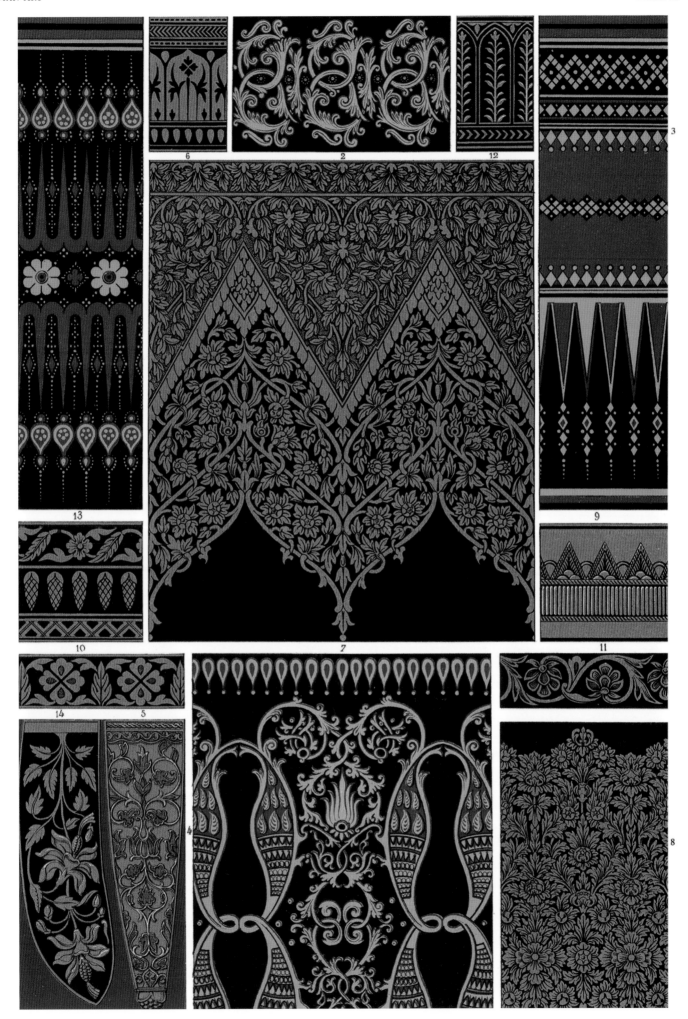

Continuous plant motifs

Embroidery, book decoration, niello and
cloisonné enamel

    1 Embroidered fabric;

 2–23 Ornamental edges and backgrounds to
        handwritten books;

24, 25 Cloisonné enamels;

26, 27 Patterned embroidery;

28–31 Niello designs.

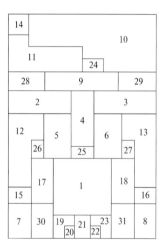

Contemporary ornamentation

Without going into the details of general stylistic features, this lists the sources of the motifs shown in the plate:

1 Painted wooden stand;

2 Footwear with embroidery and sequins on velvet;

3 Footwear sewn with gold and pearl discs on velvet;

4, 5 Decoration on a dagger. Cloisonné enamel and gold on an onyx background;

6, 7 Cup on a stand;

8, 9 Ornamental edges to handwritten books;

10, 11 Palmettes: fabric decoration borrowed from book ornamentation;

12 Tray;

13–15 Cups;

16–19 Decoration on objects made from papier mâché.

PLATE 37

Appliqué work. Plant motifs

The large fragment is a piece of Indian cloth with cloth appliqués trimmed with white thread. In this particular form of patchwork the white outline delineates all the ornamental elements, both large and small. It stresses the internal division of the decorative composition, and at the same time the stems which branch out from the bunches of flowers seem to vibrate, depending upon the intensity of the background colour. This thread, which forms a continually twisting coloured pattern in the borders, serves the same dividing function as the metal partitions in cloisonné enamel. It connects all the colours together and unites them in a single chromatic note. The irreproachably symmetrical picture confirms the Indian passion for continuous decoration. The design becomes alive and mobile by being divided into the main fields of colour, but the technique of appliqué work does not allow any form of relief in the embroidery, and the dull texture of the cloth lacks the sheen that is characteristic of silk.

Stylistically, the four motifs in the border belong to the time of the Great Mughals, as does the motif on the tent cloth (lower part of the plate). All five forms of decoration go back to the miniatures in 16th-century manuscript books.

PLATE 38

Decorative designs

All the fragments presented here are taken from a series of page illustrations with historical or romantic scenes and form a cycle to which we unfortunately do not have the key. They were probably created during the 16th century.

These motifs are encountered principally in the interiors of the houses that often appear on these pages. The firmness and clarity of the compositions turn the décor into something of exceptional artistic significance.

Plate 39

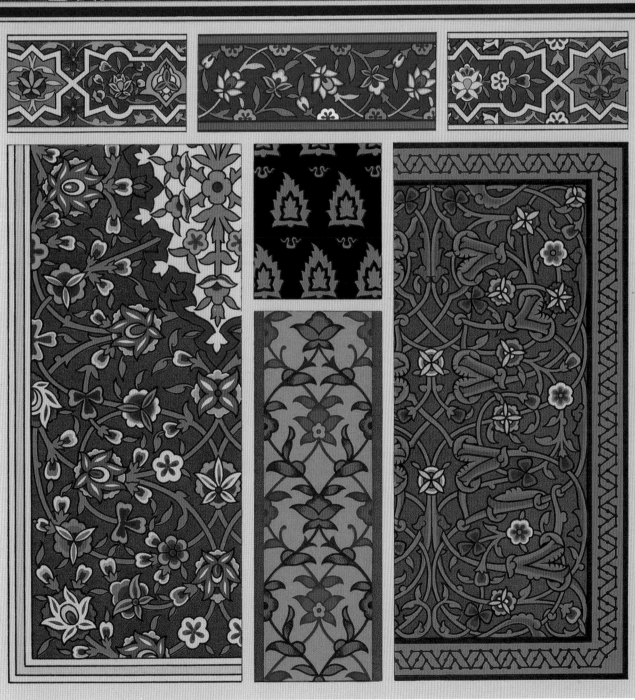

Decorative designs

These motifs, which are drawn from Mughal miniature painting in 16th-century manuscript books, demonstrate a decoration that has an extremely interesting richness and precision.

The intensity of the colours and softness of the backgrounds set off the most uncomplicated motifs whose simple repetition creates a décor of striking serenity. The central rosette is divided into five segments and displays all the features that are typical of primitive rush-weaving: decorative work using squares of one size. There is an increasing interest in this type of decoration as it dates to the 16th century.

Polychrome painting. Continuous borders

The motifs presented here are taken from the same source as plates 39 and 40, and this plate, which shows borders, completes the series. Borders were one of the main elements of Persian decorative art; as a rule they decorated friezes and door or window lintels, and it was rare for woven curtains to be made without an ornamental edge.

This type of ornamentation, with its precise forms and magnificent compositions was very popular in Persian ceramic art, and occupied a fitting place in the diverse polychrome decoration of manuscript books. To complete its study we would like to make use of the rich source of 16th-century miniatures by showing very detailed fragments from them in the plate.

It is not just variety in the palette that we can see: the paintings themselves are bold and refined. The backgrounds of some borders are painted with indigo, and in India, where the light is very intense, indigo is usually combined with black and often replaces it. This helps the unity of the decoration, and this unity was the fundamental principle of the decorative system in India during the time of the Great Mughals. The motifs of the borders are assembled so skilfully that they fill the whole space with a continuous pattern: the interwoven tendrils of plants or swirling streams of smoke against a background of plant ornamentation (cf. plate 42).

Book decoration. Double interlacing

This page from a 15th-16th-century Koran, which glitters with all the magnificence of Eastern decoration, requires closer attention to the method of ornamentation that breathes life and movement into it. It is an expressive and detailed example of the system of double interlacing that is not often encountered in decorations.

This system of decoration consists in applying a regular and graceful interweaving of plants, typical of Persian and Indian art of the period, onto a field and then superimposing a completely different interlacing of strips of varying widths with ends shaped like tongues that form spiral knots (either individual or in bunches). This type of ornamentation is called 'curling smoke': the ornamental bands wind through the whole composition as wisps of smoke that interweave in arbitrary spirals and melt away into space (in particular because of the tongues that shrink to nothing). The ornamentalist perhaps wanted to express the feelings of a person looking at a motionless pattern through the puffs of smoke from his pipe. The wisps join together on the border and become symmetrical, but still remain light and spontaneous. They are light blue and twist capriciously in the corner of the central section, whereas they are bronze-brown in the other section of the décor. The 'curling smoke' motif is typical of the system of ornamentation during the time of the Great Mughals.

43 INDO-PERSIAN ART

Book decoration

This decoration from a page in a 15th-16th-century Koran is distinguished by its truly 'Asiatic' splendour. If we can imagine this ornamentation becoming part of the decoration of a magnificent carpet, we will perhaps start thinking of this type of book decoration as not just an illumination, but direct proof of a real object.

In essence the principle of this décor coincides with the system of decoration on architecture: it has both the refined character that is a feature of Eastern ceramics, and an original method that was a favourite of both the Persians and the Indians, the interweaving of two ornamental shapes that create a double coloured pattern. Each time the gold and black backgrounds penetrate past each other they form a finished picture with a white outline that makes it stand out clearly from the background.

By comparing this plate to the preceding one we can see that the decorations come from different sources. The double interlacing on plate 42 (the background with plant patterns; the net at the top with its 'curling smoke' motif resembling the movement of spider-like insects on the smooth surface of a pond) seems to have been put together without any real system. The broad border on this plate does not have any interweaving wisps of smoke, and the picture is firm and clear. At the same time, we cannot help noticing the differences in colour; both patterns are sumptuous and produced by one hand, but they are not identical.

PLATE 43

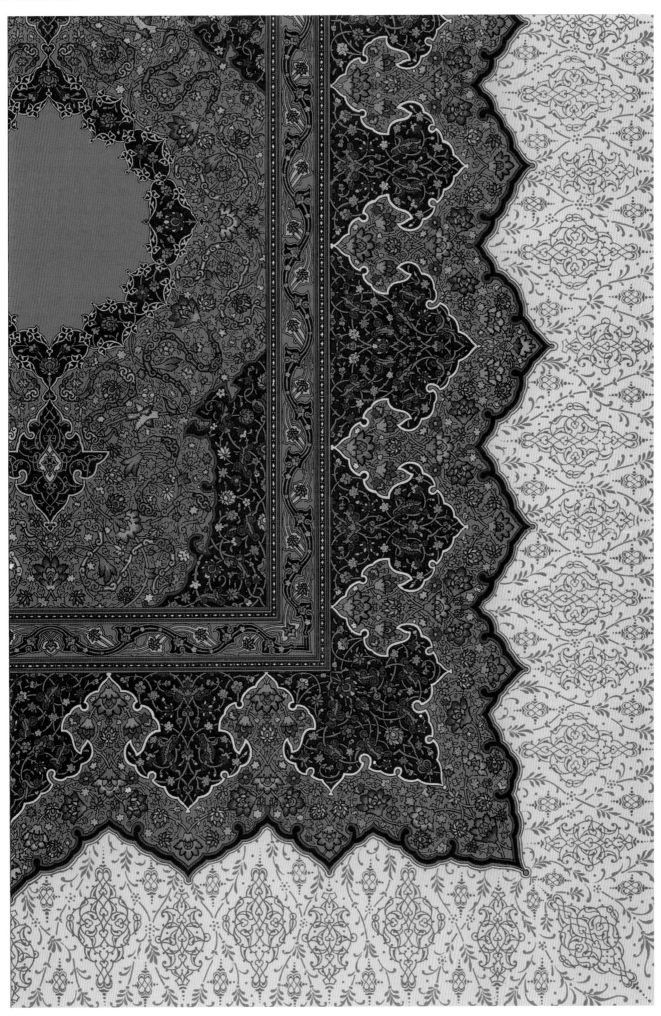

Book decoration. Cloisonné enamels

The four ornamental motifs are drawn from the decoration of a richly-illuminated Koran that was illustrated by Mir-Imad, the chief calligrapher of Shah Abbas I and the author of charming arabesques on the edges of the manuscript (cf. plate 55). The beautiful Persian dagger (the end of the hilt, the hilt itself and the upper part of the engraved blade and sheaf are shown in the plate) is of the type of weapon that is a true work of art. The elephant ivory is inlaid with thin wire in the shape of plant tendrils, and part of the decoration uses the old technique of cloisonné enamel. The dagger in its sheaf is 29cm long.

The second dagger, which is also decorated with cloisonné enamel, was made in India. It comes from Rajputana, where the best Indian enamels were made, and perhaps the best in the world. There is no better proof of this than this magnificent weapon with its amazingly harmonious decoration and rich range of colours. The dagger is 44cm long.

Book miniatures
Copper with niello decoration

(1–5) Fragments of book miniatures.

Motif 1 is a very complex work that represents a decorative window lintel; the silk curtain in the opening is slightly raised, allowing the viewer to see (in the original) a half-length portrait of an Indian prince of the time of the Great Mughals. Part of the composition displayed here (apart from the silk curtain) is repeated in the lower part of the plate and completes the surround to the window. This is the standard type of framing for a miniature portrait. The décor follows the architectonic principle of the external decoration of windows, and was in accordance with the main law for wooden and stone constructions that dictated the dividing of the frame into four ornamental panels.

Motifs 2–5 are drawn from manuscript books, and each motif is defined by a border. These borders look as if they are woven, and the broad bands of decoration seem like appliqué work that has been placed on an embroidered background and outlined by a white thread. They look just as effective in a larger scale and are ideal for the ornamentation of patterned fabrics.

Finally, motif 6 represents a continuous ornamentation for a frieze; it is engraved on the copper surface and decorated with a niello design.

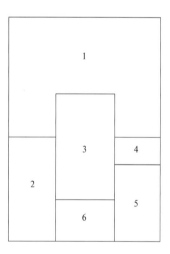

Printed fabrics
Plant and zoomorphic designs

So-called 'Persian' fabrics, which the West has loved for a long time, still play an important role in the production of everyday goods. These types of fabric created a sensational demand when they were first produced in Europe in the 18th century. For a long time it was normal in both East and West to keep repeating old designs of Eastern patterned fabrics. This was not meant to deceive the customer: new imitations replaced the old originals that were no longer available, and in this way prevented the decline of the genre.

This plate brings together fragments of Eastern fabrics in whose decoration a genuine Persian style is joined in places by the art of the Indian subcontinent. These fabrics demonstrate a flower ornamentation that includes the depiction of animals, birds and even the human figure done in a manner that lies somewhere between naturalism and decorative conventionality. The motifs are sometimes positioned freely, as if by accident, and sometimes form a symmetrical pattern (bottom left).

PLATE 46

47 PERSIAN ART

Niello patterns

The black background of the ornamentation
is achieved by a combination of metal alloys
applied on a hatched engraving (1). The pattern
looks richer and more harmonious in the
originals than in reproductions.

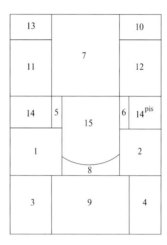

1, 2 Decorated backgrounds of a cup;

3, 4 Decorated backgrounds on a basin
for washing;

5, 6 Background with a regular design;

7–12 Edge of a cup;

13 Border of a snuff-box;

14 Edge of a cup;

15 Cartouche in the decoration of a cup.

PLATE 47

Brass articles with gilding and precious stones
Copper articles with gilding, appliqué silver and niello

The fragment filling the lower left corner of the plate (14) is part of a sumptuous brass dish with gilding and precious stones. The use of brass rather surprised Europeans as they did not consider it to be a 'noble' metal.

The comments for plate 59 about engraved motifs on copper in Arabic art give an idea of the great significance that Eastern masters gave to decoration on metal surfaces: depressions made with an engraving needle and the outlines of motifs in relief were filled with niello. Among the motifs engraved on copper in the plate are patterns that are very similar to the ornamentation of Arab craftsmen (cf. plate 59), and it is sometimes difficult to say where the differences lie. It is a delicate matter, and in some instances all one can do is simply accept the attribution given which is perhaps linked to the shape of the article.

Both in plate 59 and here (1) we can find a depiction of two birds placed in a medallion; they are in a heraldic pose that is traditional for Ancient Persian and Syrian ornamentation. This motif decorates a brass cup with silver engraving where medallions in the shape of quatrefoils flow into a beautiful design. It is divided into zones (13) that have been left blank in this plate since the original engraved subjects, for all their elegance, have not the slightest connection to the ornamental surrounding. The medallions could contain the most varied compositions including, despite being forbidden by the Koran, the figures of heraldic animals mentioned in plate 59.

PLATE 48

Tile facing

The principal building material in Central Asia was the adobe brick, and architects covered the brick surfaces of buildings with marble, stucco and, above all, an elegant facing consisting of rectangular slip-glazed tiles placed very close together. Their magnificent pattern becomes even richer and more striking since each tile is a standard decorative unit that can occupy a vast space that is only limited by the edges of the building. The nature of the décor was dictated by the Koran, which forbade the reproduction of anthropomorphic or zoomorphic motifs. The traditional ornamentation that we can see here belongs to the period when, after being ruled by the Arabs for many centuries, Persia recommenced an independent existence under the aegis of the Seljuk dynasty (1037–1193).

1 Magnificent fragment of the upper part of a *mihrab* in an abandoned mosque in Damascus. 54cm high;

2 Fragment of a tile panel. 24cm high;

3 Border with a continuous pattern. Each horizontal tile is 25cm long and the joint runs through the centre of the palmette;

4 Border with a continuous pattern. Each horizontal tile is 14cm long and the joint runs through the top of the flower;

5 Tile forming the base of a continuous border; 32cm high. In the Sèvres Museum, France;

6 This expressive fragment consists of outer and inner borders and a field with a plant pattern enclosed within a frame; it is in essence a continuous pattern. The tile of the outer border is 22cm high (from one joint to the next), and the height of the corner tile of the inner border is 25cm; the joining line runs through the middle of the rosette. The size of the square tiles with the repeating pattern is 25 x 25cm.

PLATE 49

Slip-glazed ceramics
Blue, green and white

1 Plate with flat base and raised lip.
   Diameter 32cm.
   The glass-like glaze was not fired like normal
   glazes but was laid on top like lacquer;

2 Corner motif, most likely continuous,
   although the central joining line is shaped
   like a bow;

3 Border with a continuous pattern.
   Each tile is 16cm long;

4 Border with a continuous pattern.
   The length of each horizontal tile is 24cm.
   The joining line goes through the centre of
   each rosette;

5 Border with a continuous pattern.
   The length of each horizontal tile is 15cm.
   Found in an abandoned mosque in Damascus
   (the mosque had been turned into a
   gunpowder magazine);

6 Border with a continuous pattern.
   Each horizontal tile is 17cm long;

7 Border with a continuous pattern.
   The length of each horizontal tile is 24cm;

8 Border with a continuous pattern.
   The fragment is 16cm long;

9 Vertical panel.
   The height of the tile is 29cm.
   The joining line goes through the points of
   the cartouches.
   For its origin, cf. 5;

10 Tile facings divided into panels.
   The height of the fragment with its green-
   white border (not reproduced) is 32cm.
   For its origin, cf. 5;

11 Meander ornament.
   Height 6cm;

12 Outer border with corner tile.
   The fragment is 32cm long.

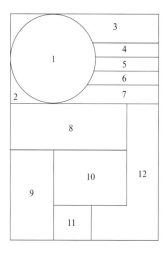

PLATE 50

Tile wall facing
External and internal decoration of
buildings

Motifs 1, 13, 16 and 17 represent fragments
of the décor of the sultan's palace in Konya
(Iconium), the capital of the Rum, or Seljuk,
Sultanate. Unlike the Ottoman Turks, the
Seljuks did not object to the portrayal of people
and animals.

The border in the upper part of the plate (1) is
full of plants drawn in an almost naturalistic
way.

Motifs 16 and 17 are fleurons intended for
decorating the inner sides of the supports for a
stucco cornice. They all differ in form and are
probably hand-made.

The remaining motifs are from the décor of
a mosque in Tabriz (Azerbaijan). Although
the Koran forbids the decoration of religious
buildings with gold, in both the mosque in
Tabriz and the mosque built in Bursa by Sultan
Murad I, the ruler of the Ottoman Empire, the
walls and columns were finished with gilded
ornamentation. The Green Mosque (Yeşil
Mosque), so-called because of the colour of the
glazed ceramic tiles on the minarets, was built
in Bursa at the command Sultan Mehmed I,
the grandson of Murad I. Both the external and
the internal walls of the mosque are faced with
Persian tiles decorated in relief.

Tile facing

An ancient tradition of the peoples of Asia was to face buildings with glistening ceramic tiles both on the inside and the outside. The walls and roofs of the wooden buildings of the kings of Phaeacia (mentioned in the *Odyssey*) were covered with sheets of metal, and the same was done by the Medes, followed by the Chaldeans, Phoenicians and Assyrians. In another tradition buildings were made of brick and the walls were faced either with worked stone slabs decorated with a polychrome relief or with large slip-glazed tiles.

14 – Square tile (40cm x 40cm), a standard decorative unit. It was placed in four rows consisting of 16 tiles so that one square could form a pattern 160cm long either horizontally or vertically;

5 – Motif of the same system, with a standard decorative unit: two squares place correctly and two placed upside down form a standard decorative unit that is placed in a square.

Motif 9 is formed in the same way.

Chromatic tones can be found only in motif 6, where they do not in the least violate the principle of pure colours, but merely provide a way of strengthening their vibrancy. Facing tiles were made in all sizes and were even used to decorate furniture.

Of course the decoration is varied in character and is done in a light and free manner, but the monochrome colouration makes it more restrained (2).

1	2	3
4	6	8
5	6	9
5	7	9
10		11
12	13	14	15	16

PLATE 52

53 PERSIAN ART

Ceramics

The motifs shown here give a full impression of the decorative system that was used widely in the production of Persian artefacts. As a rule it is based on arabesques which are often combined with plant motifs drawn in a more or less naturalistic way, and roses, marigolds, tulips, hyacinths and others are easily recognisable. Sometimes some form of fantastical being is placed in the middle of a decorative composition (such as the bird at the centre of the magnificent plate at the top).

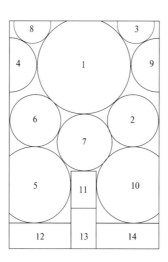

1–10 Dishes and plates;

11–14 Slip-glazed tiles.

Slip-glazed ceramics

The principle of this ornamentation — sharp lines and an expressive colouration, and no trace of relief-work or carving — hardly needs further endorsement. Some of the peoples of Asia Minor who possessed a deep understanding of colour remained true to this ancient decorative style and preserved only its purity of colour. Persian masters were very successful in varying a limited number of standard decorative units, in particular arabesques and stylised plant forms. Although it is impossible to sense the inspiration and excitement of the original décor in the examples shown in this plate, the reproductions still help us to evaluate the bold chromatic relationships under the transparent layer of glaze. Finally, as size also plays a large part in this type of décor, we include the diameters of nine of the plates shown (7–8 are wall tiles from the Omar Mosque, or Kubbet es Sakhra, the Dome of the Rock): 40cm (1), 38cm (2), 28cm (3), 27cm (4), 30cm (5), 37cm (6, 10), 40cm (9) and 12cm (11).

55 PERSIAN ART

Book decoration
Marginal decorations

The decorations on the fields of the manuscript are from a beautiful hand-written copy of the poems of Saadi (the calligrapher was Shams and it was illustrated by Mir-Emad) produced during the rule of Shah Abbas. Saadi, who was born in Shiraz in 1184 and lived to be 102, was one of the greatest Persian poets. The French writer La Fontaine borrowed the theme of his fable *The Cricket and the Ant* from him, although Saadi had a nightingale rather than a cricket.

The light and graceful ornaments shown here tell us that their author was not some mere artisan. Each motif is a logically completed composition resembling a precious decoration with an enamel finish. The large, elegant flourishes of the pattern are cleverly placed so as to balance the intensity of the coloured background that is visible in the spaces between them. At the same time the richness of the décor is increased, without taking away its lightness, by the sections formed by intersecting lines and filled with a coloured pattern.

In two of the motifs shown here the plant decorations develop in one plane. Two other examples demonstrate a double interlacing of the type that we saw in plate 42: interwoven plants covered with a network of curling streams of smoke. It is treated in the spirit of polychrome cloisonné enamel with a preponderance of a beautiful blue colour, lapis lazuli, which Persia supplied to the whole world. The religious ban on depicting people, animals, insects and even natural forms did not of course affect the ability of an artist with the talent of Mir-Emad to stimulate excitement and elevated feelings in the viewer. A genuine master will always find a way of forcing the material to reflect his inner world.

Book decoration

These ornaments can be seen on the pages
of two different manuscript copies of the
Shahnameh, an epic poem about the ancient
kings of Persia written by the poet Abul-Qasim
Ferdowsi (c. 940–1020/30). The poem contains
about 60,000 couplets; the poet worked on
it for thirty years and dedicated it to Sultan
Mahmud Ghaznavi.

PLATE 56

57 PERSIAN ART

Carpet making
Continuous ornaments

The 'flower' carpet with the wide border belongs to the heyday of Persian art (16th century). The naturalistically treated flowers that were so popular in Persia are insignificant here: the scene is devoted to stylised motifs that display the variety of the Eastern palmette in all its fullness. The amazingly beautiful colour range is typical of Eastern carpet making.

The nine regular motifs taken from book decorations (two manuscripts of the *Shahnameh*; cf. plate 56) are formed of original geometrical shapes, although this type of Persian ornamentation could never really surpass Arabic or Moorish work.

Carpet

The plate shows the central field and the border of a Persian prayer rug that stand out for their bold elegance of line and the perfection of their palette. Its cloth base is covered by a decorative appliqué in the same material and the edges are embroidered with silk. The mutual influence of Indian and Persian ornamentation in the field of carpet making is confirmed by the rhythmic repetition of flower patterns on black and white backgrounds along the edges and on a black background in the corners of the central field.

PLATE 58

Inlay
Monochrome ornamentation

After engraving the outline of a design with a chisel, the skilled Eastern metal worker would build up low sides along the grooves; he would then insert a strip or thread of gold or silver and hammer it into the opening. The polished surface was embossed. A simpler method of engraving consisted of scratching outlines around a convex decoration, and in this case the depressions were filled with niello.

Inlay is one of the most ancient ways of decorating metal. However, if we attempt to date the oldest vases in all their variety — made of copper, bronze or other alloys, decorated with inlay and engraving, covered with ornamentation and emblems, girdled with Arabic inscriptions surrounded by arabesques and interlacing — we are unlikely to see further than the 12th century.

A large number of engraved metal articles exist that were created for Muslim princes, and even for the Frankish barons in the Latin colonies of Syria. There were two main decorative schools at the time: one was in the city of Mosul (al-Yasira) on the Tigris, and the other was the Syrian school with large jewellery workshops in Damascus and Cairo. The first school sprang up in Mesopotamia; this was a region where the Muslim spirit soon lost its fanaticism, and its most striking feature was the continued depiction of humans and animals. However, the Syrian craftsmen in Damascus and Cairo remained true to pure ornamentation, including inscriptions, and it is only towards the middle of the 13th century that we find articles from the Syrian school that portray heraldic animals and birds. Some of the vases at that time were made for the European market, and they are decorated not just with anthropomorphic motifs, but also with Christian subjects and inscriptions.

This type of decoration was typical of many articles, including enormous basins, cups, flasks, candlesticks, lamps, trays, inkpots and many others.

Book bindings

This plate shows part of the binding of an extremely large Koran (104 x 52cm). The book decorations in the following plates indicate a certain blending of the Persian and Arabic styles, but in this plate we can see a purely Arabic style with its severely geometrical structure. The main motif is formed by a combination of the strict geometrically drawn rosettes that Arabian craftsmen loved so much. The eye is involuntarily attracted to the 'accidental' geometrical shape which appears at the point where two rosettes of different sizes intersect, and which binds them together. Here the actual geometrical construction suggests various combinations of double heptagons, thus eliminating any of the monotony that would seem to be a feature of this genre. The motif at the bottom centre of the plate occupies the corner section of the border of the same binding. The other ornamentations decorate its inner and outer sides.

PLATE 60

61 ARABIC ART

Book decoration
Rosette ornamentation

The ornamental motifs on this plate show that in addition to the complete absence of pictures of living beings, since this was forbidden by religion, another characteristic of Arabic art was the cogency of the geometrical structures. We can find here typical features of Arabic ornamentation, such as the constantly twisting lines that radiate out from one centre (the rosette that forms the centre of the plate). The combination of a stylised flower ornament with a linear ornament and the way that the former becomes an integral part of the latter is an indication of Persian influence.

PLATE 61

Inscriptions in ornamental surrounds
Book decoration

The ornament of coloured rosettes, which
is taken from the same Koran (cf. plate 60),
continues to stress the dominant style in this
type of book decoration. Ornamental motifs
surround inscriptions in Kufic script (an early
form of Arabic writing) that are placed between
the 114 *suras* (or chapters) into which the text
of the Koran is divided. Examples of Kufic script
are shown in the two fragments on either side
of the central rosette.

The nature of such ornaments makes them ideal
patterns for producing enamelled jewellery
decorations.

The influence of the Persian decorative style
on Arabic ornamentation has already been
mentioned, but here traces of the influence of
the Byzantine style are just as obvious (cf. the
fragment in the bottom left corner of the plate).

63 ARABIC ART

Sacred inscriptions
Book decoration

Each of these complete ornaments comes from a magnificent manuscript copy of the Koran (the prophet Mohammed called it the *Book of Glory*) of immense size: 100 x 50cm. The decorated inscriptions in the original were each at least 30cm long. In fact the manuscript, which dates from the 15th or even the 14th century, can be taken as the fruit of Arabic art purely because the text is in Arabic; the actual decorative style is Persian, and a remarkable Persian style at that!

Inscriptions of the type shown in the plate usually stand before each of the 114 *suras* of the Koran. Arabic inscriptions were often written in Kufic letters; as far as can be judged, this primitive Arabic alphabet was invented in the ancient Chaldean city of Al-Kufa (Iraq). 'Rectangular Kufic' is easy to recognise: its elegantly balanced and bold lines combine with firmness and angularity to make a striking contrast to the graceful plant motif twisting round them. Kufic letters often became an ornamental motif in their own right. The actual inscriptions were so decorative that in the

Middle Ages and Renaissance European artists, forgetful of the symbolic meaning of the words that appeared in the halo above the head of Christ, often used them in the decoration of Christian works.

Marginal decorations on the fields of manuscripts change according to the contents, and an ornamentation that includes just single rosettes could be called 'stellar'. We have reproduced one of these twinkling stars that is emitting beams of light vertically, as well as two similar stars that are throwing out horizontal rays. The last illustration contains part of the sacred text. The codified word that has been set in motion by the Heavens seems like the shining track of a shooting star. The text confirms that the most amazing things in the realm of the stars can be predicted. The symmetry of the decoration embodies the order of the Heavens, a powerful and endless universe.

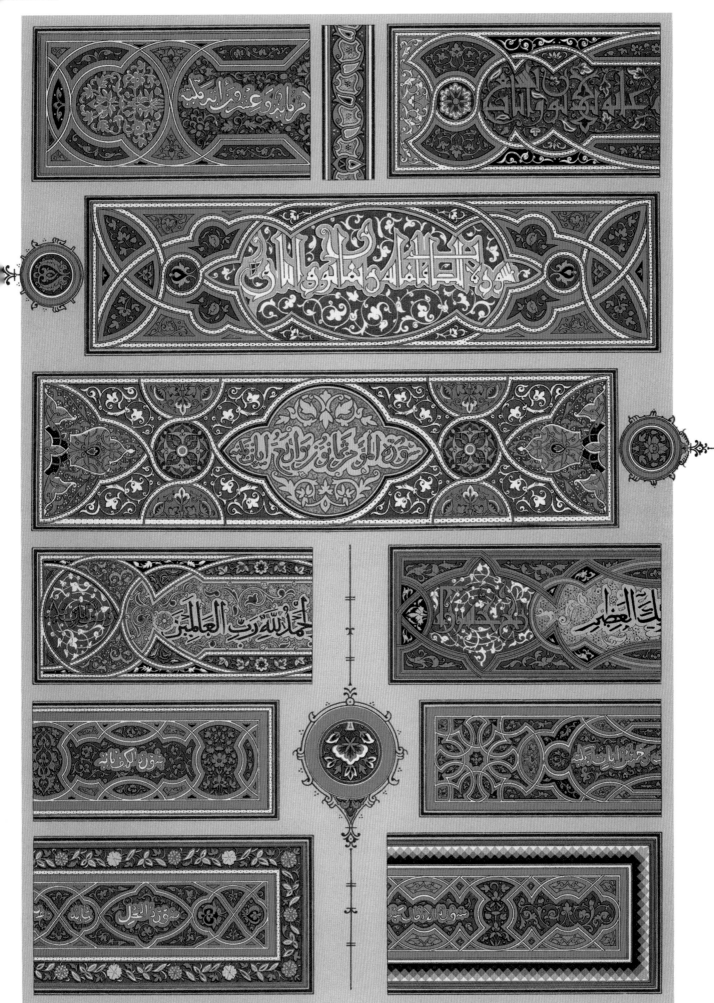

Book decoration
Decorated inscriptions

This plate is a continuation of the previous one.

Of particular interest is the large-scale ornamentation of various forms of the Kufic script used in most inscriptions: they either stand in proud isolation or make a gentle contrast to plant forms, and all are outlined by the double blue lines that we have seen before.

The tradition of decorated inscriptions arose in Persia back in ancient times. These miniature decorative compositions are in fact one aspect of a general type; they are the links of an ancient chain, of a complex system where decoration underwent specific alterations, especially as a result of the religious ban on depicting people and animals. It was as if the artist's wings were clipped, and it was only through the introduction of Arabic writing to replace Old Chaldean that decoration could be freed from the traditions that time had sanctified. However, the principle of decoration stayed the same, and the 'Arabic' manuscript from which we have taken these motifs is above all a product of Persian art. At this point it is important not to forget that the actual term 'Arabic art', i.e. ascribing all the architectural and decorative achievements of Islamic countries to the Arabs, was hotly debated by some specialists who believed that justice had to be done by admitting the kinship of the Byzantine and Persian styles.

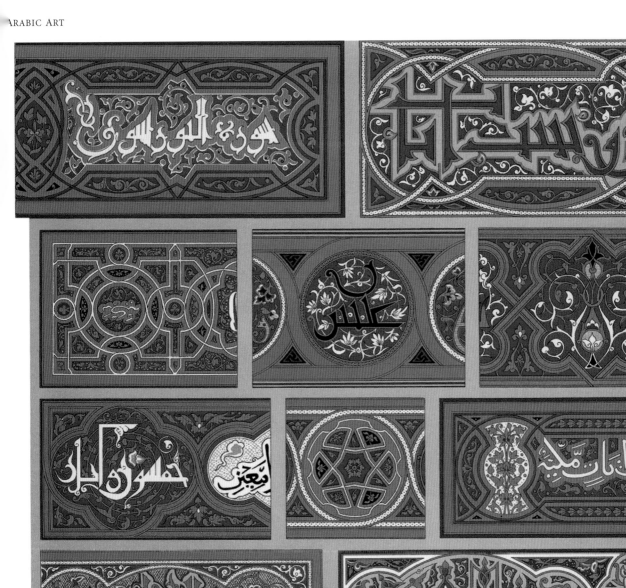

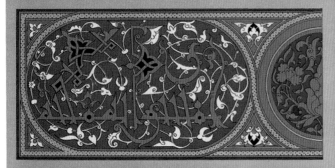

Ceramic mosaics and slip-glazed bricks

The Arabic architecture of Algeria, from which these motifs come, is remote from the old traditions of the 8th–9th centuries: proof of this is provided on the one hand by the famous mosque in Cordoba, and on the other hand by the Ibn Tulun mosque in Cairo. At the various stages that Arabic architecture passed through, specialists can see changes that are so typical and important that their origin must be sought in political events. The first signs of these changes appeared in the 11th–12th centuries, and when 14th-century ornamentation and mosaics are studied an architectural style is revealed that is called 'Moorish' or 'African'. The architectural monuments of Algeria confirm stylistically and chronologically that both Algeria and Spain were flooded with foreign craftsmen.

The geometrical compositions that are turned into drawings by pen and ruler belong to the type that specialists call 'Syro-Arabic'. The examples shown here tell us that the Moorish elongated and angular interlacing is built on the basis of either a triangle or a hexagon, or a square or an octagon.

Motif 6, in which straight lines give way to curves, is a quite whimsical type of ornamentation that is, in fact, strictly organised.

Motif 5 demonstrates an even more intricate type of décor in which the artful allocation of colour within the limits of a single-level interlacing creates the illusion of two superimposed levels; the large motifs in the corners of the square seem to be held down to the background by a white mesh (with a fifth element in the centre).

1 Fragment of a very striking ceramic mosaic that covers almost the entire dome of the minaret at the Sidi bu-Medina mosque near Tlemcen (Algeria);

3, 4 The massive doors of the former palace of the Tachfinya madrassa (Tlemcen, 1335–1340) were also decorated with a remarkable ceramic mosaic and artfully laid-out tile facing;

5, 6, 8 Decoration on the doors of the madrassa in Sidi bu-Medina: the exceptionally beautiful ceramic tiles are in an excellent state of preservation;

2, 7 Interesting examples of slip-glazed bricks that form characteristic compositions depending on the method of laying. Both motifs are from the décor of the ruined 14th-century mosque at Sidi ben Issak.

66 MOORISH ART

Mosaics and slip-glazed tiles

The motifs shown here originate from the decoration of the Alhambra fortress in Granada and the Alcazar palace in Seville (Spain). They are indebted to the Arabic decorative style for their geometrical purity. Some of them, those with flower ornamentation, already belong to the Hispano-Moorish system of decoration. By means of simple combinations of the same type of ornamentation, individual tiles form a rich continuous pattern that the ornamentalist will always find interesting.

PLATE 66

67 MOORISH ART

Architectural decoration

These motifs are from the Alhambra, the magnificent castle of the Moorish kings in Granada. This is the site of the consummate expression of a style that borrowed decorative components from Byzantium and then developed them with unusual brilliance and breadth. A striking feature of the Moorish system of decoration, and its great virtue, (we are talking about architectural decoration) is that the bold lines of the ornamentation obey architectonic principles and that individual details create a complete whole. This is why these ornaments play their part in the strength of the buildings that they decorate, despite their low relief.

PLATE 67

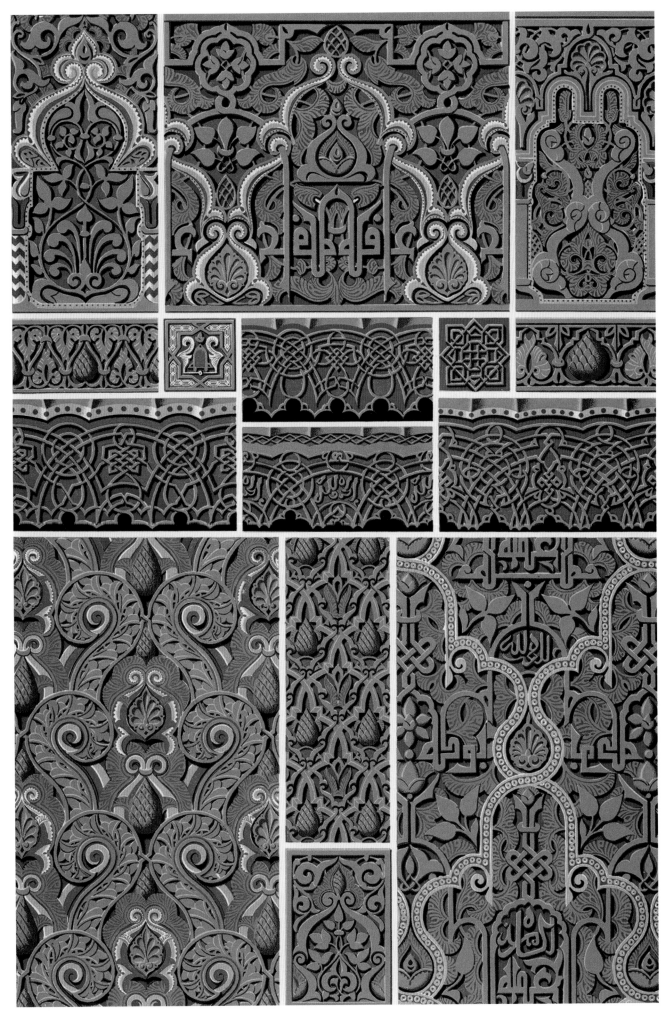

Wall tiles
Painted and slip-glazed terracotta
Tesselated work

The main role in decorating architectural structures was played by ceramics. Wall tiles were made from ordinary clay, and after careful preparation and firing they became identical, beautiful, clean and strong, but still porous. The surface was then covered with a layer of china clay, although sometimes before the china clay was applied they were decorated with a relief or incised pattern and the depressions were filled with glazes of various colours. The decoration was then outlined with a pigment containing divalent copper that formed a black outline around the drawing and did not allow the glazes to spread, mix or run (rather like the technique of cloisonné enamelling). An alternative was for each brick to be glazed separately after which a complete mosaic decoration was built from them.

The decoration reproduced here is nothing less than an example of the decay of Persian art. This process increased steadily as the art of the Ottoman Empire fell under the influence of French painters and sculptors. They were invited to Turkey by Sultan Ahmed III, who was known for his love of magnificence, to carry out special work for the ruler and were accompanied by structural engineers. As a result of this close contact Ottoman craftsmen adopted to a certain extent the European décor of the period from them: this was the time when the *style Pompadour* was flourishing in France. Tendrils, twisting lines and rocaille combined with strict traditional interlacing to give the décor a pretentiousness and splendour that fully suited Ottoman tastes. The magnificent motif in the upper centre of the plate is the only decoration on a rectangular panel. The four small motifs to the left and right of it are details of masonry discovered in the ruins of architectural monuments in Cairo. The two smallest motifs with the inverted designs painted alternately in light and dark tones belong to a particularly refined type of decoration.

Frescoes, mosaics and book decoration

The motifs are shown in chronological order:

1–5 Frescoes in the Hagia Sophia (Church of the Holy Wisdom – 6th century) in Constantinople; their style is related to the Greek style;

6 Mosaics in the Church of St George (5th–6th centuries). Salonica;

7–16 Frescoes discovered in Constantinople (7th–8th centuries);

17 Enamelled border;

18–28 Book decoration (7th–8th centuries) showing some divergence from classical examples;

29, 30 Decoration of a manuscript book produced for Emperor Basil the Macedonian (c. 860AD);

31, 32 Book decoration;

33, 34 Mosaic decoration from Palermo and Monreale (Sicily, 12th century)

35–40 Fragments of book decoration.

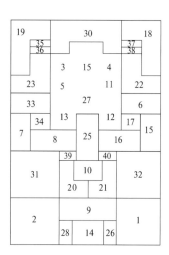

PLATE 69

Book decoration, 8th century

The 38 motifs shown in this plate belong to an extremely interesting period of transition from the Graeco-Roman (Pompeian) style (whose characteristic features can be seen in Nos. 2, 3, 5, 7, 10, 11, 13, 18, 29, 30 and 32) to the specifically Byzantine style. All the motifs are taken from hand-written Gospels, the main refuge of medieval miniaturists and ornamentalists.

1–26   The Godescalc Gospel from the Church of Saint Sernin (Toulouse). A manuscript copy of the Gospels in Latin, completed in 783 by the scribe Godescalc for Emperor Charlemagne (Paris, French National Library);

27–38   Codex from Saint-Médard, or Gospel from the Abbey of Saint-Médard (Soissonns), in Latin (French National Library, Paris).

PLATE 70

71 GRECO-BYZANTINE ART

Frescoes and mosaics, 9th–12th centuries
Book decoration

2–4 Motifs from a Greek manuscript of the four Gospels, Acts of the Apostles and Epistles illuminated in Asia Minor circa 800. The décor, which is painted either straight onto parchment or onto a gold background, has something in common with the clear-cut system of ornamentation used in Ancient Greece, and it is often only the type of flower or fruit that separates the rational development of the twisting plant elements from similar decoration on Ancient Greek vases. The repetition of one and the same motif (often a very small one) over the entire surface, or part of it, brings back memories of Indian decoration, and it was a very widespread artistic device of the time. Ornamentalists displayed an exceptional ability to avoid the unnecessary play of concentric lines, as can be seen from motifs 2 and 3, and from the circles and semicircles in the large mosaic fragment (1). Moreover, examining large- or small-scale decorations will convince us that the systems of ornamentation of the eastern or western Greek schools were similar in many respects, and we can say confidently that both the master who produced headpieces and the mosaicist were guided by a generally accepted principle of tactically organised freedom of design and soft colouring. The artists who preferred gold backgrounds were not merely varying the monochrome effect; on the gold mosaic backgrounds that were the favourites of Byzantine artists, the colour range to be used for the decoration was strictly limited both in the number of colours and in their chromatic variety. Their experience is worth the attention of modern designers.

1 A very large mosaic on the ceiling of a chapel in the Basilica of St Mark (Venice) which was built in the 9th century. In the light of what has been said about the main features of the style of the Greek school of decoration, we must stress the importance of this example; it was created in Byzantine style, which was more severe than the style of the Eastern school. Because of its restraint, this mosaic surpasses even classical decoration;

5, 6 Border in the shape of a portico framing a text in a manuscript from Grenoble Library. It was illuminated in the 10th century, possibly in Lombardy, under the influence of the Greek style; the manuscript is ascribed to the Greco-Lombard school (650–1100);

7, 8 Interwoven ribbons on fields, representing the right-angle bends of a Greek meander. These intricate versions of a classical motif appear in a German manuscript dating to the first half of the 12th century (the so-called *Gospel of Louis César de la Baume le Blanc, duc de La Vallière*);

9 Motif in the style of the 12th-century Norman school.

Greek decoration, 4th–6th centuries
Painting of building materials
Monochrome decoration

1 Part of a door made of sycamore from a Coptic church in Old Cairo. The church is dedicated to St Helena, the mother of Emperor Constantine;

2, 4, 6 Marble open-work panels from the Church of San Vitale (Ravenna). The white marble pattern stands out gracefully against the dark, almost black, background.

Motifs 2 and 6 are decorated openings in a wall; 4 – decoration of a stone floor. All three motifs are based on the principle of a continuous pattern, although they are confined by borders that are also full of ornamentation;

5, 7 Rectangular windows with open-work decoration. The compositions are distinguished by their varied decorative effects that were intended to fill up completely the whole window opening; 5 – a geometrically rectilinear ornamentation (meander); 7 – stylised plant fronds combined with zoomorphic heraldic forms;

3 The circular dormer in the façade of the Basilica of Santa Maria Maggiore (Rome) belongs to the type of window that is found in church facades. The circular windows of Roman basilicas were the prototype of the Gothic rose window. The most widely varied types and colours of material were used, and the earliest examples were found in Greece and the Arab countries. Early Greek architecture demonstrated the used of stone and brick, sometimes black and white and sometimes white and red alternately.

The Cathedral of San Vitale was built at the same time as the Hagia Sophia in Constantinople and is an important topic for study. It has been definitely established that San Vitale was constructed under the guidance of Greek masters and the Hagia Sophia was built by two architects from Asia Minor, Anthemius of Tralles and Isidore of Miletus.

As a rule the woven patterns and plant motifs of the period were not in relief. Delicate, sharply outlined and elegantly entwined, they had their individual characters which are then found in most architectural monuments in Europe in the 12th century.

1		
2	3	4
5	6	7

73 CELTO-BYZANTINE ART

Types of decorative painting,
6th–9th centuries
Jewellery decorations with enamel,
10th century
Colour in Romanesque architecture,
11th century
Book decoration

Three features that characterise motifs 1, 2 and 4 justify the use of the term 'Celto-Byzantine' when applied to them: plant motifs in a sumptuous Byzantine style, a human figure in the Greek manner and Celtic interlaced ribbons either with or without the inclusion of zoomorphic elements. This is also confirmed by the origins of the manuscripts that they decorate: Sweden, Denmark, England and the Rhineland in Germany.

Careful study of the marginal decoration shows that it is not merely the invention of the illuminators, but is the work of masters who specialised in the various types of ornamentation of the time, whether hieratic painting in a sanctuary, frescoes or mosaics in a church, an inscribed panel in a frame or enamelled gold decorations. Motif 1 is a fine example of this

last: it was created by a hand that knew all the secrets of the craft and appears on a page of a Psalter as irrefutable testimony to the heyday of the jewellery art of the time.

It was not just the influence of the Celtic ('insular') decorative and ornamental style that brought the Byzantine tradition back to life. It is obvious, for instance, that the depiction of the human figure goes straight back to the fading traditions of antiquity; it is also clear that, in the opinion of archaeologists, motifs such as 2–4 represent a direct link between the expression of physical beauty (as the classical Greeks understood it) and spiritual beauty (as it was understood by the Christian masters who painted the catacombs in Rome, and their successors: the mosaicists and artists of the start of the Middle Ages).

Mosaics, inlay, niello and frescoes
Byzantine style

The sources of the ornamental motifs shown are:

1–4   Churches of St George, St Demetrios and
       St Sofia in Salonica (Greece);

5, 6   Cathedral in Ravello;

7, 8   Cathedral in Monreale (Sicily);

9, 10   Chapel in the Zisa Palace, Palermo
        (Sicily);

11   Capella Palatina, Palermo;

12–19   Greek manuscript books;

20–22   Ornamental motifs (19th century).

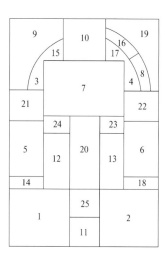

Byzantine ornamentation of the
11th century

The decorations shown here are of great interest both from the historical and the artistic points of view. With one exception, they all come from the most remarkable manuscript copy of gospel texts, the *Apocalypse of Saint-Sever* (French National Library, Paris). The exception is the fleurons (top centre), which have been taken from another Greek manuscript.

What is very important is that although these ornaments come from little-known sources, they give a clear idea of the Byzantine influence on Arabic art; this was not such a rare phenomenon at a time when victorious civilisations took and assimilated the art of the peoples that they had conquered.

The red and yellow leafy pattern on a pink background (1) and the other plant motifs (5–9 and 13–17) are characteristic examples of the outline depictions and generalised forms that were typical of Arabic ornamentalists who treated them with exceptional freedom and simplicity, even in more complex compositions.

PLATE 75

Mosaics, enamel plant patterns in filigree sourrounds and embroidery

1–7   Mosaics from the chapel of La Zisa in Palermo (Sicily);

8–11 Cloisonné enamels in a filigree surround: setting made of precious stones (binding of an Evangeliary in the Louvre);

12–19 Fresco motifs from the Theoskepastos Monastery (beginning of the 18th century) near Trabzon (Turkey).

The last group shows sumptuous fabrics sewn with pearls and precious stones. The love of the Byzantines for magnificent fabrics went so far that as well as using them for making clothes they even used them for footwear. The passion of the time for exuberant and graceful work led John Chrysosthomos to say that 'today's goldsmiths and weavers inspire our admiration.'

Mosaics of the 12th century

The sixteen motifs from mosaic decorations come from the following sources:

1–12 Capella Palatina in Palermo. When they conquered Sicily the Normans found a highly developed architecture there. The Norman King Roger was carried away by it and invited Byzantine architects, who by this time had already adopted the architectonic system of the Arabs, for his own building work. Thus during the period when the Normans ruled Sicily a particular architectural style developed that combined eastern richness with elements of Byzantine culture.

One of the most beautiful surviving basilicas was built at Roger's command; this is the Capella Palatina in Palermo (1130–1143), decorated in regal splendour with marble and mosaics, and with its lancet arches and Islamic stalactite vaulting;

13–15 La Zisa Palace in Palermo (1154–1160);

16 Palace in Salerno (Italy).

Murals on walls and floors

10, 15, 16, 18, 20 Fragments of a mosaic floor in the Basilica of Santa Maria in Cosmedin (Rome). This 'decorated' church (from the Greek κοσμεω – to decorate) owes its name to the splendour with which it was decorated in 728 by Roman craftsmen at the orders of Pope Adrian I. The entire floor of the nave is clad with porphyry and a precious marble mosaic;

9, 11–14, 17, 19, 21 Mosaic work using rare marbles together with jasper, porphyry and serpentine. The mosaics are in the sanctuary of the Monastery Church of St Fleury (nowadays Saint-Benoît-sur-Loire), which was built in 1067, and were brought from Italy at the direction of Cardinal Antoine Dupré. On his instructions considerable restoration work was carried out in the church during the 16th century;

1–8 Geometrical mosaics with an enamel inlay. They are similar to the mosaics in the Capella Palatina (Palermo) that date to the first half of the 12th century. The mosaics shown here decorated the Church of Santa Cesarea (Rome).

1		2	
3		4	
5		6	
9	7		11
10			12
13	14	8	15	16
17	18	19	20	21

Tesselation, 14th–15th centuries

The first twenty motifs show mosaic ornaments, made of pieces of elephant ivory and wood, which decorated the *Poissy Altarpiece*, a genuine masterpiece in the 14th-century style. This magnificent altar rail was donated by Jean de France, Duke of Berry, and his wife Jeanne, Countess of Auvergne and Boulogne. The Duke of Berry (1340–1416), who was the brother of Charles V and uncle of Charles VI, was a famous collector of his time. An inventory of his property compiled in 1416 mentions many pieces of ceremonial equipment, precious stones, objects from the natural world and curios;

his library contained magnificent manuscript books, including three Books of Hours, one of which was the *Très Riches heures du duc de Berry* that was illuminated for him by the famous Limbourg brothers.

21–27 Tesselated ornamental motifs made of pieces of elephant ivory on chests (from about the same time);

28–31 Marquetry pattern (15th century) that decorates the archbishop's throne in the Church of Sant'Ambrogio in Milan. Although individual motifs are chronologically close to the Renaissance, stylistically they still belong to Byzantium. The reason for this is that at the heart of the modest technique of marquetry there is a certain conservatism that stops it from reacting promptly to changes in ornamental style.

1		3		2	
	28		29		
21	25	22	23	26	24
4	6	7		8	9
5					27
10		15	16	11	
12	14	18	17	13	
		19			
30		20	31		

PLATE 79

Book decoration
Borders and fleurons, 8th–12th centuries

The corner motifs shown in the table belong to what is called the 'Period of Exfoliation' that occurred in England and Normandy between 800 and 1200. This type of decoration (and it is magnificent decoration!) was developed with great success by a completely independent Anglo-Saxon artistic school enclosed within the walls of two monasteries in Winchester, St Swithun's and New Minster. It is believed that the Winchester school was founded by Abbot Dunstan, who was himself an experienced illuminator and one of the most respected English bishops of the 10th century. The output of this school was known universally as *Opus anglicum*. In looser terms this style can be defined as a free imitation of the decorative and ornamental style of the Eastern Empire. A leading scribe and miniaturist during the second half of the 10th century was Godeman (Godemannus) who created the *Devonshire Benedictional* (it was in the library of the dukes of Devonshire at Chatsworth), also known as the *Benedictional of St Æthelwold* (it was produced in 963–984 for Bishop Æthelwold of Winchester).

The border decorations are taken from two manuscript books that historians ascribe either to Godeman himself, or to a craftsman of his school. One is in the *Benedictional of Archbishop Robert* (produced for Æthelgar, Abbot of New Minster, who died as Archbishop of Canterbury in 989); the other is in the *Missal of Robert of Jumièges* (also known as the *Missal of Robert Champart* or *Robert of Normandy, Archbishop of Canterbury*). On being exiled from England he took both manuscripts with him to Jumièges, a Benedictine Abbey of which he had previously been the head, and where he died between 1052 and 1056.

Celtic ornaments of the 7th–9th centuries

'Celtic' is the term that modern art historians usually apply to a style which is also called 'Anglo-Saxon'. Some believe that it resulted from the mixing of Scandinavian and Byzantine elements. It is also considered to be a local style that was created by the insular genius of the primitive inhabitants of the British Isles. The early period of this style is characterised by a complete absence of plant motifs and by a concentration on simple geometrical forms: curls, spirals, bell shapes and ribbons that form complex interlacings. Book decoration is not linked to the text, and the Irish miniaturist does not illustrate the text, but decorates it.

7TH CENTURY

1, 3, 5–7, 11–13, 25, 28–30 Gospel from Durrow: symbols of the evangelists and decorated pages (Trinity College, Dublin);

4, 33 Frontispieces of the Gospels of St Mark and St Luke;

26 *Lindisfarne Gospel*: decorated page (British Museum, London);

22, 31 Frontispiece of the Gospel of St Luke.

8TH CENTURY

18 *Commentary on the Psalms* by Cassiodorus 'manu Bedae' (by the hand of Bede) *David and Goliath* (Cathedral Library, Durham);

8, 24 *King David*;

2, 14 Gospel of St Mark with symbols of the evangelists (Monastery Library in St Gallen, Switzerland).

9TH CENTURY

6 Gospel in Latin: decorated page and *Praise of Christ* (Monastery Library in St Gallen, Switzerland);

10 Manuscript Gospel: *Crucifixion of Christ* (Monastery Library in St Gallen, Switzerland);

27 Psalter of John the Evangelist (Cambridge, England): *David and Goliath*, *David kills the Lion* and beginnings of Psalms 1 and 102.

Like most of the motifs mentioned above, the small ornamentations (15–17, 19–31, 32) also originate from manuscript books in the Bodleian Library (Oxford, England), the library in St Gallen and the library of Trinity College (Dublin).

PLATE 81

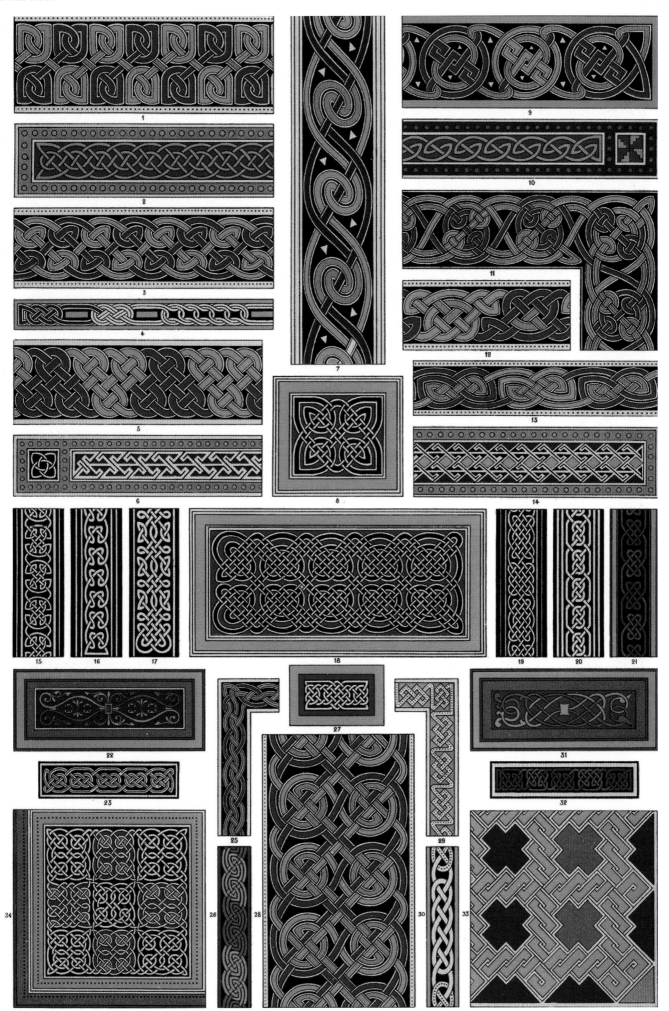

Ribbon interlacing and writhing dragons
Book decoration, 7th–9th centuries

Unlike the severe geometrical designs of Near Eastern ornamentation, Celtic ribbon intelacings create a play of lines whose interwoven images, sometimes straight and sometimes curving, turn them into the fruit of a fascinating and logically thought-out caprice. This organised freedom of line was created by a true master, and it gave birth to striking patterns that represented a step from simple ribbon interlacing towards complex geometrical oramentation combined with plant fronds and the stylised twisting figures of animals. From the historical point of view it is not even a step, since both types of decoration continued to exist and develop simultaneously.

These highly-stylised 'animal style' motifs, writhing dragons (*drakslingors*) whose complex interweavings look so striking on rune stones, were used even more widely on metal articles of the 7th–9th centuries on the island of Gotland (Sweden). The motifs decorating the Irish manuscript books are of the same origin.

Archaeologists suspect that the appearance of bronze in Scandinavia circa 1000 BC is linked to the arrival of a Celtic tribe that brought with it both the metal and the type of decoration described. Whatever the case, the ribbon ornament and the elongated bodies of fantastical animals appeared on Scandinavian weapons and jewellery at the very beginning of the Iron Age.

7TH CENTURY

Motifs 1 and 4 are from a Gospel of St Matthew;

Motifs 3, 7, 9, 10, 12, 17 and 19 are from the *Durrow Gospel* (both in Trinity College, Dublin);

Motif 6 is from a manuscript in the British Museum (London).

8TH CENTURY

2, 5 – motifs from another Gospel of Matthew;

8 – from the *Lindisfarne Gospel* (beginning of the 8th century);

11, 13 – from the *Mac Durnan Gospels* in Lambeth Palace;

15, 16, 18, 20 – from manuscripts in the Monastery Library in St Gallen (Switzerland);

PLATE 82

Celto-Scandinavian ornamentation,
7th–9th centuries
Decorated letters

1 Part of the first page of the Gospel of
Mark from the *Codex Aureus* (Stockholm
Library, 7th–8th centuries). The text is
written in uncial script, as was usual at the
time. The first group consists of three
Greek letters and forms a monogram of
the name of Christ. The monumental
details that surround the monogram and
weave themselves into the first line of the
text produce an impression of richness
and elegance which reminds us of precious
decoration on gold brocade. The artist has
avoided monotony by varying the motifs
and using all the resources of Scandinavian
ornamentation. Celtic interlacing appears
in all its forms, and is supplemented by
Byzantine-style pictures of birds and
animals that seem almost to be struggling
in its curls. Sometimes simple plant motifs
stand out in their purely Byzantine clarity
and logic. Part of the space is covered
with spirals that represent the continual
movement of the sea's waves, or even
whirlwinds or whirpools, which (like other
natural phenomena) the Chinese managed
to represent so convincingly;

2 Another monogram of the name of
Christ, this time with a lengthened first
letter, appears on the first page of a Gospel
of Matthew (8th–9th centuries, Monastery
Library in St Gallen, Switzerland). We
can see here the zoomorphic interlacing
that is so common on rune stones, as well
as geometrically rectilinear decorative
compositions placed diagonally that
remind us of Chinese decoration. The rows
of evenly spaced dots in the strips that
divide the decorations are another feature
of this style.

Motifs 7–9 are taken from the same
manuscript;

3–6 Latin initial Q, letter O, double spiral
ornament and border with continuous
interlacing from the Durrow Gospel (7th
century, Trinity College, Dublin, Ireland).

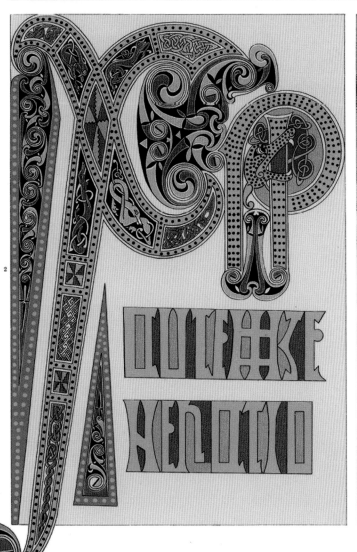

Book decoration, 8th–10th centuries
Gallo-Frankish and Anglo-Saxon schools

The types of Byzantine plant interlacing and
Celtic ribbon interlacing shown here were
used both separately and together, and we will
merely indicate the sources. All the manuscripts
were produced before 1000, and are listed in
chronological order:

8   Start of the Gospel of John ('In the beginning
    was the Word…') in the Four Gospels from
    the Church of Saint-Pierre in Liège (8th–9th
    century). Despite the graphic nature of the
    work, the decorated initials are a magnificent
    illustration of the book art of the Carolingian
    period. The original sheet is 23cm high ;

3   Initial in the style of the 'writhing dragons'
    that were carved on Celto-Scandinavian
    rune stones. It is in a Psalter (Cambridge
    University, England) dating to the 9th
    century;

7   Ornamentation on a page from the *Gospel
    of Chlothar I* in the French National Library,
    Paris. The manuscript was copied and
    illuminated in the royal Abbey of St-Martin
    in Tours. Gallo-Frankish school;

2   Upper part of a border with a depiction of
    the Saviour. Anglo-Saxon school, 10th
    century. The Byzantine decorative elements
    should be noted;

4   Border that includes similar decorative
    elements, but done more delicately. From
    the Charter of King Edgar to Winchester
    Cathedral in 966 ('Donation Charter' of
    King Edgar to the New Minster Abbey);

5   Latin initial 'I' (from 'In principio' – 'In the
    beginning was the Word…'), the first letter
    of Gospel of John. The initial represents
    'the Word became flesh' (John 1: 14). 10th
    century. The mutual influence of Celtic and
    Byzantine decorative elements is noteworthy;

1   Latin initial 'B' (from 'Beatus' – 'Blessed
    is the man…') that begins the Psalms of
    David. Anglo-Saxon school, c. 1000. Celtic
    ornamentation combined with figurative
    pictures in the Byzantine manner;

6   Border with a continuous motif from the
    same source.

Celtic ornaments, 7th–11th centuries

Table 81 and the first twelve motifs in this plate exemplify the first period in the development of the Celtic style, where purely linear geometric compositions predominate. However, in motifs 13, 15 and 16 (8th–9th centuries) we can see the heads of fantastical animals that have been woven into the decoration, and as we move forward into the 9th and 10th centuries we can see how the lines gradually lose their extreme stylisation and mathematical regularity; forms become freer and something living appears that has been borrowed from the variety and unpredictability of nature itself. Motifs 18–33 (10th–11th centuries) appeared during this period, which is known as the 'Period of Exfoliation'. Finally, four magnificent isomorphic initials (34–37) demonstrate an indivisible and faultless combination of fantasy and symmetry.

7TH CENTURY

1–6 *Durrow Gospel* (Trinity College, Dublin);

7, 8 *Book of Kells* (Trinity College, Dublin);

9, 10 Royal manuscripts (British Museum, London);

7TH–8TH CENTURY

11 *Canterbury codex aureus* [Purple codex written in gold] (Royal Library, Stockholm);

8TH CENTURY

12 *Gospel of Abbot Thomas* (City Library , Trier);

13 *Commentary on the Psalms* by Cassiodorus (Cathedral Library, Durham).

8TH–9TH CENTURY

14 *St Chad Gospel* (Lichfield Cathedral, England).

9TH CENTURY

15 *Psalter of John the Evangelist* (Cambridge, England);

16, 17 *Mac Durnan Gospel* (Lambeth Palace Library, England).

10TH CENTURY

18 Gospel in Latin (Trinity College, Cambridge);

19–21 *Codex Vossianus* (Bodleian Library, Oxford);

22 *Benedictional of St Æthelwold* (British Museum, London);

11TH CENTURY

23, 24 Large Psalter in Latin (Public Library, Boulogne);

25–33 *Arundel Psalter* (British Museum, London);

34–37 Decorated initials from a Psalter from Saint-Germain-des-Prés (French National Library, Paris).

Mosaics and paintings of the Gallo-Roman
and Romanesque periods

9, 13   Mosaics of the Gallo-Roman period
that were discovered in Bielle
(Pyrénées-Atlantiques) in 1842; they
are now almost totally destroyed.
These magnificent mosaics are made
of small (5–6mm) cubes of stone,
marble and brick. The reader must
remember that due to the small size of
these reproductions it is impossible to
show the network of lines that separate
the cubes on their white cement base;
at a distance they look like a veil on a
delicate face, toning it and reducing the
brightness of the colours so that they
mingle strikingly. As an example, if
the black and red cubes are looked at
outside the composition they have a
rich, saturated shade. However, when
they are united with the others they
gain a touch of white, and this brings
harmony to the relationships of colour
in the decoration without causing
any harm to the strong lines of the
composition. When the background
is black (2) the lines become grey and
sufficiently bright, but less precise and
less saturated. The effect achieved does
not run counter to the technique of
painting, but is completely unacceptable
for mosaics: the deep black forms 'holes'
that distort the surface;

7, 11   Mosaics from Pondoli near Girona
(Pyrénées-Atlantiques). The baths that
these motifs decorate are a remarkable
example of Gallo-Roman decorative art;

3   The border of the sole surviving
fragment of a Gallo-Roman mosaic
(15cm x 15cm) discovered at a cemetery
in Taron (Pyrénées-Atlantiques) in
1860. The mosaic was mounted on a
pink base. The border is filled with a
pattern laid out in a masterly manner;
it has not survived;

2, 5   Fragment and continuous motif
(12th century, Romanesque style) in
the decoration of the church in Sorde
(Landes), of which only the apse (end
of the 11th century) now survives. The
church was built in the Byzantine style,
but the mosaic is considered to belong
to a transitional Romanesque period;

1, 4, 6, 8, 10   Borders and a fleuron from the
decoration of the *Bible of Martial of
Limoges*. The décor reflects the French
Romanesque style (950–1200);

12   Ornamental motif from the Psalter
of the Grenoble Bible. 12th century,
Romanesque style.

PLATE 86

Mosaics in the Gallo-Roman and
Romanesque styles

4, 5 Mosaics from Pondoli near Girona
(Pyrénées-Atlantiques). These
interesting examples of Gallo-Roman
decorative art were discovered in the
ruins of Roman baths;

1–3, 6 Mosaic from the church in Sorde
(Landes). This church was built in
the Romanesque style (end of the
11th century) and only the apse
has survived. The mosaic reflects a
transitional Romanesque style in
which characteristic Byzantine features
predominate. The elongated figures
of animals (1) are in heraldic poses.

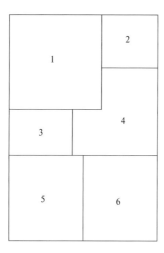

PLATE 87

Bas reliefs. Metal working. Painted
decoration
French schools, 11th–14th centuries

PROVENÇAL SCHOOL.

1, 2 Bas-reliefs from the cathedral in Viviers
(Ardèche), Carolingian period. The
single-altar chapel on the upper floor is
surmounted by a dome made by Salardu.
The individual horizontal rows of the
stone cladding are decorated with graceful
moulded friezes, plant motifs and stylised
zoomorphic motifs.

POITOU SCHOOL.

The principle of the ornamentation goes back to
the classical palmette.

3, 4 Wrought-iron decoration on the doors of
the Church of the Holy Sepulchre in Neuvy
(Indre). This circular church was finished
in the 11th century and rebuilt in the 13th;

5–7 Paintings in the church of the former
Abbey of Saint-Désiré (Allier). The apse
dates to the end of the 11th–beginning
of the 13th centuries and the crypt
(the underground chapel) from the
9th–10th centuries.

BURGUNDIAN SCHOOL.

8, 9 Carved borders on the wooden doors of
the church of the former abbey in Charlieu
(Loire), 11th–12th centuries.

The only parts of the church to survive
are its portal, one of the finest examples
of Romanesque architecture in Burgundy,
part of the covered arcade that was
rebuilt in the 15th century and one or
two buildings that were once occupied by
the prior.

Motif 8 – meander with pearls;

Motif 9 – double interlaced ribbon.

PLATE 88

Painted decoration
French schools, 11th–14th centuries

Continuation of the preceding plate.

1–7 Painted friezes from the church of
the former Abbey of Hambye (Manche)
which was founded in 1145; part of
the stone walls that surround the
abbey have survived. Judging from the
architectural style of the mortuary,
the church was built in the 13th century.
Both the walls of the mortuary and those
of the Chapter House and covered arcade
were covered with paintings.

Motif 3 is a horizontal frieze and the
others are ceiling friezes.

ILE-DE-FRANCE SCHOOL.

8, 9 Painted decoration from the church of
the former Abbey of Saint-Jean-aux-Bois
(Oise), dating to the first half of the
13th century.

Motif 8 is on the arch of a tomb and
motif 9 is on the end of a vault rib;

10, 11 Painted decoration in the Sainte
Chapelle (Paris), which was built
during the time of St Louis by Pierre de
Montereau (or Montreuil), 1242–1247.
Some parts of the building underwent
alteration in the 15th century, during the
reign of Charles VII. The yellow colour
indicates gilding;

12 Painted frieze from the Church of
St-Jean in Poitiers; it was often called
a temple because of its classical
pediment. The church, which dates to
the 6th century, was originally the town
baptistery. The ornament is a meander
in the classical style;

13 Painted frieze from the cathedral in
Clermont-Ferrand (Puy-de-Dôme,
Auvergne), 14th century;

14, 15 Painted decoration in the Church of
St Philibert (Tournus), 13th–14th
centuries. We do not have any reliable
information about this architectural
monument, but the paintings shown
here (one of them with a classical
motif of acanthus leaves) speak clearly
of the approach of the Renaissance.
There is unlikely to be a more striking
example of this style than the meander
with its fantastical and even symbolical
depictions of animals, and the cross at
the centre of each bunch of grapes.

PLATE 89

Book decoration
Romanesque style, 11th–12th centuries

These ornamental motifs are drawn from
two manuscript books. One of them, the
Commentary on the Apocalypse by Beatus, is
written on a half sheet and reproduces enlarged
miniatures from another old manuscript
(possibly 8th century). The second manuscript
is a Gospel in the same format; it is richly
illuminated with a wide range of ornamentation
that is typical of architecture and painting in
the 11th–12th centuries. The Gospel was created
in the scriptorium at the Abbey of Luxeuil
(Haute Saône), a famous monastery founded
by St Columba.

Each of the four Gospels opens with a page
that is coloured purple or blue and painted with
fantastical animals in the style of the decoration
on silk of the time. These coloured pages seem
to anticipate the appearance of the miniatures
that are scattered throughout the text. At that
time it was usual to separate one Gospel from
another with a piece of silk or a sheet of thin
parchment with miniatures in the style of
tapestry decoration.

The ornamentation belongs to the
Romanesque style, in other words Byzantine.
The energetic lines of the deeply cut leaves and
the combination of naturalistic and fantastical
shapes represent the final metamorphosis of
classical ornamentation; they still gravitate
towards architecture and especially towards
the decoration of the round arch. However, it is
only in the 13th century that the imitation of
the local flora, trefoils, four-lobed rosettes and
the curves of bishops' crosiers are replaced by the
Gothic style of decoration. Motifs 1–16 are in the
Commentary of Beatus and the remainder are in
the Luxeuil Gospel.

PLATE 90

Mosaics: coloured paste and smalt
Marble mosaics, 9th–13th centuries

With the exception of the large initial (12), all the motifs shown here decorate the Basilica of St Mark in Venice (976–1071); a considerable amount of the decoration was added later. In its architecture and decoration St Mark's Basilica belongs to the second period of Byzantine art (9th–12th centuries); the third period is reckoned to coincide with the Venetian conquests.

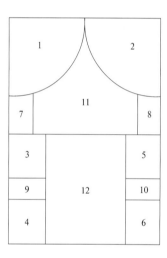

The two rosettes (1, 2) are among the most intricate elements of the decoration. Coloured glass pastes and smalt placed on a gold background create the illusion of a relief. These beautiful mosaics, which probably date to the 12th century, decorate the cathedral's portal.

The vertical and frieze borders (7–10) are made of polychrome glass paste or smalt. The transparent background allows their amazing dynamism to stand out.

Motifs from a mosaic floor (3–6, 11) made of marble. Their method of composition is based on tessellation; this is a quite conservative technique and probably explains why they resemble classical decoration more than most.

Motif 12 is taken from the decoration in a manuscript of the 12th or early 13th century.

Book decoration, 8th–13th centuries
Plant tendrils and emblems

3 Ribbon interlacing in the Celtic style
from the *Gospel of Charles I*, a manuscript
that was produced in the 8th century in
the former monastery and royal priory
of St Martin des Champs in Paris. Gallo-
Frankish school in its heyday, 700–950;

2 Latin initial *E* from a manuscript of
German origin dating to the second half
of the 11th century. This Latin Gospel was
copied for the superior of Luxeuil Abbey
in Franche Comté;

1, 4 These fragments of borders on the pages
of Harley manuscripts (Harley Collection,
British Museum) are magnificent
examples of 12th century calligraphy. The
ornamentation is close to the style of the
wrought-iron decoration of the period,
and therefore the very neutral colouring is
confined to the background;

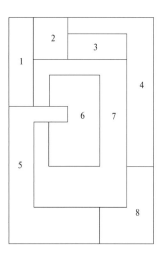

5, 7 Marginal borders from another Harley
manuscript, a two-volume Bible dating
to the end of the 12th or beginning of the
13th century. The richness of the severe
leaf ornamentation is supplemented by
the introduction of emblematic features.

Motif 7 edges the first page of the *Book
of the Prophet Jeremiah*, and in the original
the ribbon that the prophet is holding has
an inscription in Latin: *Verba Ieremie*
(The Word of Jeremiah). At the beginning
of the *Book of Jeremiah* God says to the
prophet: 'I make you this day a fortified
city, an iron pillar, and bronze walls
against the whole land…' as a promise that
Jeremiah will remain firm and unshakeable
in the face of trials. The illustration
confirms this: the prophet knows that God
is on his side ('For I am with you, says the
Lord, to deliver you'). The miniaturist has
transformed the dragon which Jeremiah
is trampling underfoot into a magnificent
decorative motif: it is alive and talking,
since the rich branch-like ornamentation
crawling out of the monster's jaws is the
tongue of evil;

6 Fragment of a border that it is easy to
restore and present in completed form.
The motif is from a 12th-century prayer
book from the former Abbey of St-Maur-
des-Fossés in the Diocese of Paris;

8 Part of the border decoration in a prayer
book from the church of the Abbey of
St-Denis, which dates to the 13th century.

Book decoration, 8th–12th centuries
Plant motifs, vertical friezes, borders, etc

The motifs are listed in chronological order.

16 From the *Bible of Emperor Chlothar I.* Gallo-Frankish school, 750–800;

15, 21, 30 From a manuscript in Latin, 900–950;

6, 7 From a manuscript in Latin, 980;

1, 4 From a manuscript in Latin. Graeco-Lombard school, 1100;

8, 10 From a manuscript in Latin, 1100;

9, 11, 17–29, 31–33 From a three-volume in folio *Biblia Sacra* (Holy Bible). Graeco-English school, 1150. It is the work of Manerius of Canterbury, a scribe and illuminator of the Canterbury school.

Motifs 17 and 33 should be viewed together;

Motif 17 is the completion of the decoration. The manuscript is considered to be a rare and valuable example of the Graeco-Saxon style of the period. The ornamentation has some similarities to the *Æthelgar Manuscript* in the Rouen Public Library. However, Manerius's work contains many ingenious and mature artistic solutions that can be explained as the introduction of new forms of decoration (cf. 17 and 23, 22, 29). It can be called an Anglo-Saxon miniature enriched by French influence, with the addition of Byzantine ornamental motifs.

Motif 25 also reprents a new form: it is essentially Byzantine, but treated in an openly Saxon way that anticipates the beautiful borders which include bishops' crosiers in the stained-glass windows of French cathedrals. A bishop's crosier is shown in motif 32;

2, 3, 5 From a manuscript in Latin, 1150;

12–14 From a manuscript in French, 1190.

PLATE 93

Embroidery, frescoes and enamels

1–4   Silk fabrics embroidered with gold (12th century) from a tomb in the Abbey of Saint-Germain-des-Près (France);

5–8   Frescoes (13th century) in the Chapel of Notre-Dame de la Roche (Seine et Oise) and the Dominican monastery in Agen (Lot et Garonne);

9–15   Frescoes in churches in Amencharods-Roda [Södra Råda?] [Аменчародс-Рода] and Edshult (Sweden);

16–27   Enamels from the treasury in Aachen;

28, 29   Fragments of book decoration.

11	4	12		
5		6		
9	1	10		
7		8		
28	3	29		
16	13	18		
	14			
17	15	19		
20	2	24		
21		25		
22		26		
23		27		

PLATE 94

Graeco-Syrian fabric ornamentation

Eastern fabrics were extremely popular in Western countries from the very beginning of the Middle Ages, and the finest were obtained from Constantinople, Jerusalem and some Greek towns. Until the end of the 13th century West European weavers were no more than apprentices to their Eastern counterparts, and almost all the fabrics made on their looms were imitations of Near-Eastern examples. Nobody at the time dared to give up Greek and Egyptian styles and try to bring something new into the decoration. If we remember the cloth called *camocas* (heavy satins with an embroidered pattern that were produced in the 14th century), we cannot help being surprised that stylistically the decoration often turns back to the ornamentation of a much earlier period.

1, 2 Decoration on the hem and field of a chasuble that is preserved in the church in St-Rambert-sur-Loire. The decoration includes a pattern of half-rhombuses in lilac and dark red, producing a purple effect; the lilac stresses the lines of the folds. This beautiful example of patterned fabric exemplifies all the old richness of Byzantium;

3 Fragment of a border with a continuous pattern composed of almost naturalistically drawn plant motifs with depictions of a lion and an eagle alternately filling the spaces between them. This decoration on the hem of ecclesiastical vestments is probably of Byzantine origin, although it is difficult to say exactly where they come from;

4 Cloth from the treasury in Aachen Cathedral. The pattern clearly indicates that the cloth was intended for the robes of an ecclesiastic, although the ornamentation does not go beyond individual pagan types of decoration. Over the centuries multi-coloured silk fabrics enriched with gold thread and even sewn with pearls have been used for ecclesiastical vestments;

5 An example of figured velvet for the clothes of a noble; it was used for making the long tunics that knights wore over their shirts of mail from the end of the 12th century.

PLATE 95

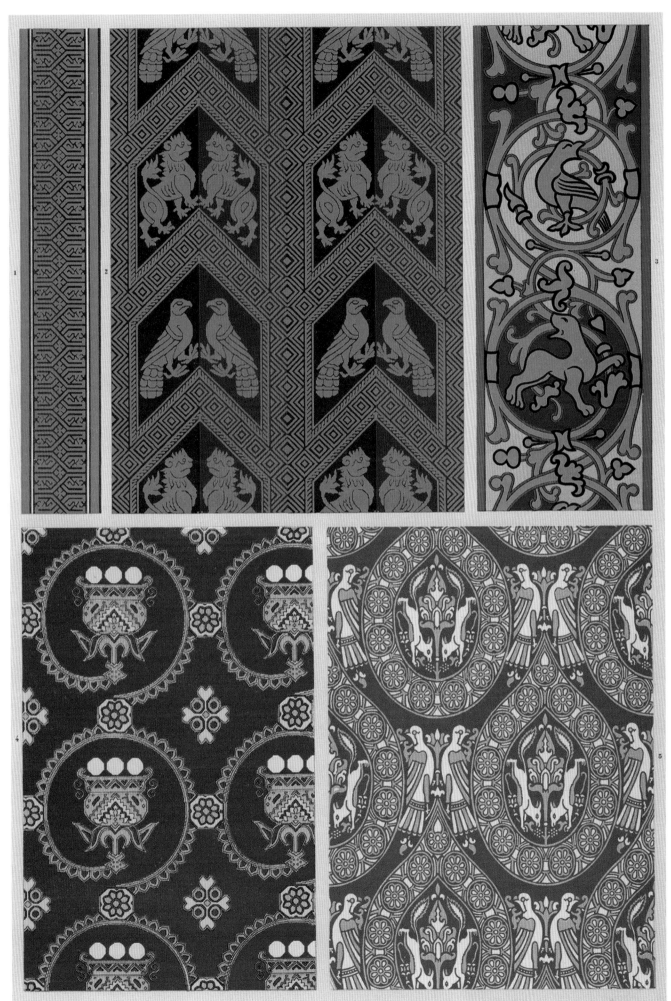

Precious European fabrics in the Eastern style

Top: fragment of 15th-century silk brocade that appears in a picture by Marco Marziale (Cantarini Gallery, Venice). The woven decoration on the white satin background reminds us of the ornamentation of the time of the Great Mughals: the twisting plant motifs bring to mind the skilful ornamental compositions on Persian tiles, yet the flora is mainly of Indian origin. This fabric with its subdued blue pattern which is continuous without being monotonous, and its slightly animated colour, belongs to the entrancing type of silk brocade known in the Middle Ages as *sarcinet* or *sarrazines* (Saracen). The fabrics produced in Europe differed considerably from those that were imported directly from the East to medieval Venice; the city maintained close links with the countries of the Near East, and it was their weaving factories that supplied the whole of Europe.

The central of the three fragments at the foot of the plate is taken from a picture by Giottino in the Uffizi Gallery (Florence) and shows part of the dress of an ecclesiastic. The decoration in the Byzantine style is woven with gold and silver thread on black and red velvet. The inscription is sewn in silver. The palmette motif has a symbolic meaning: a person who managed to overcome all trials and remain true to God was awarded a garland of palms. During the Middle Ages ecclesiastical vestments were often decorated with inscriptions in Latin; it is more rare to find one in Greek.

The fragments on either side of the central motif are taken from pictures by Italian primitives of the first half of the 15th century (Florentine Academy of Arts). The red velvet sewn with gold thread (left) is decorated with a stylised flower pattern. Plant and zoomorphic elements form a continuous complex composition on green velvet, which is also embroidered with gold (right). There is still a hint of the East and Byzantium, although the decoration already belongs stylistically to a transitional period. Until the middle of the 14th century all fabrics that appear in pictures and frescoes are in the Byzantine style; this is indicated by the symmetrical positioning of geometrical ornaments, stars, fleurons and rhombuses. In nine cases out of ten the main colours, apart from gold, were crimson, in other words the purple of antiquity, or a saturated light green (veronese). In the dynamic poses of the cockerels we can see the birth of a new decorative tendency that announces the beginning of the realistic treatment of what is portrayed. This decoration appears on the clothes of a person in the picture: in the early Christian symbolism that was typical of the paintings in the catacombs of Rome, two cockerels in heraldic poses represented the allegory of the battle for faith and martyrdom. Italian primitives still belonged to the group of painters who had recourse to decoration as an artist language.

PLATE 96

Book decoration of the 14th century

Ornamental motifs drawn from the *Gospel of St Thomas Aquinas* (French National Library, Paris). The illustrations are the work of 14th-century Italian miniaturists. The actual ornaments are distinguished by a boldness and accuracy that immediately remind us of engraving on metal or other decorations on flat surfaces. What is important from the artistic point of view is that they testify to the transition from the Byzantine style (modified by Arabic influence) to the Renaissance.

PLATE 97

Stained-glass windows, 12th–14th centuries

1–5	Chartres Cathedral;
6–12	Bourges Cathedral;
13–15	Cologne Cathedral;
16	Church of St Cunibert, Cologne;
17, 18	Soissons Cathedral;
19–23	Le Mans Cathedral;
24–26	Lyon Cathedral;
27–29	Angers Cathedral;
30–33	Church of St Urbain, Troyes;
34, 35	Strasbourg Cathedral;
36–38	Rouen Cathedral;
39	Cathedral in Sens.

There can be no doubt that these stained-glass windows were created when this genre of religious decorative art was at its peak. As we are unable to reproduce their glistening transparency, we would like to recommend these ornaments with their beautiful combinations of colours as models for the sort of work that is very popular today.

PLATE 98

Stained-glass windows, 12th–14th centuries
Plant motifs in a Gothic window

1, 2   Borders. Cathedral in Angers;

3, 9, 14–16, 24, 27, 28   Borders. Cathedral in
Bourges;

23, 29   Stained-glass background. Cathedral in
Bourges;

5, 7, 18   Borders. Chartres Cathedral;

10, 11   Borders. Church of St Remi, Reims;

6   Stained-glass field. Church of St Remi,
Reims;

20, 22   Borders. Cathedral in Sens;

12, 13, 17, 26   Stained-glass background.
Cathedral in Sens;

25   Border. Cathedral in Soissons;

4, 21   Strasbourg Cathedral;

8   Reims Cathedral;

19   Stained-glass background. Chapter
House in Salisbury Cathedral (England).

During the 12th–14th centuries stained glass formed an integral part of church decoration and had only one purpose: to embellish the work of the architect. Up until the 15th century painting on glass did not have its own special significance.

Decoratively, stained glass usually consisted of two areas with opposite functions. The border followed the line of the arch and was not meant to let too much light through. It was here that the artist had to use all his powers of observation and his knowledge to achieve the desired result. The pieces of coloured glass that were intended for the background (usually blue and red, but sometimes green) were both dull, so as to reduce the brightness of the light, and also doubled so as to increase the intensity of the colour. It was normal practice to cover the glass in the border with a layer of paint so that it was opaque. The decoration of the central part of the oriel was dictated by the window's main function, to let as much light as possible into the building. If a subdued effect was wanted, the artist would follow the decorative principles of patterned fabrics where coloured motifs, either embroidered or appliqué, were placed on a background of white silk that was marked with small designs in the Eastern style (23).

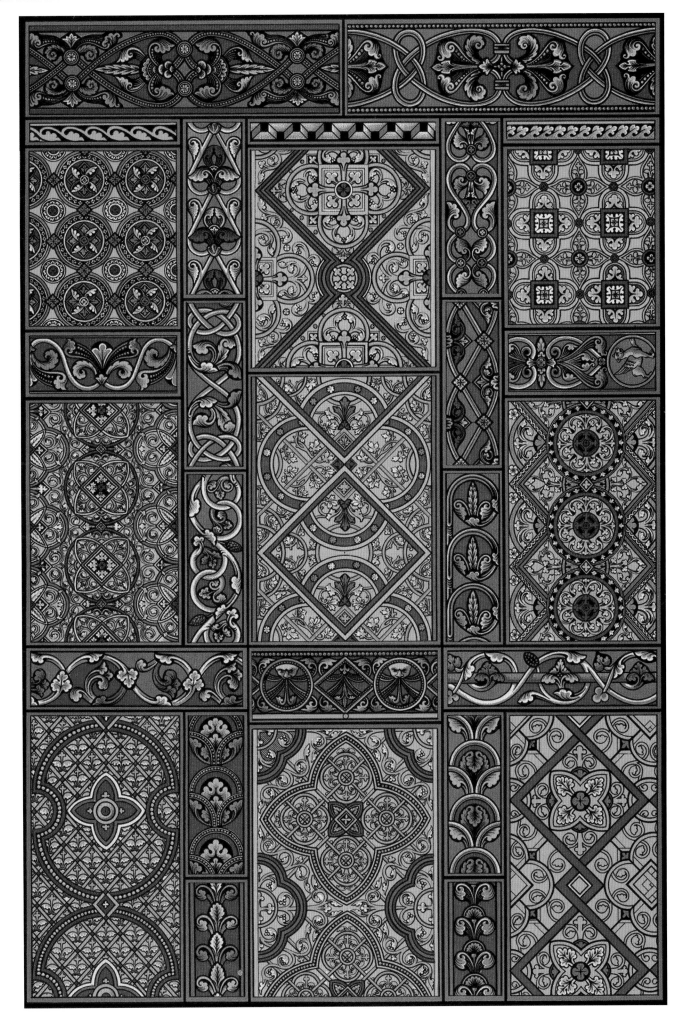

Grisaille stained-glass windows,
13th–14th centuries

1–23 Cologne Cathedral;

24–27 Ornamental fields from a monograph
about Bourges Cathedral;

28–31 Strasbourg Cathedral;

33–35 Chartres Cathedral;

36–39 Bourges Cathedral;

32, 40–42 Cathedral in Tournai.

The 13th century was the golden age of stained glass. Its simple and noble ornamental style dominated the whole of the next century until it gradually began to decline in the 15th century as the décor became overloaded. This can be seen in the stained glass made in 1475–1500 for the cathedral in Tournai.

Slip-glazed tiles, 12th–14th centuries

Right up to the 12th century the floors and walls of grand palaces were covered with mosaics or squares of coloured stone — jasper, porphyry, marble, etc — or stone blocks covered with a glaze and a painted decoration. It was only in the 13th century that slip-glazed tiles came into wide use.

Combinations of tiles can be very interesting to the artist and ornamentalist. The most widespread examples of tile decoration are shown:

12TH CENTURY

1, 16, 17, 21, 25 Laon Cathedral;

2, 3, 7, 9, 10, 12–15, 24, 31–33 Rouen Museum;

4 Abbey of Saint Lô;

5, 22, 27 Cathedral in Saint-Omer;

8, 19, 29 Fontenay (Côte d'Or);

11 Cluny Museum, Paris;

18 Town Hall in Reims;

20, 26 Troyes;

23 Louvre, Paris;

28 Troyes (Archives of the Department of Aube);

30 Law Courts, Rouen.

13TH–14TH CENTURIES

34–43 Manuscript books

(French National Library, Paris).

1–8 Individual tiles with a complete motif;

9–12 Edging tiles;

13–29 Tiles laid in squares in fours to produce a complete pattern;

30 Hexagonal tiles laid in fours around a central square to create a new pattern;

31 Three tiles laid in groups of nine to create a large complete pattern;

32 Four tiles laid in groups of sixteen to create a large pattern;

33–43 Examples of regular patterns on individual tiles.

PLATE 101

Book decoration

Most of these motifs, which are taken from a 14th-century Italian manuscript book with miniatures by Simone Memmi, continue the theme of plate 97 and demonstrate the same free manner; however, the stylised plant forms are becoming more varied, and depictions of people, birds and animals are included more often.

The remaining motifs, which are also of Italian origin, present standard 15th-century marginal decorations and initials from *The Twelve Caesars* by Suetonius and *The History of the Emperor Justinian*.

Continuous monochrome ornamentation
or its imitation, 12th–15th centuries.

4 This type of ornamentation decorates
many objects of the time of Louis IX. The
imitation of the relief decoration
on the wrought-iron doors of the
Cathedral of Notre Dame in Paris is
simply staggering. At the same time the
Paris school drew inspiration from the
East. The Crusaders were struck by
the sumptuous plant ornamentation that
the Byzantines had drawn from Greek
models, and soon made it very popular
throughout France. Craftsmen such as
Biscornet, the creator of the decoration on
the doors of Notre Dame, worked skilfully
and confidently in this genre;

1, 2 Fields of a 14th-century Latin bible
decorated with a traditional plant
ornamentation. The intricate interweaving
and the fantastical zoomorphic figures
shine in silver
and red;

6, 7 Example of one of the forms of
manuscript ornamentation that was
widespread in France during the second
half of the 12th century, i.e. at the end
of the French Romanesque style;

13 Regular pattern of plant motifs made in
Italy (possibly in Florence) circa 1400;

11 Usual type of marginal decoration
for manuscripts in the 14th and 15th
centuries. The manuscript entitled
Manipulus florum (Bouquet of Flowers),
from which this motif is taken, was
illuminated in France circa 1420;

3, 5, 12, 14 Plant motifs on frescoes and stucco
moulding in the church and former abbey
of Saint Antoine de Viennois (Isère), 15th
century;

10 Motif from a 15th-century manuscript;
it includes leafless plant forms and
creates a genuinely harmonious type of
ornamentation;

8, 9 Magnificent motifs of leaves using
traditional flora characterise the style of
book decoration that was widespread in
Italy towards the end of the 15th century.

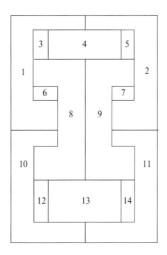

PLATE 103

Enamel designs based on motifs from
Italian book decoration

Thanks to the enamel paintings of the 10th century we have the chance of getting to know the various technical processes of enamelling, even though genuine articles dating to the Middle Ages are very rare. By the 10th century gold- and silversmiths were able to combine in one object the transparent or opaque enamel of the background (using either champlevé or cloisonné techniques) with painted enamel above which a layer of translucent colourless enamel was applied.

We would like to show here one more method of producing enamel, one that was intended for decorating glass; furthermore, this technique was traditionally ascribed to an earlier period. The process consisted in producing an engraving on a sheet of colourless crystal in such a way that the bottom of each groove was wider than the top. Gold leaf was put into the opening and folded slightly over the lip of the groove, so as to produce something like a box into which glass paste was then placed. After being fired at a temperature lower than the melting-point of the crystal, the object was ground until it was smooth; finally, pieces of purple, green or blue foil were glued to the reverse. The foil gave colour to the transparent glass, while the transparent enamel patterns stood out clearly on the suffused gold backing.

1, 3, 5–9, 11–13 Marginal decoration from a manuscript copy of the *Small Missal for the Mother of God* (from the Monastery of Santa Maria Magdalena, Siena).

The manuscript dates to the 15th century;

2, 4, 10 Motifs taken from the *Book of the Order of St Catherine* (Siena Library).

The medallion (4) includes the arms of Siena.

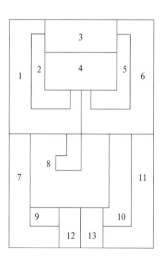

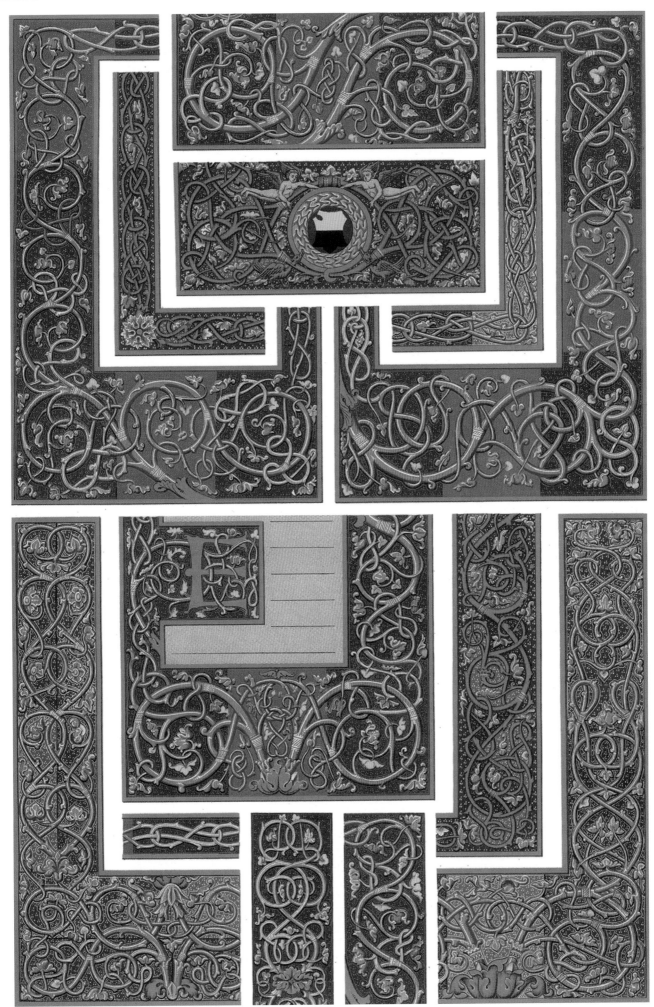

Embroidery and appliqué work.
Motifs from frescoes, 15th century.

Twenty-two ornamental motifs decorating
fabrics and drapery. Their apparent simplicity
springs from the strikingly effective combination
of gold with one, two or three local colours:
either a gold pattern glistens on a coloured
background, or a coloured pattern shows
expressively on gold. Most of the decorations are
taken from manuscripts in the French National
Library in Paris.

1–6 Manuscript books
    (French National Library, Paris);

7 Sainte-Chapelle in Bourbon-
    l'Archambault (commune of Moulins);

8, 9 Church stained-glass windows
    (Moulins);

10 Manuscript book
    (French National Library, Paris););

11, 12 *Chronicle of Monstrelet* *
    (French National Library, Paris);

13 *The Book of Hours of Anne of Brittany*
    (Louvre, Paris);

14–17 Manuscript books
    (French National Library, Paris);

18–19 *The Golden Legend*
    (French National Library, Paris);

20, 21 Manuscript book
    (French National Library, Paris);

22 *Schoenborn Book of Hours.*
    * Monstrelet was the provost of
    Cambrai and the author of the *Chronicle*
    (1400–1459).

Stylised plant motifs and fleurons,
15th century.

The examples of plant motifs, which are too
numerous to list their sources, are taken from
15th-century manuscript books.

The ornamentation was usually inspired by
local flora, sometimes by its simplest forms and
sometimes by arbitrary combinations of stylised
plants or by combinations of plants and animals
and even human figures that seem to grow out
of their leaves.

Medieval ornamental artists were very successful
in creating these fantastical combinations where
the imagination continually varied the elements
of a composition with the same freedom of
invention that characterises this genre. Certain
individual repeating forms can in fact be
identified, such as the various forms of holly leaf;
this motif was widespread in book decoration
and ornamental casting.

PLATE 106

Book decoration
Flower ornamentation and gems,
15th century.

These twenty-five motifs are also drawn from
manuscript books.

Although one or two of the motifs reproduced
are made in the fanciful and capricious manner
that was so dear to the medieval illuminator,
the ornamentation is in a graceful and restrained
style that is easy for modern manufacturing
to imitate. From this point of view it is worth
noting the practical value of the jewellery motifs
(8–25).

1, 2 Book of Hours
(French National Library, Paris). The Latin
text dates to 1398; the miniatures are later
and are ascribed to Israel von Mekenen (?).

3, 4 *The Golden Legend*
(French National Library, Paris).
Miniatures by Jean Fouquet;

5, 6 Manuscript books (Arsenal Library, Paris);

7 *Schoenborn Book of Hours*;

8–25 The jewellery motifs originate from
decorations on the fields of a copy of
the works of Seneca (French National
Library, Paris).

PLATE 107

7

3

1

6

5

2

8 – 25

4

Book decoration, 15th century.

The motifs shown here should be viewed as completely original creations of French and Flemish art, dating to before the arrival of the Italian influence, and representing a specifically French Renaissance. From the decorative point of view the range of plant elements — stem, leaves and flower — is drawn gracefully, cleverly and elegantly.

1–10 *Book of Hours of the Marquis of Paulmy* (Arsenal Library, Paris);

11, 12 Manuscript book;

13, 14 Book of Hours with miniatures by Israel von Mekenen (French National Library, Paris);

15–18 Manuscript books (Arsenal Library, Paris).

Painted and gilded wood, 15th century
Gothic rose windows and panels

These decorations on furniture belong to the late-Gothic style which is known as Flamboyant Gothic because of the inclusion of flame-shaped tendrils in the décor. The expressive ribs of this period were usually prismatic in shape, with a thin convex edge. Sometimes flower elements poke out from this edge and seem to branch off from the main stem; sometimes they fill up the gaps in the open-work trellis. Often the spaces in the corners and between the arches are richly decorated with plant forms treated in a realistic manner. This style is also known as 'flowery'. The rules that guided the ornamentalists of the period when producing large works also dictated the technique that was used for wood carving.

A common type of decoration during the closing phase of the Gothic style was the blind arch, which is represented in this plate by two vertical panels. Their colour range creates the illusion of genuine open-work. The Gothic rose window was also often imitated in architecture, but 15th-century 'roses' cannot be categorised because of the unprecedented multiplicity of combinations of trefoils and quatrefoils, continuous and dotted lines and other decorative elements that make up the complex compositions.

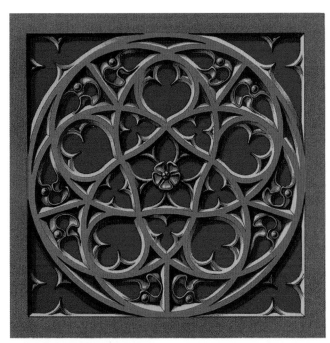
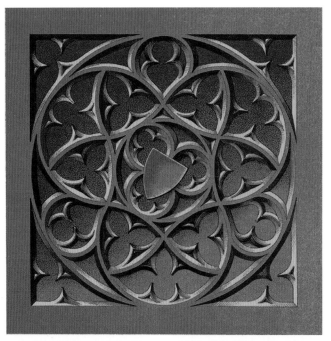
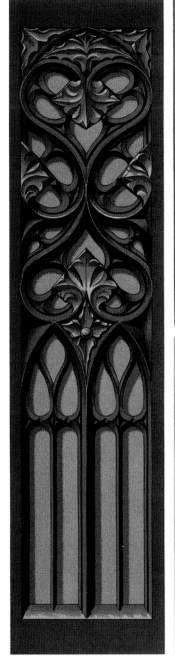

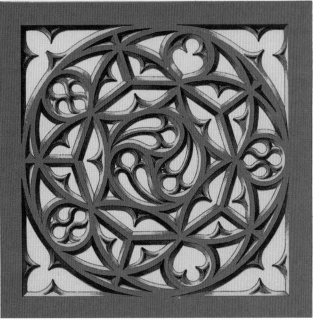

Painted and gilded wood, 15th century
Fragments of furniture
Hanging blind arches, panels and
'balustrades'

1 Panel divided up like modern windows.

   Shield with heraldic lilies in the centre;

2 Double arcature with pendants. Imitation
blind arches were a common type of
decoration on very large surfaces, and in
most cases they were doubled;

3 Panel imitating a window with a large
decorative arch divided into two parts,
each containing a pair of lancet arches.
The upper decorative arch is surmounted
by a spire that widens as it rises; there are
fantastical animals with dragons' bodies
and horses' heads and necks on both sides
of it;

4 Massive panel decorated with an oak
branch and acorns. The exaggeratedly large
leaf is an example of the artistic manner
that wood-carvers of the time used when
they transformed real objects through
their fantasy. The motif is completed by
the depiction of a miniature dragon;

6–8 Borders of the type that architects call
'balustrades'. Motifs 6 and 8 are decorated
with fretwork and surmounted by
serrations. It was only in the final phase
of the Gothic style that it became usual to
decorate rainwater gutters in churches with
this type of balustrade. The 15th-century
examples shown here are decorated with
an abundant lace ornamentation using all
possible combinations of lines. Motif 7 is
a wood carving with coloured shading to
strengthen the illusion of open-work;

5 Continuous pattern produced according to
the same principle.

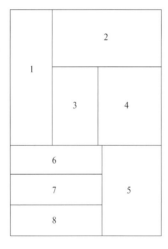

PLATE 110

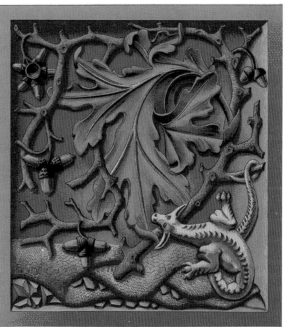

Wood carving with paint and gilding,
15th century.
Furniture decoration and decorative panels.

Most of the motifs shown here are similar to
the rose and balustrade ornamentation in plates
109 and 110.

For all the diversity of the compositions, the
artistic principle remains the same and achieves
its greatest effect in the fretted work of the finials
of the furniture (bottom centre of the plate).
By the end of the 15th century finials had already
lost the crenellated friezes (which resembled the
embrasures of medieval fortresses) that were the
characteristic furniture décor in the 13th–14th
centuries. Hanging arches were surmounted
by added open-work ornamentation, although
this type of decoration invariably imitated
stone carving. It was as if the furniture makers
did not understand that they were holding a
new material and were faced by a new purpose;
in reality they still produced carved stone for
cathedrals.

The one exception, and a very pleasant one, is
the example in the top centre of the plate. The
woodcarver's independent mind and undoubted
taste that show through in literally every element
of the motif are worth the closest attention.
The imitation of blind semicircular arches is in
harmony with the most characteristic feature
of late-Gothic decoration, and we are apparently
looking at an emphatically architectonic form.
However, we cannot help noticing that the
master has managed to free himself from the
jaws of so-called logic. In fact, what is there
in common between artistic carving and laws
that deprive creativity of any individuality? The
anonymous carver has found a magnificent
solution to this question.

Architectonic decoration
Carving and painting, 15th–16th centuries
The human figure in hieratic decoration

Three distinct ornamental motifs are shown in this plate:

2, 8–11 – fragments of gilded carving on wooden furniture. These are additional examples of the type of décor shown in plates 109–111.

All four plates contain drawings that have been copied in a strictly geometrical style from photographs.

1, 4, 6, 7 – reliefs based on book miniatures.

3, 5 – compositions of a religious nature in which the human figure occupies the central place. They are subordinated to the traditional scheme that was inspired by the architecture of the period, and in particular to 13th–14th-century stained-glass windows; their compositions were so closely linked to all three phases of the Gothic style that it is rare for studies not to have a special chapter dedicated to the most skilful ornamentalists of the Middle Ages. Using oils, tempera, honey or gum arabic, Flemish artists and masters of the Cologne school painted religious subjects on wooden panels or the leaves of triptychs, and for a long time these paintings followed the decorative scheme of glass-painters; the cartoons for stained-glass windows served as patterns for hieratic poses.

PLATE 112

113 RENAISSANCE

Panels, friezes and borders

The motifs shown here decorate the famous *Rouen Book of Hours* 'Printed for Simon Vostre, bookseller and inhabitant of the city of Paris'; the first edition dates from 1508.

As a rule these early works of the French Renaissance have a twofold origin. On the one hand they form an integral part of the Northern art that held sway in France during the Middle Ages, and on the other hand they are already being influenced by the Italian manner that soon began to prevail in the field of the arts. However, the French style dominates in the ornamentation of the *Rouen Book of Hours*, and it is only in one or two motifs at the bottom of the plate that signs of Italian influence can be seen.

We have been able to reproduce this masterpiece in colour due to one circumstance that often occurs in connection with incunabula. For publishers like Simon Vostre, Antoine Vérard and others, books were printed on thin parchment and then coloured by hand so as to give the appearance of authenticity, and to fool the purchaser who imagined that he was buying an original.

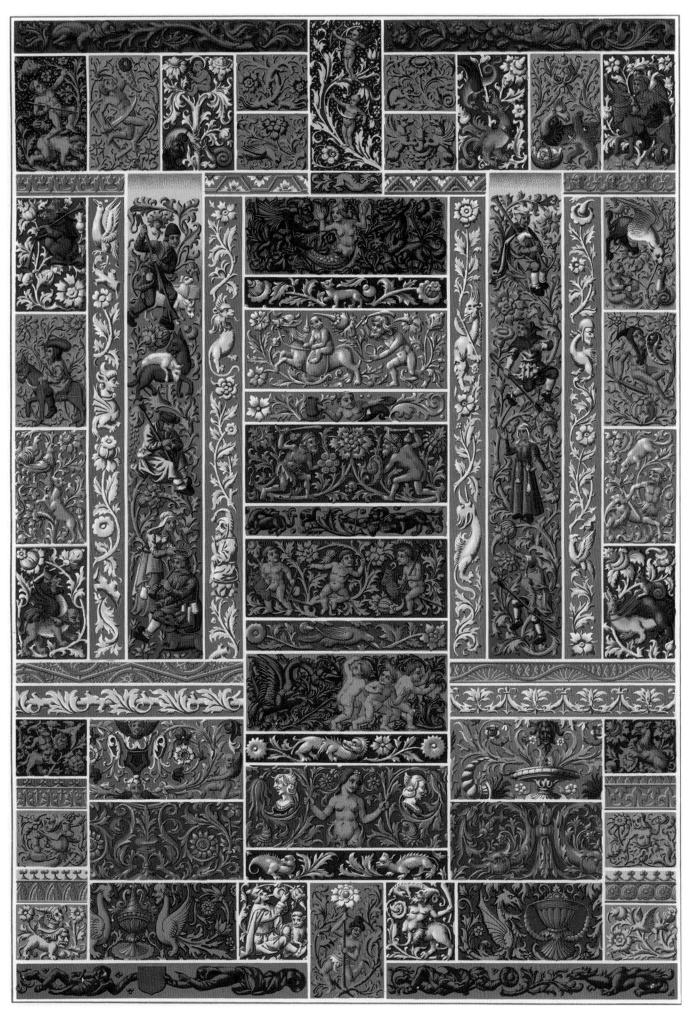

Goldsmithing and jewellery.
Copper, silver, enamels and precious stones.
16th century.

Four types of jewellery decoration are shown in the plate:

1.
2, 5, 7, 8, 14, 16, 21, 45 – diadem-shaped haloes for *panagias* (a *panagia* is a small circular icon depicting the Mother of God, and it is worn on the breast by priests as a sign of their senior rank). Two diadems were suspended from the *panagia* by small rings (8). The convexity on the obverse of the diadem forms a halo around the head of the Child Christ who is clinging to the Virgin's shoulder.

2.
Pectoral crosses:
12, 18, 24 (obverse and reverse),
20, 22, 28, 29 (obverse and reverse),
30, 32, 34 (obverse and reverse),
33, 39 (obverse and reverse),
36, 37, 40, 42, 44 (obverse and reverse).

The first two groups, which occupy most of the plate, are reproduced from the originals at two-thirds of their actual size.

3.
Elements of an artistic décor that goes back to Old Russian manuscripts of the 16th century, i.e. the same period as the jewellery decoration whose flower motifs are close to the décor of painted enamels (1, 3, 4, 6, 9–11, 13,15, 17,19, 23, 25, 27, 31, 35, 38, 41 and 43).

4.
Finally, 26 is the precious binding of a manuscript from the end of the 17th century in the Moscow Armoury Palace. It is the Bible of Tsarina Natalya, the second wife of Tsar Alexey Mikhaylovich and the mother of Peter the Great.

PLATE 114

115 OLD RUSSIAN ART

Book decoration, 16th century
Interlaced flowers

In Plate 114 we have already met 16th-century Old Russian jewellery decorations with their graceful flower motifs that look as if they have been seized from living nature, and their variegated enamels that harmonise with the warm radiance of gold and silver and remind us of a flowering steppe. The numerous examples of interlaced flowers reveal in all its fullness something that can seem hypothetical when it comes to jewellery decoration. The ornamentation of the braid, the actual nature of the flower motifs and the softness of colouration allow us to determine the main type of décor. At first this new field of study gives unconvincing results, but we can see very clearly how this basic type develops into one of the most successful decorative solutions; the impression of splendour is created by the simplest of means. The motifs have been taken from three manuscripts and provide examples of the final metamorphosis of the Celtic ribbon interlacing, from which the Slavs immediately removed the zoomorphic elements.

Motifs 9 and 11 demonstrate the combination of flat ribbons or bands that was still in use, but thanks to its rounded and symmetrically placed decorative knots, motif 9 represents an interlaced ribbon shaped like plants, and this is emphasised by the schematic flower motifs growing out of the corners. The interlaced ribbons in motif 11 have lost the plant-shaped knots, but even so there is a schematic flower in the upper corner and rich vegetation in the lower.

2, 12 and 14 are motifs from the second manuscript. The Celtic interlaced ribbon is still the main feature of the decoration, but its geometrical nature indicates Arabian or Persian influence. Even so, the Russian craftsman has contributed his mite with the help of the naturalistically drawn stems growing out of the lower corners of the last two motifs.

The remaining motifs are drawn from the third manuscript: they demonstrate a fresh artistic manner that achieves exceptional expressiveness in motif 6.

Book decoration, 14th century
Monochrome painting

As early as the 12th–13th centuries there were craftsmen working in Old Russia who were completely independent of foreign influence, whether Greek influence or the influence of Italian stonemasons sent for by Prince Andrey Bogolubsky to build the Cathedral of the Assumption in Vladimir (1158–1161). Old Russia's links with the Greek world were cut short by the Mongol invasion, and therefore Old Russian ornamentation owes its originality to this artificial isolation: its individuality has nothing in common with either the Byzantine style or the Romanesque that developed from it.

In the motifs shown in this plate the Celtic and Scandinavian influence is so obvious that we will not spend any time on it. However, it is worth noting the specific method of organising and placing the interlaced plants and zoomorphic elements which superimposes a special, specifically national, imprint on well thought-out ornaments that represent something rather more complex than mere vignettes. Indeed, the ornamental motifs are closely linked to a logical decorative structure (which can be used when working with forged metal articles). It can also be seen in the ornamental script of Old Slavonic inscriptions: their role in Old Russian decoration is similar to that played by Kufic writing in the decoration of Persia or the Arab world.

Old Russian manuscripts were produced from the 11th to the 18th centuries, but originality in book decoration can only be observed in the 12th–16th centuries. From the beginning of the 18th century Russia came under the influence of Western styles, but it is still interesting to see how national traits were transformed as they passed through the crucible of foreign influence, and how the national genius expresses itself.

PLATE 116

117 OLD RUSSIAN ART

Decorative motifs, 12th–15th centuries
Liturgical books and embossed metal
Panel with monochrome decoration

For several hundred years the development of Old Russian decorative art was in part held back by imitation of Western art.

As an expression of the inborn talent of the people, Old Russian art per se finds its place again on embossed vessels with magnificent patterns, on jugs and pot-bellied samovars that are encircled by zoomorphic decorations and on the matt silver of emblems bearing Old Slavonic script. The worth of this national decorative style is now universally recognised, and despite its architectonic character, it is fully suited to working with precious metals.

The capabilities of this genre are demonstrated by the decoration of church patens: we can see rosettes (4, 7) and borders (8, 9); their rectilinear surfaces covered with a laconic pattern of tendrils (11, 12), corner motifs (1, 10) and fleurons (2, 13, 17, 18, 20, 21); initials (15, 16) and ornamental details (3, 5, 6, 14. 19, 22). Most of the motifs date from the 13th–14th centuries, and some of them (7, 10, 13, 17, 19, 20, 22) spring from Eastern decoration and are from the 15th century.

Engraved and embossed rosettes and
borders of patens

The character of this type of decoration
dating from different historical periods and
demonstrating different stylistic treatments
is extremely interesting in that under all
the superimpositions of foreign influences
it remained a means of expression for the
distinctive talent of Old Russian craftsmen.
Each symmetrical motif is an element of a well-
organised decorative creation, and even the most
capriciously twisting pattern follows a strict
compositional logic and is easily recognised.
The pattern remains rhythmical both when
the decorative scheme is modified and when
there is a change in the degree of opulence.

From the above we can assume that, as people
with good taste, the craftsmen of Old Russia
gave way easily to foreign influence; they were
unable to resist the attraction of new artistic
solutions which, as in our case, were being
grafted on to the old ones. Fully convinced that
they were perfecting the national style, these
craftsmen unfortunately undermined its viability
by including Eastern or Western ornamentation;
even so, they subordinated foreign motifs to
their own national taste. The various decorative
formulas were used so skilfully that it is usually
easy to recognise Old Russian work, despite the
stylistic transformations.

Embossing and book decoration
Panels, borders, loops, decorative knots
and fleurons

Although these decorative motifs are already
less closely linked to the so-called national
style, they are still of great interest. As a rule
they are well thought-out and beautifully made;
at times you can see in them what might be
described as the last ripples of the influence of
Ancient Celtic interlacing, sometimes enriched
by Byzantine stylistic overlays and sometimes
enlivened by a network of Eastern arabesques.
Most of these motifs remind us of top-quality
forged metal articles, or putting it another way:
they reveal a well-considered striving towards
maximum maturity of conception and towards
variety of decoration. The components of this
sort of decoration are by nature even primitive,
but in different combinations they produce
an impression of striking magnificence. A
composition resulting from imagination does
not leave any place for imitating natural forms,
and consequently it is not a question of either
a developing or, even more so, a dying art.
The motifs find renewal in themselves thanks
to the play of the imagination of the skilled
ornamentalist who endowed them with a specific
unity: at its basis is always the in-built intuition
of the people as it strives for originality, clarity
and rhythm, and for the production of the
simplest and the most complex decoration.

Embossing
Knots, corners, borders and background
motifs

This is the seventh plate of the series dedicated to Old Russian decorative art. Despite the differences of type, a certain unity characterises all the examples shown here. The ornamental background interlacings have the appearance of the logical shape-generating combinations that are needed to create a genuine compositional integrity, for example a wooden structure with open-work, one of the favourite types of decoration for a wood-carver. Achieving stylistic unity while using changes in style was something that depended upon the ornamentalist himself; this is all the more important since, due to their geographical location, Old Russian craftsmen had to choose between two basic cultural influences that, even if they were not totally incompatible, differed in many respects. Whatever the influence from Asia Minor might be, the decoration of Old Russian gold and silver articles does not have the slightest resemblance either to the decoration of Persian ceramics or to traditional Indian isolated motifs; neither the asymmetrical plant tendrils in the cloisonné enamels produced by Chinese and Japanese masters nor in particular their scattered flower motifs on porcelain and lacquerware are features of Old Russian decoration. When they imitated ornamental patterns (like the ones in the plate) whose components give an impression of the carved wood that was the normal and favourite decoration in the 16th–17th centuries, Old Russian craftsmen were acting according to national intuition, despite the fact that this led over the course of three centuries to regrettable metamorphoses in their original style.

Embossing and border corners

This plate completes a series (cf. plates 117–121) of Old Russian metal articles based on drawings from a work dedicated to the history of Russian ornamentation that was published by the Stroganoff Institute of Technical Drawing in the 19th century. The plate gives practical information that is useful for people working in this field, and the variety of forms and sizes can satisfy literally any requirements. Having finally freed themselves from any traces of pre-Christian traditions, some motifs betray elements of Eastern decoration while others remind us of European work of the late 16th and early 17th centuries. Sometimes an authentically Russian tectonic clarity of form and ornamentation can be seen in them, and this stresses the object's structure. We have already mentioned that all the compositions are endowed with a consistent national style and high artistic merits that, while accentuating the changes to the original style, still emphasise its presence which can be felt in the distinctive logic of the decorative plant 'grid'. This dominant feature is also typical of the schematic plant motifs inspired by 15th-century European examples that Old Russian goldsmiths included in their decoration.

In the hands of a skilled goldsmith embossing could turn into sculpture. The individual decorative details reproduced in this plate show that even strictly symmetrical Old Russian decoration is never monotonous; symmetry is a feature of every ornamentalist's soul, but this symmetry is alive and vigorous!

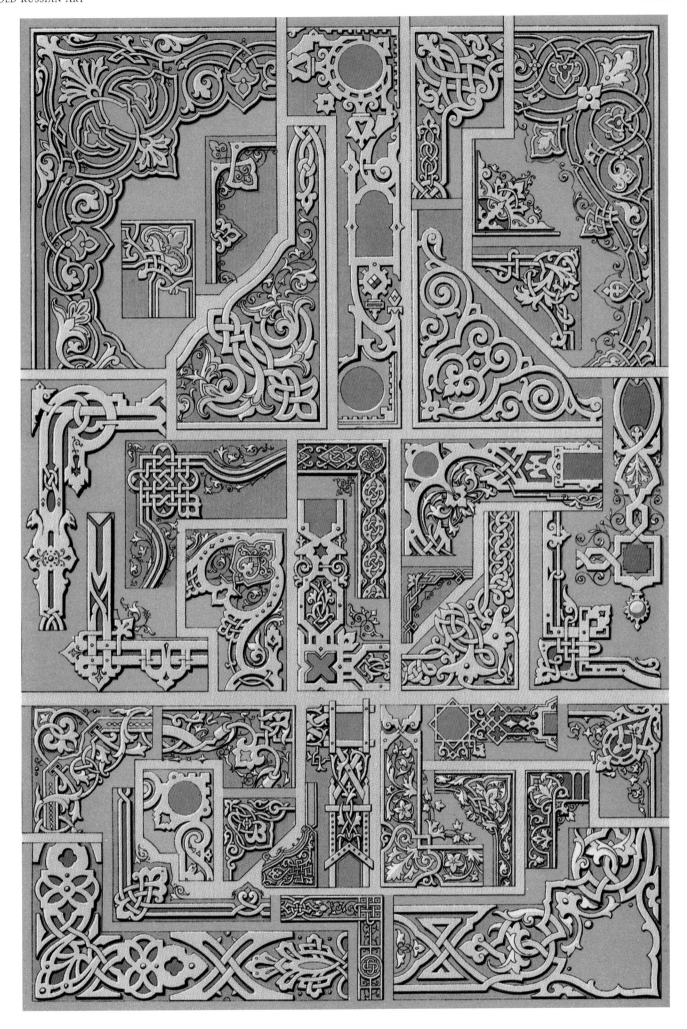

Book decoration

The motifs shown here are drawn from a 16th-century Gospel, but it is very clear that this decorative style appeared considerably earlier. We only have to compare the ornamentation in the plate with three motifs from the decoration of a Greek manuscript that was illuminated in Asia Minor circa 800 (cf. plate 71: 2–4; examples of Greek book decoration modified by influence from Asia Minor) to be convinced of the true antiquity of individual ornamental features. It is particularly clear that the influence of Asia Minor is having a greater and greater effect on Armenian ornamentation, yet it is also significant that despite the undoubted Indo-Persian influence Armenian craftsmen managed to develop their own style. Ultimately Armenia's neighbours probably also made their own contribution to the final result. In the decorative systems of Armenian masters we can find a certain logic that stresses the complex plant interlacings which are close to the Old Russian decorative style. An additional and very important point is that having brought all these complex elements together and by combining daring with elegance and a refined manner, the illuminator was no longer a 'scribbler', but a first-class artist whose vignettes could become magnificent models for people working in metal and jewellery.

The definite similarity in the decorative systems used by Armenian and Old Russian masters (cf. plate 115) is emphasised by the use of a similar colour range.

PLATE 122

Marginal book décor in the style of enamel jewellery decoration, 15th century.

The motifs shown here go back very clearly to the décor of precious Italian decorations of the 15th century and together with some examples of Flemish jewellery art they create a series of genuine jewellery articles or painted jewellery decorations that have been included in the decoration of books. We are thus looking at a historical 'treasure chest' dating to the 10th–13th centuries, and we can trace the evolution of a purely European use of relief to make decoration stand out. There is an obvious contrast to the traditional principle of Persian and Indian ornamentalists who had a predilection for colour: multicoloured enamel was used to give the simplest forms and most uncomplicated patterns a homogenous shining surface. At first the introduction of relief went slowly, but after craftsmen began setting gems, using embossing with various degrees of relief, which sometimes turned gold and silver into pure plastic arts, and finally after they introduced filigree work — which became very popular — the jewellery of the period lost any similarity to Ancient Egyptian or Classical decoration. The motifs shown here speak for themselves: the low-relief embossed decoration is fundamentally different from gold open-work foliage which has turned into pure plastic art and stands out effectively on a background of black velvet.

PLATE 123

Book decoration

These motifs decorate a collection of antiphons from the cathedral in Siena and belong to the hand of Girolamo da Cremona, a prolific ornamentalist of the end of the 15th century. The Italian biographer Giorgio Vasari mentions him at the end of his account of the life of the artist Boccaccio: 'At that time there was a miniaturist called Girolamo living in Milan. His works could be seen both in Milan and throughout the whole of Lombardy.' Girolamo was considered one of the finest miniature-painters; his ornamentation is free and expressive, and this puts it considerably above the work of his contemporaries. It might seem that the artist is taking a deliberate step backwards towards the classical style, but it is a step that is unequalled for its originality. Both the ornamental motif of the bull's head and the one-headed chimera with two bodies take us back to Greek antiquity. Indeed the architect Paccard used similar motifs when restoring the Parthenon.

125 Renaissance

Precious articles with enamelling,
15th–16th centuries

This and the following plates present a
series of book decoration motifs from Italy
and Flanders. The marginal decorations of
manuscripts from the end of the 15th and
beginning of the 16th centuries were created by
illuminators who had studied under goldsmiths
in Italy. The typical features of this decoration
separate it from others, and this is precisely
in accordance with the principles of jewellery
art. It demonstrates remarkable accuracy in its
artistic expressiveness in which the decorative
scheme, while setting off the intricate curls of
the scribe, is always subordinate to a certain
logic: a medallion or buckle that is included
in the overall composition often graphically
demonstrates its original nature, even if it exists
outside any link to the other ornamental motifs.
Knowledge of the famous manuscripts of the
cathedral in Siena and especially of the pages
illuminated by Liberale da Verona, who arrived
in Siena in 1466, tells us that the artist chose
a very special type of marginal decoration for
large-format manuscripts. He includes jewellery
decoration in the ornamentation, and places
each one separately as if it was in the window of

a jeweller's. The jewels that Liberale depicts are
still full of classical reminiscences (concerning
the picture) and demonstrate the full range
of technical means of the time: coloured
transparent enamels on relief-work, painted
enamels on an enamel background, the inclusion
of pearls (which da Verona's disciples used
continually, sometimes combining them with
gems) and so on.

1–3, 10–12, 16, 18, 19, 21 Church books from
the cathedral in Siena.
Collection of church hymns and psalms
(the *Gradual*) and the *Antiphons*;

7, 22 Manuscript from the cathedral in
Florence;

5, 6 Roman prayer book, 15th century;

4, 14, 17, 20 Prayer book, end of the 15th
century;

8, 9,13,15 Breviary of Cardinal Grimani

(decorated with inclusions of Flemish
jewellery).

Jewellery decoration with enamelling,
15th–16th centuries

The motifs of Flemish origin that are shown
in the plate (4, 8, 13, 14, 25, 29, 30, 32, 34, 39,
40, 42, 52, 67) are from the famous breviary of
Cardinal Grimani in the library of the Basilica
of St Mark in Venice. They appear on pages that
were illuminated by Hans Memling, who placed
jewellery decoration on the edges not just as
components of a decorative composition that
sprang from his imagination, but also simply
for his own enjoyment, because of their beauty.
Memling was born in Germany between 1433
and 1435, and became a citizen of Bruges in
1465; he was a soldier in the Burgundian army
and fought at the battles of Morat, Granson
and Nancy. He is known to have illuminated
the prayer book of Philip the Good, Duke of
Burgundy, and it is quite likely that the jewellery
that he depicts was actually part of the fabulous
wealth of Emperor Charles the Bold, the
successor of Philip the Good.

Among the items of Italian origin reproduced
here it is easy to identify applied jewellery
decoration:

2 – gives the appearance of a decoration for a
bodice (transparent enamel on relief-work);

21 – belt pendant to replace a rosary.

In addition to brooches of all types and sizes,
earrings, hair pins and simple buttons, we can
also see several items of religious significance
that were once attached to rosaries.

7 – a substantial religious plaquette showing
the Lamb of God, made using the technique of
Limoges enamelling.

Finally, the central place is occupied by a Gothic
initial *M* from the hand of Liberale da Verona
(27). It has three structural elements, and the
middle one seems to be cut short so as to include
the Virgin Mary and Elizabeth in the scene of
the meeting of Mary and Elizabeth within the
structure of the initial.

Book decoration, 15th century
Florentine school

The five vertical borders from a manuscript by Martianus Capella (*On the Marriage of Mercury and Philology* and *On the Seven Disciplines*) were, like all the decoration in this manuscript, produced by the famous Florentine miniaturist Attavante. In the 15th century Italian miniaturists were very different from painters; even if miniaturists did at times outdo painters in the perfection of their work, the specialisation of the miniaturist was very narrow. Attavante stood out especially among them, and with his own hands he turned a second-rate decorative art into a great one (although small-scale). In 15th-century Italy the works of classical authors were constantly being re-copied, and the need arose for miniaturists who would turn away from the pictorial range of the medieval illuminator — realistically drawn plant motifs and the plant 'mesh' of the late-Gothic period — so as to create a truly harmonious setting for classical texts or texts that were inspired by classical literature, using graceful arabesques whose purity, clarity and balance became the essence of the new style. Florentine miniaturists were the first to pay homage to classical influence by including such decorative features as jewels, coins, intaglios, cameos and nude mythological figures in the borders.

In manuscripts like the work of Martianus Capella, where Olympia is shown in Florentine dress, anachronistic clothes have become yet another powerful source of decorative magnificence. This is especially noticeable in the fifth vertical border where beautiful plant volutes in grisaille on a gold background are enlivened by polychrome figures in medallions. By drawing inspiration from the masterpieces of classical sculpture that he could study in the Medici collection Attavante was fighting more for purity of line than for visual effect. His deeply Attic elegance and his ardour betray a great yearning for Ancient Greek art rather than for Ancient Roman art.

Book decoration, 15th century
Florentine school

In this plate, which is a continuation of the previous one, we can see new decorative motifs with which Attavante varied the pages of the famous manuscript. Despite all the prolific artist's mastery, he certainly cannot be called original. Although a contemporary of the precursors and the founders of the Italian renaissance, in reality he resurrected ancient decorative formulas; he made their charm stand out through clear, graceful lines, but without, however, showing any initiative of his own (apart from in ornamental details). His main merit as an ornamentalist lies in the refined plant 'mesh'.

The composition includes figures of putti painted in lightly-modelled flesh tones which make the mythological characters, that have replaced the draped figures of the medieval period, stand out with brilliant clarity against the rich coloured background. The light and airy backgrounds of the portrait medallions and in the spaces between the initials, combined with the polychrome portraits themselves, make a sharp contrast to the dark backgrounds and monochrome foliage which imitates bas-relief. If we add to this enamelled arms, coloured gems hidden among the leaves, a lone delicate pearl and finally borders with a simple pattern, we have a complete set of the means with which Attavante achieved the noble expressiveness of his ornamental mastery.

Painted decoration in Italy at the start
of the 16th century
Florentine school

We would like to complete this plate with a
number of ornamental details from various
sources so as to show some very important
motifs in all their fullness.

These motifs (1, 14, 15: initials; 4, 7, 10:
fragments of 'broken' initials) are among the
finest of their type. They were created by Monte
di Giovanni (or Monte del Fora), a famous
master of the Florentine school who worked
between 1500 and 1528. He was another
professional miniaturist who had studied under
goldsmiths; he was also an eminent mosaicist,
and it is this that explains the striking sweep of
Monte's work. As the mosaicist possesses only
very limited artistic means, he knows that variety
in polychrome decoration is achieved not so
much by the range of colours as by the choice of
a dominant note, and this has to be done so that
real variety is obtained. With this in mind it is
worth noting that in the initial *M* (14) the artist
has preserved the central structural component

so as not to clash with the composition of
the scene in the background. This and other
compositions by Monte di Giovanni are taken
from a manuscript in the cathedral in Florence.

2, 6, 8, 9 – Motifs from a Siena collection of
church hymns and psalms dating from the
period of Liberale da Verona.

13, 16 – motifs that are more modern in style,
taken from the pages of the *Antiphons* of the
cathedral in Florence, and illuminated by
Antonio di Girolamo.

The beautiful motifs in the top centre (3) and
11, 12 and 17 are from a manuscript in the
Carthusian monastery in Pavia;

5 – ornamental motif from the prayer book of
Pope Clement XII.

PLATE 129

Marginal manuscript decoration of the
15th–16th centuries
Isolated flower forms and symbolic motifs

The idea of decorating architectural structures with naturalistic plant motifs arose during the Flamboyant Gothic period. Manuscript illuminators turned to the same pictorial means and drew inspiration from the same sources.

During the second half of the 15th century and the beginning of the 16th they managed to give this type of decoration a quite specific character and charm by combining natural forms with individual artistic liberties.

The motifs usually took the form of a lone flower or fruit, and were scattered freely on the marginal backgrounds so as to frame a miniature or more often a text sprinkled with vignettes. All the plants here are easily recognisable, and we can gaze with genuine enjoyment at the curly cabbage leaves, prickly thistles, roses, stocks and poppies of our gardens, the sweet peas of our fields, as well as borage, pansies, forget-me-nots, violets, field daisies and many others. Everything is familiar to us, even the insects and the birds!

PLATE 130

Decoration of Eastern-style tapestries
Italy, 15th century

We are looking at two of the most interesting examples of tapestries shown on canvases by Renaissance masters; the paintings are in the Academy of Fine Arts in Ferrara and the Florentine Academy. The arras with the black background appears in a painting by Ghirlandaio and the velvet tablecloth is on a canvas by Carpaccio. Both designs have been produced according to a traditional Eastern decorative layout.

The arras with its woven ornamentation has a slight resemblance to marquetry: the serene pattern is created from continuous geometrical motifs and seems luxuriant. These humble motifs, which are graceful and varied, do not become lost against the black background because of the play of white points that completes the décor.

A quite different appearance is presented by the velvet tablecloth where the embroidery makes the arabesque decoration stand out. The border is composed of a series of identical motifs and their mirror images. The ornamentation is strongly influenced by Persian ornamentation: the arabesque changes easily into a plant form in the hands of Persian ornamentalists. The same applies to the central medallion, although the surrounding motifs do betray a certain Byzantine influence. This splendid fringed tablecloth is a true masterpiece of its kind. Excellent taste can be sensed in the rich embroidery of the border with its slender, well-defined stems that slide through the knots of flowers and trefoils. The colours of the arabesques give them a decorative expressiveness that is all the more obvious since the artist has had the happy thought of using only gold thread (apart from in the central medallion), and the rich velvet background remains untouched in its magnificent uniformity.

Architectonic settings
Precious decorations with enamelling
Book decoration, 15th–16th centuries

Because of the growing interest in ancient culture, 15th-century Italian artists had a passionate interest in classical architectural structures, and this inevitably spread to book decorators. Architectural motifs were included more and more often in the plant compositions of borders and fields. Their role continued to grow from the end of the 15th century, and by the 16th century they had become very popular in France. However, book decoration, and especially borders with architectonic features produced on thin parchment, borrowed their characteristic features above all from the jewellery art of the period.

Jewellery work in the second half of the 15th century was fundamentally different from the gold and jewellery work of the 13th–14th centuries, not just in form but also in the end to the use of multi-coloured *champlevé* or

opaque enamel on carving or relief. In the examples of large jewellery articles shown here, the decoration has been produced using the painted enamel technique that flourished in Limoges during the 16th century. We can see both transparent and opaque enamels, glass on a foil backing, semi-precious stones *en cabochon* and pearls worked in relief. Silvering was combined with gilding, and metal was embossed in every known way from high relief to bas-relief; niello and inlaying were especial favourites. Finally the work was richly decorated with coloured semi-precious stones such as cornelian, porphyry, lapis lazuli, serpentine, jade, from which the details of this miniature architectonic composition were assembled.

PLATE 132

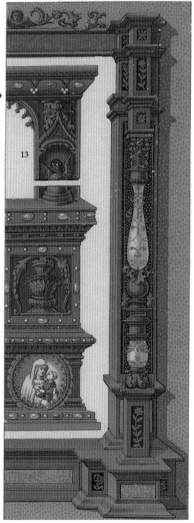

Frescoes and arabesques by Raphael
Rooms in the Vatican, 16th century

What can one say about these miracles of decorative art that are also miracles of ideal art? By giving space in our book to some fine frescoes that were painted by Raphael's pupils under the guidance of the master himself, we are certainly not getting away from the subject: we are merely widening its limits by including the most sublime expression of ornamental creativity. These gigantic compositions are more than ornaments, but at the same time they are ornaments. Whether linked by unity of theme or, as here, at the whim of entrancing imagination, they are still guided by an all-encompassing vision and answer all the demands of decorative effect.

The vertical sections on either side of the plate are filled with the main subjects: on the left are the four Seasons with their attributes, both expressive and poetic, and on the right are the three Fates holding the thread of human life in their hands. The central part of the plate contains various ornamental motifs from the same source.

PLATE 133

Grotesques
Decorative painting in the Vatican

The term 'grotesque ornament' comes in all probability from classical frescoes showing fantastical creations — flower ornamentation and figures that were half bird and half woman — that were discovered during excavations (circa 1500) of Roman buildings, and which were called *grotte* (grotto, cave or room in a hill). Their design is based on a passion for the miraculous, on human nature's powerful need to leave the sphere of its life and to transport itself to the magical world of the imagination. This universal need, which is born in a person as naturally as thought and poetry, develops more intensively among peoples whose civilisations have been created by heterogeneous elements from different origins. All the ornamental motifs are present in Raphael's frescoes, apart from the 'trophies' (in the centre of the plate), which have been taken from a manuscript book with miniatures by Giulio Clovio (Arsenal Library, Paris), and two grisailles with gilding on blue backgrounds on either side of the figurative composition on a black background (in the bottom row of the plate) that were found during excavations at the Casa Taverna (Milan).

Plate 134

135. RENAISSANCE

Engraved articles made from elephant ivory

The motifs shown here fit in with our subject because of the polychrome ornamentation using black and white tones. Sometimes black becomes the background for a pattern that is marked out by a line made of pieces of elephant ivory, and sometimes it makes the picture stand out and gives added detail. In other cases black is used for the lines that mark out the design on a white ivory background.

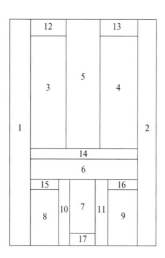

1–4 Fragments of the decoration on ebony furniture. The motifs on the panels and vertical friezes of this magnificent example are taken from Raphael's frescoes in the Vatican;

5 Decoration of a chair with outline engraving from the same source;

6 Motifs from sketches by Agostino Veneziano;

7–11 Ornamental motifs;

12, 13 Decoration on a chest;

14–17 Continuous ornamental motifs.

Architecture as an ornament
The human figure in a traditional setting
Painting and miniatures,
15th–16th centuries

1 Part of the decoration of a manuscript copy of Dante's *Divine Comedy*. The rich ornamental motifs cover the frontispiece of *Paradise*: the arched entrance leads away into a perspective that was replaced by a miniature in the original;

2 Part of the decorative surround for a page in a 15th-century manuscript. The motif is based upon a vertical row of alcoves, each of which contains a picture of an angel playing a musical instrument of the time;

3 The architectural background plays an important role in the depiction of St Helena who, according to legend, found the True Cross. An accented perspective is used to increase the height of the panel;

4 Part of the surround to a 16th-century miniature. The fantastical architecture bears the imprint of the Italian style. It shows double pillars on either side of the miniature; they are connected by a graceful arch surmounted by a narrow cornice, and below them there is a narrow step on which the pedestals of the pillars are resting;

5 The decorative surround to a page and the miniature are linked by a striking perspective. The motif is from the same source as 4;

6 A vertical panel from the brush of Israel von Mekenen. The composition testifies to the artist's lively mind: the depth of perspective is considerably greater than the depth of the alcove, but by skilfully uniting the vaulted arches in the upper part of the panel the artist has managed to create a visual impression of a classical alcove;

7, 9 Details of settings for miniatures in a 16th-century manuscript;

8 A vertical panel depicting a main figure standing out against the background of an architectonic frame linking the saint in the foreground to an enchanting landscape in the middle distance;

10 Painting on a vertical panel that resembles the leaf of a triptych. The same decorative system is used as in 8, but in a simplified form. The stone wall rises to the middle of the figure's breast, and she is connected to a landscape which takes the level of the wall as its starting point.

Book miniatures, 15th century

1, 2 Frontispiece of the manuscript book *Roman History in Extracts from the Historical Works of Paulus Orosius (Historia Romana excerpta ex libris historicis Pauli Orosii).*

These remarkable miniatures are by a pupil of Raphael, Giulio Clovio, who according to Vasari was very successful in Italy. The precise lines of the Italian style also appear in the other three ornaments (3–5) that decorate a manuscript book of the works of Flavius Josephus (Mazarin Library).

Book miniatures and murals

The works shown in this plate belong to
the most remarkable period of the Italian
Renaissance miniature. Giorgio Vasari speaks in
the most rapturous terms about the Florentine
masters of this form of art: Stefano, Gherardo
and Attavante (or Vante) are the ones who stand
out especially among the others.

1 Prayer book (for a requiem) that
belonged to Pope Paul II. 1450;

2 Manuscript from the library of Matthias
Corvinus with miniatures by Attavante
or Gherardo. 1492;

3–7 Book of antiphons (psalms and excerpts
from the Sacred Scriptures or the Bible
that were performed during a church
service) from Florence. Miniatures by
Attavante, 1526–1530;

8, 9 Missal (for daily use) with miniatures
ascribed to Attavante di Gabriello;

10, 11 Manuscript with miniatures by Attavante
from the library of the noble Barberini
family, Rome;

12, 13 Details from decorative frescoes by
Raphael in the Vatican. They may have
been painted by his pupil Giovanni di
Udino;

14, 15 Miniatures from a prayer book that
belonged to Cardinal Cornari. Ascribed
to Raphael;

16–19 *Lives of the Dukes of Urbino*. Vatican
Library. Rome;

20–24 From a Book of Hours with a calendar
dating from 1554. Terento Monastery.

Book decoration, 16th–17th centuries

Most of the motifs shown here (1, 3–5, 7, 9,10, 12, 13, 17, 19) decorate two pages of a prayer book which belonged to Cardinal Pompeo Colonna, Archbishop of Monreale and Viceroy of Naples, where he died in 1532. They demonstrate the skill with which the ornamentalist of the period turned freely to pagan sources to create the décor of a deeply Christian manuscript. Without in the least offending the client's personal convictions, he spread out before him a whole world of pictures that were the particular favourites of the educated Italian of the Renaissance, someone who loved the classical past: architectural monuments, coins, intaglios, cameos and, of course, mythology.

The miniatures in the Cardinal's prayer book are traditionally ascribed to Raphael, although this seems unlikely apart from the fact that the choice of motifs and compositions sometimes recalls the paintings in the Stanza della Segnatura in the Vatican.

The miniature motif in the top centre (2), a decorative vertical band separating two columns of text, and the initials (14, 15) are from the prayer book of Pope Pius II, which was illuminated about 1450. The marginal miniatures illustrate scenes from the Holy Scriptures, New Testament or Acts of the Apostles.

6, 8, 16 – two borders and an initial from a manuscript copy of the works of Pliny the Elder (16th century);

11 and 18 – fragments of marginal decoration in a prayer book that belonged to Cardinal Cornaro.

Book decoration, 15th–16th centuries
Jewellery motifs

Apart from the initial that occupies a central place in the plate, all the motifs shown here are taken from one source, an Italian manuscript known as the *Aragon Book of Hours*. Its décor reminds us of a goldsmith's work decorated with pearls and precious stones. During the 15th–16th centuries the profession of goldsmith was considered essential for anyone undertaking sculpture, and future sculptors were supposed to follow a course of study under a specialist in gold-working. The great sculptors Brunelleschi, Donatello, Pasolino and Luca della Robbia were highly-qualified goldsmiths.

In all probability the person who illuminated the *Aragon Book of Hours* also received a similar training, since the choice and execution of the motifs inspired by Roman antiquity and Renaissance gold-working indicate the hand of a genuine master. The examples represent a true treasure chest containing the magnificent riches of the period, especially of Milanese origin as Milan was the second-richest city-state after Venice and the home of the House of Sforza, whose passion for splendour knew no limits. Eight scribes, two miniaturists and two bookbinders worked permanently at the court of Alfonso, Prince of Aragon, whose arms decorates the manuscript. The bookbinders also included motifs of precious jewels when decorating bindings.

The initial *D* by Monte di Giovanni (1448–1529) is from the ecclesiastical books in the cathedral in Florence. Monte was an exceptional mosaicist and first-class miniaturist, and he worked on these books for many years. The initial is surmounted by a vase with realistically drawn lilies and schematic leafy motifs. At the bottom an angel is holding a magnificent decoration covered with pearls, amethysts and rubies.

PLATE 140

141 RENAISSANCE

Book decoration, 15th–16th centuries

Like many of the motifs in the preceding plate, these border motifs come from the famous *Aragon Book of Hours* which was illuminated in the 16th century.

1 Acanthus leaves with naturalistically painted flowers; pearls and gems hang down like fruit from the branches;

3 The central scene depicts Christ being mocked, and the marginal decoration is therefore based on a motif of thorn branches;

4 The fields of the manuscript are filled with supple interwoven reed stems resembling Celtic ribbon interlacing, but it is so graceful that the pattern does not seem overloaded. The jewellery decorations in this composition are almost imperceptible;

5 This pattern — poppies with green and bronze leaves alternately and almost naturally coloured flowers — does not contain any decorative jewellery motifs;

6 The only jewels are in the top centre; the border is filled with motifs of leaves, pea pods and red cinquefoil flowers;

7, 8 Parts of borders from the same manuscript.

7 – base of a gold and enamel jewellery decoration, as indicated by the polychrome colouring. This magnificent example of jewellery work holds our attention on the central part of the plate;

8 – upper part of another page of the manuscript; the decoration on a lilac background is made of oak branches with acorns, as well as strawberries and red cinquefoil flowers.

DECORATED INITIALS

9 Initial *E* from a *missale antiquum* (old prayer book) illuminated in France c. 1400;

10 Initial *E* from the *Antiphons* in the Carthusian monastery in Pavia;

11 Initial *P* from the same source;

12 Initial *E* combined with a depiction of John the Baptist.

ROSETTES AND ORNAMENTAL KNOTS

13–20 Details of a purely Gothic style taken from a collection of church hymns and psalms in Siena; the manuscript was illuminated by Giovanni di Paolo.

Finally, 2, with its alternating bunches of scarlet and blue-white flowers, illustrates a type of marginal decoration that was very widespread in the 15th century.

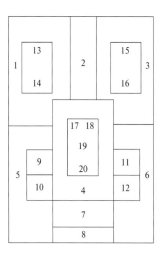

Stained glass windows with architectonic features

Stained glass windows were extremely popular in the 16th century. They differed from the coloured glass windows of the 13th–15th centuries both in style and the way that they were produced. The first people to make stained glass windows created most of their compositions with pieces of real coloured glass, and only had recourse to painting clear glass when dealing with exposed parts of the body, white drapery and individual parts of the background. By the beginning of the 16th century stained glass windows were made solely of transparent glass. The use of enamels had spread during the 15th century and the adaptation of the process to painting gradually led to the idea of achieving the same artistic effects in stained glass. From this came the lightening of tones, strict modelling and the introduction of perspective, in other words a total rejection of the flat decoration used in medieval stained glass. However, although 16th-century stained-glass windows lost the traditional appearance that had made them dependent on architecture, the colours had never before been as clear or sparkling as in these light and shining compositions, for the semidarkness of medieval cathedrals was undesirable and even harmful for secular buildings. Unlike stained glass that was made of pieces of coloured glass, where detail was sacrificed to the overall effect, the people who now made stained glass followed the principles of the Italian Renaissance and endowed their work with a different character through its great graphical and colouristic merits.

6 A border which includes the royal lilies of Louis XII and the ermine of Anne of Brittany; rose window (which has not survived) in a church in Gisors, 1500–1515;

5, 7, 8 Motifs in a church in Grand Andely, 1520.

5 – architectural motif, a very beautiful vestige of the Norman Renaissance. Southern side chapels;

7 – motif from a large rose window in the south transept, with the same decorative features as the lost rose window in the church in Gisors. It consists of two motifs, placed one above the other and repeated many times so as to form rays meeting in the centre. (The second motif, which is also on a green background, is reproduced in motif 9, plate 143);

8 – motif from the chapel of St Christophe;

1, 3, 4, 9 Motifs from the Church of St Vincent in Rouen.

4 – dated twice: 1525 and 1526;

2 Motif originating from a church in Montmorency, 1535.

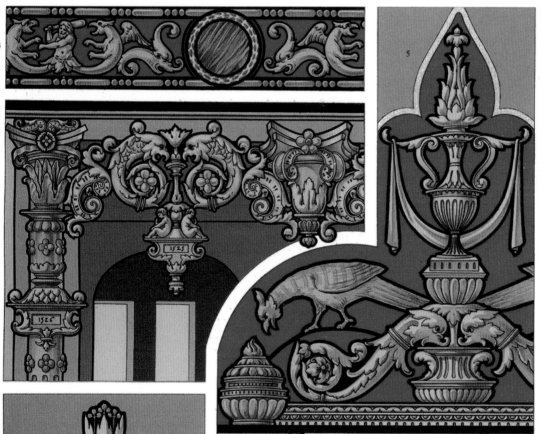

Sculptured decoration and stained glass

This plate is a continuation of the preceding plate.

The wealth of motifs makes it possible to draw a parallel with the marginal decoration on manuscripts of the same period. The nature of this decoration shows much more strongly in stained glass windows with their simpler artistic solutions and large sizes, whereas the work of the illuminator is invariably overloaded with small details. In the 16th century the people who drew the cartoons for large stained glass windows often themselves painted the glass surfaces and were genuine decorative artists of their time. Artistic schools were still very important during the first half of the 16th century, and the French stained glass makers of the period comprised a truly brilliant group of craftsmen.

7, 9, 11, 14 Stained glass in the church in Grand Andely, 1515–1520.

> 7 – part of a border in the Chapel of St Christophe;

> 6 – rose window motif in the south transept (the pair of motif 7 in plate 142);

> 14 – motif above a small door in the south façade;

8 Decorative finial from the Church of St Patrice in Rouen, 1520;

2 Panel from the south chapel near the altar in Rouen Cathedral, 1521 (dated). A typical expression of the Norman Renaissance;

13 Ornamental finial to a stained glass window of John the Baptist in the Church of St Vincent in Rouen, 1525–1526;

12 Frieze in the Museum of Antiquities in Rouen; it is possibly from the former Church of St Eloi, 1530;

10 Motif of a keystone in a stained glass window that has not survived. The fragment was included in a stained-glass window in the Church of St Crépin in Gisors, 1530;

1, 3 Motifs of a baldachin from a church in Montmorency, 1535–1540.

> 1 – part of a continuous pattern that fills the upper part of a stained glass window facing the right-hand side-altar. It is a motif of the Touraine school, c. 1540 (end of the reign of François I);

> 3 – dated 1535;

4 This architectural fragment is part of a stained glass window in the Church of St Gervais in Paris, 1535;

6 Cartouche with a polychrome lattice from the ossuary at the Church of St-Etienne-du-Mont in Paris. 1535. The motif is a final and rare reminder of the French Renaissance, an example of the elegant and free model which artists copied during the time of Louis XIII. The prototype belongs to the Fontainebleau school;

5 Part of a stained glass window in the nave of the Church of St Patrice in Rouen, 1550.

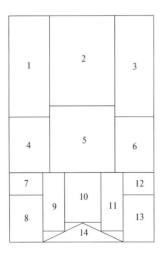

PLATE 143

French schools of sculpture, tapestry
and stained glass

This plate completes the series linked to
16th-century stained glass. Four exceptions from
the same period belong to other genres where
polychrome colouring also plays a significant
role: it is quite restrained in stone carving,
which still has a considerable depth of relief,
and more prominent in tapestries, where it
produces striking results. We will not go into
the different types of colouring used for carved
stone, tapestries or stained glass; even so, our
examples will help to explain the way that
dissimilar materials were used by craftsmen
who so often proved themselves to be true
masters in the great period of the Renaissance.

We will discuss the exceptions first:

1   – recess in the upper part of the tomb
of the cardinals of Amboise in Rouen
Cathedral, a masterpiece of the Norman
Renaissance (1520–1540);

5–7   – corner cartouche and a cartouche
included in the continuous pattern on
the border of an arras whose central
scene has the title of *Triumph*. The
monogram of Maria de' Medici in the
cartouche (7) indicates when the arras
was made, but not when the cartoon
was produced; however, the corner
cartouche with the seated figure still
belongs stylistically to the Fontainebleau
school. The tapestry with the border (5)
is part of a series of arrases called *The
Story of Artemisia* for which cartoons
were produced several times. The royal
weaving studios in Paris repeated this
series ten times between 1570 and 1660;

19   – pattern for the back of a chair.

NORMAN SCHOOL

14   Church in Grand-Andely, 1515;

6, 10, 11, 15, 17   The same source, 1520;

16, 18   Church of St Vincent in Rouen,
1520–1525;

2, 3, 9, 13   Museum of Antiquities in Rouen,
1530;

8   Church in Grand-Andely, 1535–1540;

4   The same source, 1560.

PARIS SCHOOL

12   Church of St-Etienne-du-Mont.

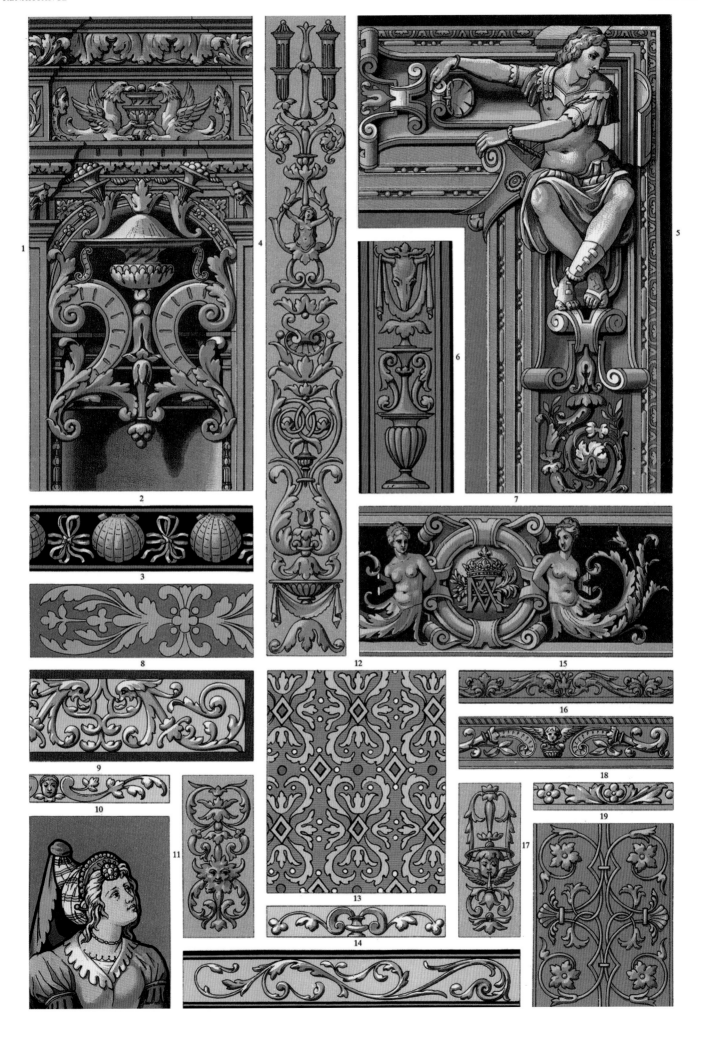

145 RENAISSANCE

Majolica and painting on glass
Italy, 15th–16th centuries
France, 16th century

1 Architectonic ornamentation on slip-
glazed terracotta (Louvre, Paris). The
earliest ceramics of this type are the work
of Luca della Robbia (1400–1482), who
was apprenticed to a goldsmith during
his youth and then became one of Italy's
leading sculptors. He invented a method
of firing a clay model in a glaze made of
lead and tin oxides mixed with potash
so as to protect it from the effects of the
atmosphere;

4–7 Two borders and two tiles that were made
at the Caffagiolo factory, a major centre
for producing ceramics in Tuscany;

8 Faience with a *sopra bianca* decoration, a
pattern in white glaze on a slightly tinted
white background. The border has a green
pattern;

9 Decorative 'lattice' of leaves on a china
plate. The first European dishes of this type
were produced in experimental workshops
set up by Cosimo the Great in the Palace
of St Mark in Florence. It was not genuine
porcelain made of pure china clay, and
the Frenchman Alexandre Brongniart, the
director of the Sèvres Porcelain Factory,
called it 'hybrid' or 'mixed porcelain'.
The trials were unsuccessful: after firing
the body of the dish sometimes took on
a greenish or yellowish hue, and the glaze
was not always smooth. The monochrome
decoration, which in our case is in pure
cobalt, was rarely a rich colour, nor did it
have a uniform texture;

10 Majolica is a form of Italian faience with a
metallic lustre. It is believed that 'majolica'
is a mispronunciation of the island of
Majorca. Demi-majolica is classified as
slip-glazed ceramics, and it owes its
whiteness to underglaze. After being
painted, the surface is covered with lead
glaze, producing a mother-of-pearl tint;

2, 3 Motifs from the period of the Norman
Renaissance: painting on glass using
grisaille on a yellow background, 1530.

2 – upper part of the altar in the church
in Grand-Andely;

3 – stained-glass window of St Crispin in
the parish church in Gisors.

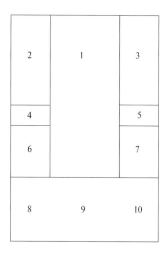

PLATE 145

Slip-glazed tiles for walls and floors

The wall tiles shown in the upper part of the plate are from Spain; they date to the time of Charles V (1500–1558), and were made in Italy. The very elegant bas-reliefs on these tiles, with their almost imperceptible convexities and depressions, are excellently made and provided with amazingly sharp compositions. The narrow ribs that stress the motif reflect light in such a way that the compositions glisten in a calm and magnificent way. The colouration is the result of a very complex technical process in which firing probably plays the main part. The work is distinguished by its faultless taste and the confidence of its lines, and the nature of the decoration makes it impossible to confuse it with Moorish work. At the top of the plate there are two examples of four identical tiles that form a large picture. The motif in the centre is a single tile that has been enlarged purely because of its beauty. The lower part of the plate is occupied by part of the tiling laid on a floor in front of a fireplace. The slip-glazed tiles were made in Italy. By using tiles of two shapes (hexagon and rectangle) the ceramicist has produced a beautiful composition that resembles the distinctive coffered ceilings of the great Italian architect Sebastiano Serlio so much that one is tempted to ascribe them to him. The relief surface of this type of tile clearly indicates their purpose: they can only be used for facing walls. Tiles with a smooth surface were also used for facing walls, but more often for laying on floors.

Book decoration

The two ornamental motifs placed one above the other in the middle of the plate are of Italian origin and taken from the famous Siena collection of church hymns and psalms (the *Gradual*). The remaining motifs are in the traditions of the French Renaissance (the Tours school) and they are interesting not just because of their decorative merits but also because they are the work of François Colombe. Michel Colombe, his uncle, was one of the most productive French sculptors of the 15th–16th centuries, and a true founder of the Renaissance in French plastic arts. He used the culture of the Italian Renaissance in his own way to introduce classical motifs into the decoration of his works. Michel Colombe was the author of the design for a magnificent funerary monument using features of Renaissance decoration (pilasters and ornamentation) that was erected in Nantes Cathedral at the order of Queen Anne of Brittany as a memorial to her parents, François II, the last Duke of Brittany, and Marguerite de Foix. We know from the archives that Colombe worked with three of his nephews who were 'great craftsmen': Guillaume Regniault carved the faces and figures from stone, Bastien François was an architect and stonemason and François Colombe was the 'painter'. Michel Colombe is known to have made terracotta models, and François painted the faces and hands, and whatever was necessary, with various colours.

PLATE 147

Cartouches

Initially the cartouche was a moulded decoration that sprang from the medieval shield with arms, an emblem and an inscription. Its numerous modifications are very interesting for the ornamentalist. Cartouches were also carved out of hard wood, polished with leather and worked in every possible way until they were transformed into the S-shaped fronds of foliage and the rocaille decorations of the 18th century, and ultimately attained the elegant lines of the Louis XVI style. The Italians only began paying the cartouche its due as an ornamental motif in the 15th century. The cartouche was the fruit of the architectural genius of European masters, and has nothing in common with the art of Asia or the East. It subordinates all forms of décor to itself.

Rather than counting the many separate examples, we are offering a series of cartouches in chronological order. This is the first attempt of its type.

15TH CENTURY.

   1 Motifs from a picture by Cima da Conegliano (Louvre, Paris).

16TH CENTURY.

  2–5 Sketch by Antonio Razzi (Louvre, Paris);

   6 Manuscript book (Arsenal Library, Paris);

 7–11 Slip-glazed terracotta reliefs painted in the Italian style (external decoration of the Château de Madrid in Paris, built during the reign of François I);

12–15, 18–21 Paintings by Primaticcio in the Palace of Fontainebleau;

26–28 Decorative surrounds to portraits in a magnificent book that was copied for François I c. 1530. French National Library, Paris);

  29 Stained glass window in the crypt of the Church of St-Etienne-du-Mont. French Renaissance, 1535. This cartouche is one of the few relics of the French Renaissance of the time. Initially it surrounded the arms of the people who had donated these windows (the windows were broken during the Reformation); we have replaced the arms with an arabesque in the same style;

  30 Stained glass window with the arms of the goldsmiths' guild in Rouen and the date 1543;

16, 17, 22–25, 31–35 Motifs of book decoration from sketches by Geoffroy Tory, Cousin the Elder and other artists of the time of Henri II.

PLATE 148

Decorative painting in the François I
Gallery
Palace of Fontainebleau

A large architectural cartouche, sometimes
supplemented by small secondary ones, always
forms the decorative centre of these magnificent
panels. Since a projecting panel requires
shallow carving, the cartouches are made
almost completely flat, and the tendrils of the
plant ornamentation that surrounds them are
very thin; in this way all the advantages of a
convex relief that their fragile nature allows can
be preserved. Thus the tabernacle medallion
with a depiction in relief of a salamander, the
heraldic symbol of François I, has to have a
low relief border, and therefore the *carta* type
cartouche surround with its twisting ends has
to be softened and even removed from the
composition of these cartouches; many of these,
because of their severe lines, seem to be made of
wood. The variety and at times perfect elegance
of the decorations, where cartouches combine
strikingly with plant motifs, form a single
homogenous element which makes the panels
into some of the finest of their type.

We can see with what taste and skill the
Italians managed to soften the usual cartouche
by enriching it with acanthus leaves and
introducing the real or mythological world
of antiquity into its decoration. With their
knowledge of how to use classical models, these
craftsmen were in no way slavish imitators.

Professionalism aided the development of
their native talent, and they worked completely
independently with the material that they
had inherited from the past. The artists of
antiquity knew nothing of the decorative
cartouche, and the varied combinations that it
gave birth to, thereby creating the foundations
for compositions with elegant plant fronds,
were never part of the repertoire of classical
decoration. The period of the Renaissance was
a rebirth, but a rebirth of a different sort: in
the hands of the skilled carvers who produced
these panels it was full of the charm of renewal
that spring brings. These talented craftsmen,
who were the direct inheritors of the classical
past and had excellent 'characteristics' that
had been instilled by their schools, had not
the slightest embarrassment in recalling their
origins; they were convinced that that they were
revealing their own personalities by introducing
their innate taste into almost everything that
the world had known from time immemorial.
Thus it was that the 16th-century Renaissance
developed a style that resembled antiquity, yet
was neither Grecian nor Roman.

PLATE 149

Carved, painted and woven cartouches of
the 16th–17th centuries

As a rule, the decorative cartouche originates
from the church monstrance which, with the
arrival of the Baroque, had become an exquisite
jewellery article looking like the sun with its
rays. The purpose of the cartouche was to
stress the inscription, symbol, or historical or
mythological person that it contained, and to
surround them with a decoration that could
be simple or intricate and accompanied by
plant motifs, figures, flowers, fruit, ribbons, etc.
Sometimes the main cartouche contains smaller,
secondary cartouches which combine with it
to form a large-scale composition. Finally, the
cartouche can be a purely architectural feature
that coincides with the main lines of the

structure; it can also be an independent item
on a background that is limited by the edges
of the panel; when used even more freely and
decorating part of a continuous field, it can
take on an airy lightness.

This plate shows:

1, 2 – cartouches from the François I Gallery
in the Palace of Fontainebleau. The ends of an
architectural cartouche of the *carta* type are
shown; it has a flat surface which curls into spiral
scrolls at each end;

6, 7 – motifs from arras borders. The cartouches
and moulded decorations are architectonic in
style and there is a magnificent colour range;

3–5 – gilded door panels (using the *sali d'or*
technique) from the same source as plate 151.

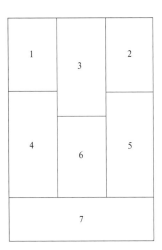

Decorative painting
Palace of Fontainebleau

The decoration shown here is closely linked to the fine arts of the period of Henri IV and Louis XIII. Its characteristic features allow us to consider it at the same time as the decorative painting of the first half of the 17th century. However, the reader must be warned that the medallions with emblems that decorate the first reception room in the Palace of Fontainebleau were made in 1834 under the direction of Charles Moench, whom Louis-Philippe had commissioned to restore the guardroom (vestibule).

We have enough material available to be able to recreate the character of the original décor. Practically everything has survived: after the canvas covering them had been removed, the pieces of card discovered on the ceiling (admittedly, most of them had turned into shreds) still had traces of ornamental motifs and flowers, 'trophies' and weapons painted in oils on a gold background. This was sufficient to make it relatively easy to return the *plafond* and frieze to their external appearance at the time of Louis XIII. The white background of the panels is adorned with an exceptionally rich decoration with delicate work and magnificent finish. The gilding was done with a special technique called *sali d'or*: hatching with pure metal on a background of a rich bronze colour created a striking effect of light. The five folding doors (either real or fake) of the guardroom were painted with compositions that commemorated rulers whose names were linked with enlarging or decorating the Palace of Fontainebleau. The two large panels show part of the decoration of a door commemorating Antoine de Bourbon, the Duke of Vendôme and father of Henri IV; on one leaf there is a portrait of the hero of the Battle of Les Andelys surmounted by the arms of Vendôme, and on the other is the monogram of Jeanne d'Albret, the mother of Henri IV, and the arms of Navarre. The two smaller panels with the monograms of Henri IV and Marie de' Medici demonstrate various emblems and mottoes. The monogram of Anne of Austria is in the bottom centre.

Limoges enamels
Grisaille

1, 12, 16, 17 Motifs from the decoration of a
cup with saucer and lid.

1 – effectively two motifs: the medallion
with the boy on a dolphin adorns the
inside of the cup, and from there the
decoration moves onto the outer surface
of the lid;

12 – border ornamented with an egg and
dart beading;

16 – painting on the stem of the cup;

17 – border on the inner surface of the
lid;

2, 14 – details of the painting on a circular
dish that was made by the same
enameller (2 – inside of the dish,
14 – outside);

3 Painting on the outside of a cup with
a saucer;

4, 11, 15 Painting on the inner surface of
the cup.

4 and 15 – two *mascarons* (cf. also plate 153,
motif 11);

9, 10 Painting on a circular dish with the date
1558 in a cartouche.

9 – border on the reverse of the dish;

5 Part of the painting on the stem of
the cup;

6 Border on a small enamelled box;

7, 8 Decoration of a water jug.

7 – decoration on the inside of the neck;

8 – base of the vessel (upper) and stem
(lower).

About 1520 the Limoges craftsmen abandoned
almost completely the old methods of painting
in enamels on an enamel background, and
began using a new technique known as grisaille,
although the old method was still used from
time to time to give variety to the decorative
effect.

During the whole of the 16th century grisaille,
or the line obtained from a process of the type
that is used in chemical etching, stressed the
features of a picture and gave the image the
clarity and firmness that, together with the use
of light, made the enamels particularly striking.
The misuse of gold leaf and flecks of gold
lowered the artistic merit of Limoges enamels,
and by the end of the 16th century their
commercial value had fallen sharply.

PLATE 152

Grisailles in Limoges enamel
Painted enamels
Embroidery and painting

ENAMELS

3 Reverse of an oval dish (54cm long). This example of painted enamel is signed with the monogram *J.C.*, which belonged to Jean Courteys (1515–1586), a Limoges enameller to whom the decoration of this dish is ascribed. Unfortunately he did not usually date his works.

The technique of painted enamel in which a layer could be applied to the reverse of a metal object (counter enamelling) was very important in preventing deformation of one side during firing. The Limoges enamellers turned this necessity into an advantage by using it when producing objects whose shape allowed the reverse side to become visible. This type of decoration could be extremely varied, and sometimes both sides were decorated the same way with gold-flecked grisaille on a dark brown background, and sometimes the reverse was in contrasting colours;

4, 5 Borders with repeating motifs on dishes.

This is the work of Léonard Limousin, the most original and most famous of the Limoges enamellers. His early works were produced mainly under the influence of German masters, and in 1532 he decorated several plates with pictures by Dürer; later he copied prints of compositions by Raphael. From 1552 he was influenced by the Fontainebleau school, and in particular the style of Niccolò dell'Albatte, one of the masters of this school;

6, 7, 14 Enamels by Pierre Courteys.

This enameller, who worked during the second half of the 16th century, dated his enamels.

6, 7 – decoration on a cup: painting on the stem;

14 – motif on the upper part of a water jug (supplemented by motif 8 in plate 152);

8 *Mascaron* on the bottom of a dish;

11 Fourth *mascaron* of the series shown in plate 152 (4, 11, 15).

EMBROIDERY AND PAINTING

1, 2 Corner motifs of book decoration made by Girolamo da Cremona;

9, 10 Corner motifs made by Liberale da Verona;

12, 13 Field and border of the cloth upholstery of an armchair;

15 Field of arras with repeating pattern. Period of Henri II;

16 Edge of a tunic. The same period.

Limoges enamels and Italian majolica

The art of painted enamels, which is close to the forms of easel art, sprang up in Limoges about 1520 and reached its peak some 20 years later. The Italian artists Rosso and Primaticcio, who worked in France, made sketches for the Limoges enamellers and helped them to produce a new art form.

The Royal Enamel Factory in Limoges was set up by François I and its first director was the court enameller Léonard, more often called Léonard Limousin (an inhabitant of Limoges). The most famous masters were the Penicaud brother (who represented the old school), Pierre Reymond, the Courteys brothers, Martial Raymond, Etienne Mercier and Jean Court (known as Vigier). Most of the ornamentation to be used in painted enamel was created by Ducerceau, Cousin the Elder and Pierre Voeiriot, but above all by Etienne Delaune (Stephanus).

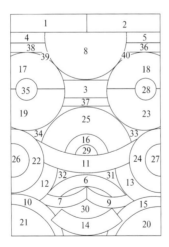

Motifs 17–40 decorate Italian majolica articles; they are generally accurately and skilfully composed, yet at the same time they do not hide their Eastern or classical origin. Some majolica dishes were so good that Queen Christina of Sweden, a connoisseur and collector of decorative art objects, proposed exchanging them for silver dishes of the same size.

Motifs in Limoges enamels:

1–3 Articles produced by Martin Limousin;

4–6 Workshop of Léonard Limousin;

7 Workshop of Pierre Raymond;

8 Reverse side of a tray with an opening in the centre.

Workshop of Pierre Raymond;

9 Lip of a dish from the same workshop;

10–13 Lip of a dish painted by Pierre Courteys;

14 Edge and rim ascribed to Jean Courteys;

15, 16 Rim of a dish painted by Jean Court (Vigier).

17–23 Majolica plates with ornamental rims;

24, 25 Glazed rims;

26–29 Monochrome ornamentation;

30–40 Grotesques, Urbino (Italy).

PLATE 154

Slip-glazed tiles

1 Pentagonal tiles;

2, 3 Pentagonal tiles (with the same border as 1);

4–8 Square tiles;

9–14 Mosaic floor in the Castle of Polisy (Aube);

15–18 Separate tiles with individual subjects from the Castle of Polisy.

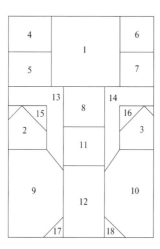

PLATE 155

Book decoration

This magnificent decorative composition (1573) is in oils on a sheet of thin parchment. It is believed to be the work of Giulio Clovio, who painted it for the enthronement in 1572 of Pope Gregory XIII (born Ugo Boncompagni). The arms of the Boncompagni family are in the large cartouche at the bottom. As something of a compromise between the medieval book miniature (from whence the naturalistic depiction of plants and animals in the border) and the more modern cartouche, the decorative composition makes use of its capabilities with the breadth and harmony that are typical of the school of Raphael to which the artist belonged. The master's hand has painted the figures of the four Evangelists in the central field, especially the figure of St John (lower right). It is impossible not to be entranced by them, even when seen outside the composition of which they are organic parts.

PLATE 156

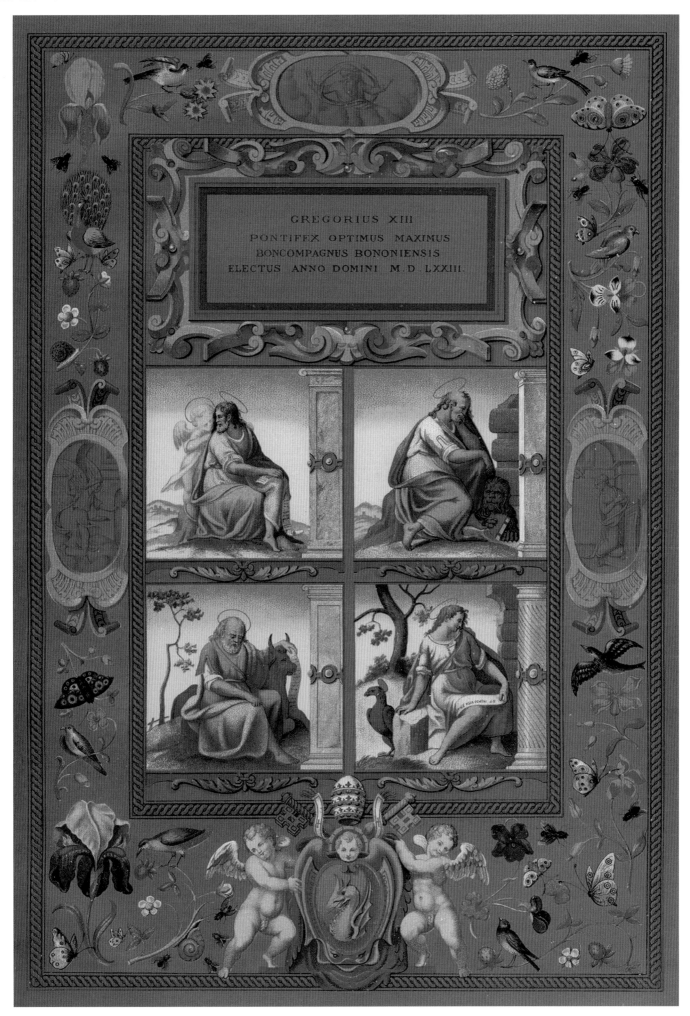

GREGORIUS XIII
PONTIFEX OPTIMUS MAXIMUS
BONCOMPAGNUS BONONIENSIS
ELECTUS ANNO DOMINI M.D.LXXIII.

Decoration of weapons
Steel and enamel, steel and niello,
embossing

The sabre and dagger hilts shown in the plate are forged from steel and decorated with cloisonné enamel on gold, and the same decoration is on the scabbard and the metal fittings of the belt. This type of decoration on a weapon is rare; the examples date from the reign of Henri II (1547–1559).

The enamel decoration is applied in such a way that the surface remains completely smooth; relief patterns are only seen on hilts with a rectangular cross-section. The blade of the sabre is Spanish in origin, but the enamel decoration on the sabre and dagger are more likely French.

The technique of *champlevé* enamel was rarely used in Italy, and if ever it was used it was for small enamel and niello patterns in which an engraved motif was filled with blue-black enamel that stood out on the dark background.

21, 22, 24 – inlaying with enamel resembling the technique of niello and enamel, although the examples are not of Italian origin.

22 – (possibly a ferrule on the binding of a scabbard) the type of weapon with imitation Eastern inlaying that was brought to Northern Italy by the Arabs who lived principally in the Sinai Peninsula. It is an example of the artistic creations that became popular from 1554 onwards through the engravings of Balthazar Silvius. The pommel with its intricate plant motifs (21) was made by the Nuremburg armourer Virgilius Solis, as was the embossed decoration (25) bearing the master's monogram in a medallion that was placed between the cross-guards of the sword.

The three ferrules on the binding of a scabbard (20, 23, 26) belong to the Rhineland school of the second half of the 16th century; the perfection of the embossing indicates the skill of their creators. German armourers also worked as goldsmiths and their work had a big influence on the decorative styles of the time.

Gold and silver articles with enamelling, jewellery

Nowadays the art of the goldsmith and enameller is almost completely forgotten in France, and the decline began after 1668. The financial crisis caused by the wars in Europe sharply reduced the use of precious metals after 1693; the massive silver services made for Louis XIV were melted down at the mint and replaced by imported Eastern lacquered goods. The end of the craft was brought closer by wide use of china and cut glass. From then on gold and silversmiths only produced various curios for the royal courts, and it was for this purpose that in 1698 by royal decree the Louvre still had the jewellery workshops of four goldsmiths, Melin, Rotier, Delaunay and Montarsy as well as the enameller Pierre Bain.

1, 2　Tips to sword scabbards;

3　Decoration of a ring in elephant ivory;

4　Part of the decoration of an agate cup;

5–7, 9, 12　Decoration of a gold cup;

8, 10, 14　Clasps;

11　Ring with a relief insert of a man's head;

13　Hilt guard of a sabre from the treasures of the Austrian royal house; it terminates in a woman's head;

15–17　Relief decoration on an ebony box from the former treasures of the kings of Poland;

18　Vase tripod;

19–26　Figured handles for vases and cups;

27, 28　Saucers;

29–31　Fragments of jewellery.

Decorative plant motifs in Flemish tapestries

Almost all the best tapestries produced in Europe during the 16th century were woven in Flanders, and their decoration represents the purest and boldest expression of the Italian Renaissance style. We do not know who were the authors of the fragments of tapestry shown in this plate, but we do know the names of the great artists who created the cartoons that came to Flanders, principally from Italy. The cycle *The Triumph of the Gods* was woven in Brussels from sketches by Andrea Mantegna, and the weavers of the same city produced Raphael's *Acts of the Apostles*. Giulio Romano created the sketches for the ten-part cycle *Scipio Africanus* with hunting scenes that were woven from compositions by the school of Dürer. Lucas van Leyden provided models for the cycle *The Twelve Seasons*. Weaving was a very expensive process and drawings for tapestries were commissioned from the most talented artists. The artistic merits had to coincide with the luxury of the time. Jean du Bellay, one of François I's generals, commented that he had seen 'four enormous tapestries of *The Victories of Scipio Africanus* (not the series by Giulio Romano) woven entirely from gold thread and coloured silk.'

1, 2, 4 – fragments of border ornamentation;

3, 6, 7, 9 – border motifs.

In some of the best Italian cartoons (especially from the school of Mantegna) similar ornamental motifs often decorated the clothing, objects and furniture shown in the central scene;

5, 8, 10, 11 – examples of this type of decoration.

In the originals:

5 – upper part of a tunic;

8 – greaves;

10 – hem of a tunic;

11 – part of the decoration for a flower vase.

PLATE 159

1

5

6

7

2

9

8

3

10

4

11

Italian book decoration

The motifs shown in plates 160 and 161 are taken from the *Antiphons* in the Carthusian monastery in Pavia. These religious books provide extremely interesting material for the student as they show the changes in ornamentation during the long period needed to complete them. The dates 1562 (book 3) and 1578 (book 12) occur in two of the fourteen books from which we have taken our illustrations, and from this it is obvious that work began a little before 1562 and was still continuing after 1569. This is proved by the examples of decorations taken from books 13 and 14, which date to the end of the 16th–beginning of the 17th centuries. Whatever might be the precise date when the illuminators started their work, it is clear that the artists who began the task drew their inspiration from the magnificent architectural decoration of the monastery in Pavia. Its construction began in 1396 under Gian Galeazzo Visconti, was continued under the dukes of Sforza and was completed circa 1542. To a certain extent the decoration on the façade of the monastery resembles the decoration on the bronze doors of St Peter's Basilica in Rome, providing a very memorable example of the mixture of pagan and Christian ornamental features that was typical of the Early Renaissance. In book decoration this phenomenon is the result of the influence of fine arts on decorative and applied arts.

The magnificent layout of the *Antiphons* is in perfect harmony with the environment in which talented miniaturists worked for almost fifty years and gradually modified the style of decoration. In following the tastes of their time, the illustrators created a historical gallery of book decoration in which the various stages in the transformation can be easily identified.

1 Ornamental motif on the first page.

Portrait of Gian Galeazzo Visconti, the founder of the monastery in Pavia;

2–4 Borders.

3   – with the date 1562 included in the cartouche.

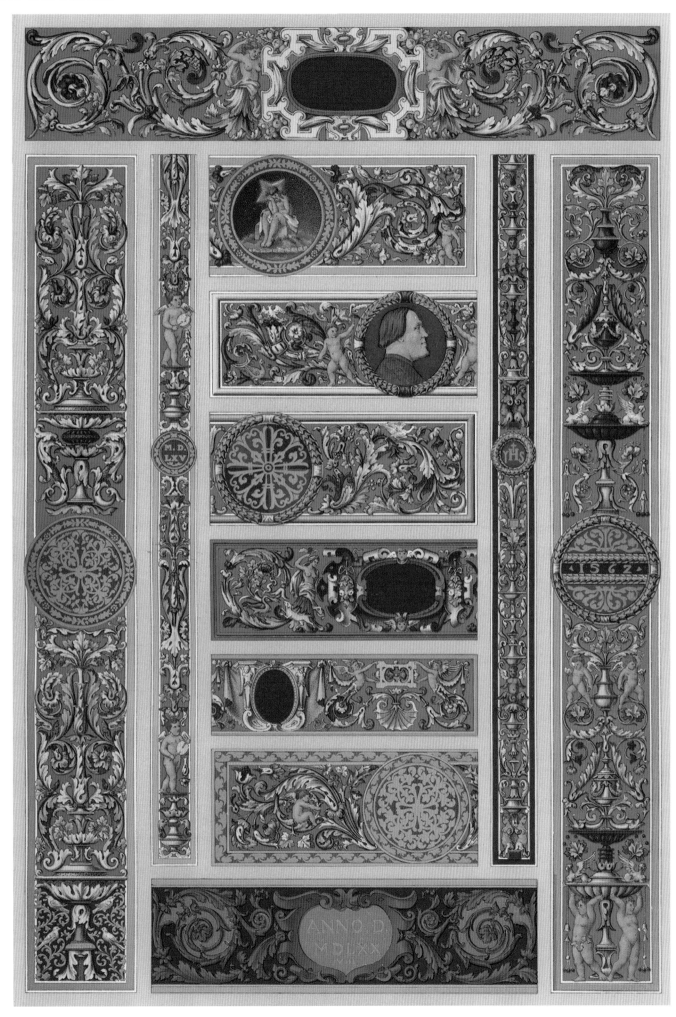

Italian book decoration

Illustrations 7–10, 13, 15, 20 and 22 are in plate 160.

5, 6   Beautifully traced initials *N* and *D*, especially 5, where we can sense the hand of an experienced ornamentalist and goldsmith. The tendency to make the picture more complex can be seen above all in the initial *D*, which is less interesting when compared to the others and with a mirror image, moreover;

7–10   Borders

8 – purely ornamental, without the inclusion of human figures;

9 – two figures of drummers and a medallion with the date 1565;

10 – the scene in the medallion represents the Saviour weeping for the sins of mankind. The way that this miniature composition with its border has been produced definitely resembles the decoration of Limoges enamels.

11–14   The initial *N* (11) exemplifies a completely different type of decoration; it was made by a skilled artist who has managed to introduce something new into it;

12 – a purely decorative motif supplemented by full-length human figures or half-length portraits (children playing with birds and garlands of flowers; two winged beings with pointed ears and pear-shaped breasts – like female fauns – growing out of the foliage);

13 – dated 1578. There is reason to believe that this new type of decoration with its polychrome colouring was produced by a foreign artist or master who had studied not in Milan but, for instance, in Bologna, as the style indicates fairly definitely;

15–18   Motifs 15 and 16 suggest a search for a new elegance and a new gracefulness of movement combined with a strict symmetry;

19–23   Motif 22 embodies the idea of a new magnificence, as indicated by the increasing role of such a decorative feature as the cartouche.

5	21	14	17
11		18	
		23	
12	19		
	6		
16			

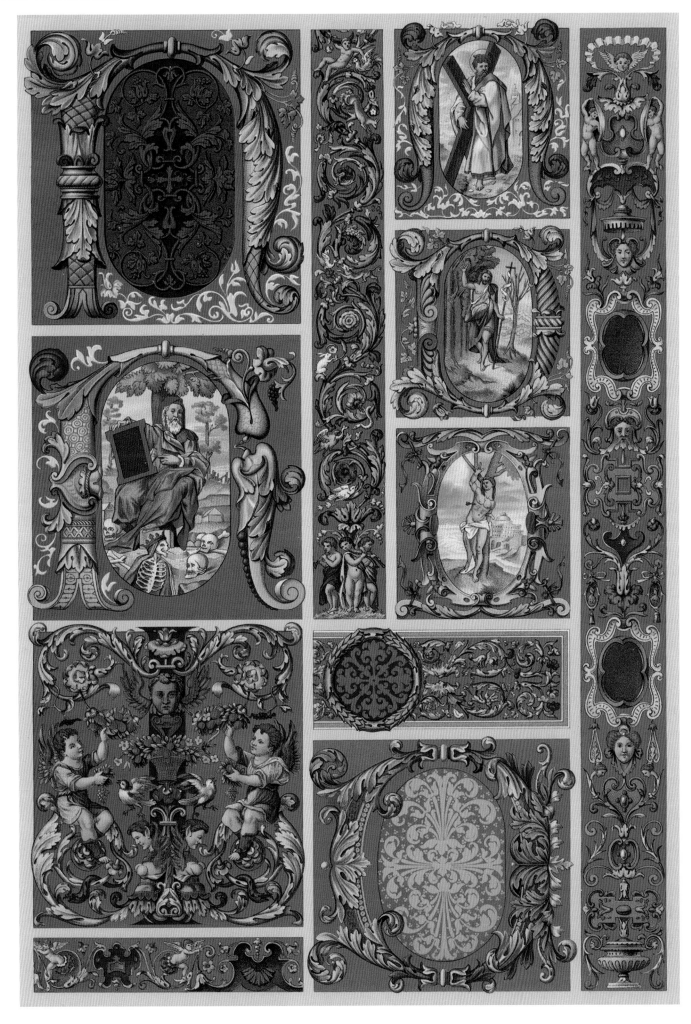

Book decoration. Wooden cartouches

The page and parts of an ornamental border reproduced here are taken from a manuscript of the *Lives of the Dukes of Urbino*. The rich decoration combines two elements that are in reality incompatible. On the one hand when creating the plant 'lattice' and placing his grotesque ornaments vertically, the illuminator was guided by the art of classical Rome as Raphael had studied it in the baths of the Emperor Titus and on the bas-reliefs of Trajan's Column, and as Giovanni da Udino had interpreted it when he decorated the Villa Farnesina with frescoes. On the other hand we can see in this decoration something that the classical ornamentalist could not have known. Whether by themselves or combined with others, the structures form a special compositional element that under the title of 'cartouche' occupied such an important place in the architectural and painted decoration of the High and Late Renaissance. This completely new component provided an excellent base for a plant 'lattice' and laid a unique stamp on European ornamental art. From the 17th century on it is very easy to date decorations from the style of the cartouches. It is difficult to identify the origin of the carved wooden cartouche shown in the plate. The one certainty is that it was not made in Italy; it may be the work of German or Flemish wood carvers who produced its flourishes so skilfully.

Foreign masters worked constantly in Italy from the 16th century on, and the famous people at the court of the great Federico da Montefeltro in Urbino included (just to give one example) Justus of Ghent (Joos van Ghent) 'whose Flemish realism was valued as highly as his colouring', and another master (provided that they are different people) known as 'Justus from Germany'.

Book decoration

The ornamental motifs shown in the plate are in two hand-written documents in Spanish; they are patents of nobility (*Carta ejecutoria de hidalguia*) issued to Juan Catano (1588) and Augustin de Iturbe (1593). The decorative composition of the documents allows us to judge about the arrival of the Renaissance in Spain.

Cartouches play a significant part, and as a rule they include human figures in a grotesque style. Special attention should be paid to the elegant and natural way that the initials in the bottom row of the plate have been produced.

PLATE 163

Carved and gilded *plafond*

This oak *plafond* with its carved and gilded decoration adorns the old Large Hall of the Parliament of Normandy (nowadays the law courts) in the Palais de Justice in Rouen.

Unfortunately it is not possible to identify either the designer or the date when this magnificent *plafond* was created. However, the hall was presumably decorated at the same time as the rest of the building. Construction of the Palais de Justice began under Louis XII and his minister, the Cardinal of Amboise, circa 1499 and continued until 1514. Moreover, to judge from the internal furnishings of the palace, there is justification for placing the decoration of the ceiling at the start of the 16th century, in other words at the beginning of the French Renaissance.

165 Renaissance

Decorative painting and wood carving.
France, 16th century

An exceptionally important and interesting point in the history of French art was the period when, because they had the chance of getting to know the Italian Renaissance and classical art, craftsmen were adopting Italian artistic motifs with amazing taste and tact.

Nowadays people are beginning to do justice to the French national school whose high proficiency and vivid originality created a magnificent basis for the conscious acceptance of classical culture as a valuable inheritance that was subsequently revived by the French with inspired enthusiasm.

As early as the 1460s French artists could boast of their original style and refined taste, and also of their deep understanding of classical forms. Their inspiration and the freedom with which they interpreted classical ideals gave them a place of honour in the stylistic art movement known as the Renaissance.

It is inappropriate to say more about how the Italian masters working at the court of François I taught their skills to the untutored French. The strength and refinement of the French national school is proved by the speed with which it mastered the Italian style.

The sources of the motifs shown are:

1–3   Stone carving
       Château of Blois, 1530;

4–7   Stone carving
       Castle of Châteaudun, 1530;

8–15 Panel edges
       Château of Blois, 1530;

16–19 Panel edges
       Chapel of Catherine de' Medici in Blois, 1560;

20–24 Book decoration in a Bible (Arsenal Library, Paris) and the *Schoenborn Book of Hours.*

PLATE 165

Ceramics with multi-coloured glazing

The dishes and ornamental sides shown in
the plate are the work of the French ceramist
Bernard Palissy. We know how much effort
the famous innovator devoted to trying to
understand the secrets of Eastern and Italian
ceramics, whose high standards he wanted to
emulate. We will not discuss here the 'rustic ware'
that made him well known. Despite their success,
the modelled decorations shaped like realistically
treated animals and plants that were applied
to large dishes did not have the slightest effect
on the artistic tastes of the time, even if they
were themselves of the highest quality. Other
works by the master, which were inspired by
Prieure, Pilon and Goujon, link his style closely
to the contemporary style, and it is this aspect
of his talent that is emphasised by the motifs
shown here. The decorative faience dish with
the pewter surround (top) is made in the style
of contemporary ornamental casting; it is based
on the large pewter dish called *à la Tempérance*
(1585-1590) by the François Briot. Palissy often
borrowed Briot's forms for his faience articles
which he covered with multi-coloured glaze.

Venetian bindings and marquetry

1 Binding with an artistic figurative subject in the central medallion (treated as a line drawing);

2 Inner binding with an ornamental pattern;

3 Three ornamental motifs using the technique of marquetry (16th-century harp).

All the motifs are of Persian origin and continue the series of examples of Eastern ornamentation. By connecting them to the period of the Renaissance we want to emphasise how, thanks to Venice's links with the Levant, vine-shaped arabesques arrived from the East and combined harmoniously with the classical tradition from the 16th century on.

Mosaic motifs on book bindings.

These examples of ornamental motifs coincide
with our theme thanks to their combination of
polychrome colouring and gilding.

Sources:

1   Bible by Robert Estienne, in folio.
    Paris, 1540.
    'The binding was made to the order of
    president de Thou, and in all probability the
    Bible was part of his library';

2   Bible, in folio
    Florence, printed by Paolo Giovio, 1540.
    From the famous Grolier Library.
    Stamped in Latin: *Grollerii et amicorum*
    ['Belongs to Grolier and his friends'].

PLATE 168

Book decoration, tooling

Motifs 1–7 are taken from a manuscript produced for Henri II (*Confirmation of the Privileges of the Notaries and Secretariat by Louis XI*) and represent the finest examples of contemporary book illustration. The similarity of these decorative compositions to the miniatures of Jean Cousin the Younger allows us to ascribe their authorship to him.

Motifs 8 and 9, which are by Ducerceau, are very close to the old murals in the Palace of Fontainebleau.

Motifs 10–15 are ornaments with silver and gold tooling and are among the masterpieces of the printing-house in Lyon.

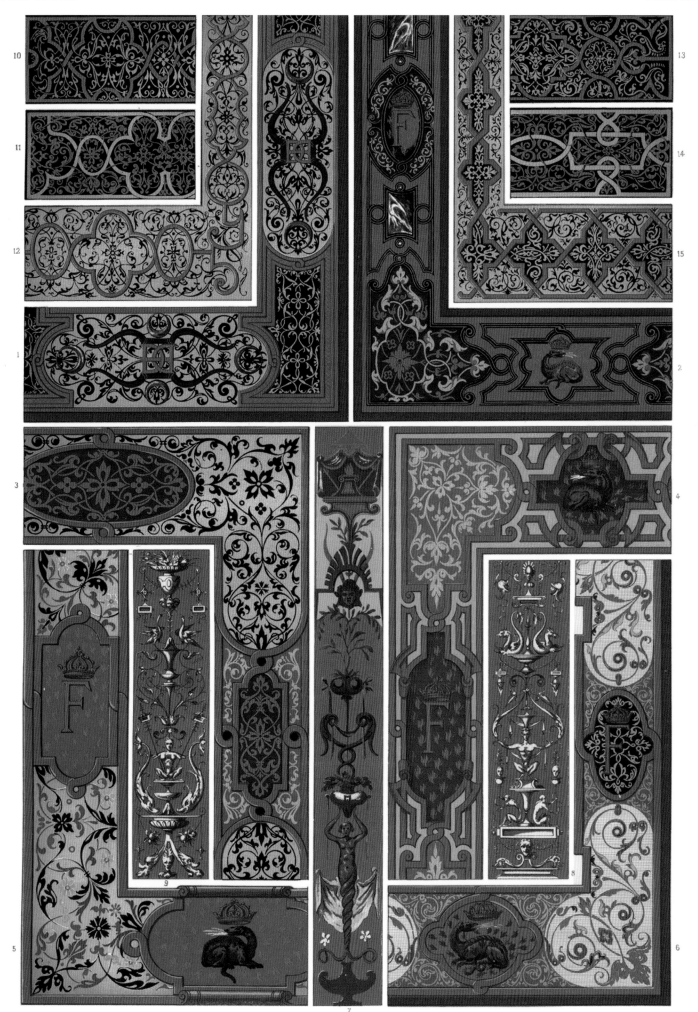

Decoration as a structure
Surrounds, cartouches and fleurons

This type of decoration grew out of delicate joinery work. It is constructed logically, despite being supplemented by plant motifs, shoots, garlands, bunches of flowers, fruit, ribbons, trophies and attributes, reptiles and molluscs, animals and even human figures, not to mention various arabesques and draperies. In a word, this type of decoration, where each element is a self-sufficient unit, is purely European in character. Its popularity coincided with the spread of the Italian Renaissance in France, although the style of our fragile structures has nothing in common with antiquity. The cartouche in particular was an ornamental resource that was unknown to the ancients.

During the first half of the 16th century the Fontainebleau school provided the country, and principally the Limoges enamellers, with models of cartouches with ends that twisted into volutes. However, under the influence of the Italian school that had received its impulse from Germany, this genre was very successful throughout Europe and increasingly took on the character of joinery work. At the end of the 16th and beginning of the 17th centuries French, German and Flemish craftsmen competed in their efforts to alter the early types of cartouche so as to give them a different external appearance, a new splendour and a new elegance, needless to say without forgetting their basic decorative principle. Countless versions of cartouches have come down to us, principally on engraved pages. Everywhere artists, sculptors (especially wood carvers) and goldsmiths used this type of ornamentation. Engravings, which usually served as examples for all craftsmen, provided rich material for creating cartouches, and it is from there that we have drawn most of our motifs.

PLATE 170

Guipure edging
Decoration of curtains and clothes

Guipure is a type of embroidery that unites appliqué work with bobbin lace. During the 16th century it was known as *passement*, and if it was placed on cloth it became a decorative edging (or cording); its precision and relief produce a striking decorative effect. Guipure was made from *cartisanne* and twisted silk. *Cartisanne* was the name given to a thin strip of parchment onto which a silk, gold or silver thread was wound to give it body. Specifically, guipure was a silk thread wound around a thick thread or cord. Mary Queen of Scots called it 'parchment lace', and this definition is confirmed by motifs 2, 3, 9, 12 and 16, where the pattern ends with an even row of dentelle. The term 'lace' can also be applied to the mesh to which the guipure is fixed, giving it the appearance of needlepoint.

When we look at the large patterns shown in the plate we can see that they were made so that the seams were concealed as far as possible.

The more delicate the work, the greater was the number of seams required, and sometimes the craftsman felt it necessary to position them symmetrically, in effect including them in the decoration. The seams are clearly visible in motifs 1, 5, 6 and 13. When it comes to open-work embroidery, guipure is the richest from the point of view of materials used: gold and silver thread, silks of various colours and sometimes feathers and precious stones.

Special collections of examples for embroidery were printed from the beginning of the 16th century, and all the European craftsmen tried to outdo each other in inventing patterns for edgings and other forms of embroidery. The popularity of guipure is closely linked to the Italian Renaissance.

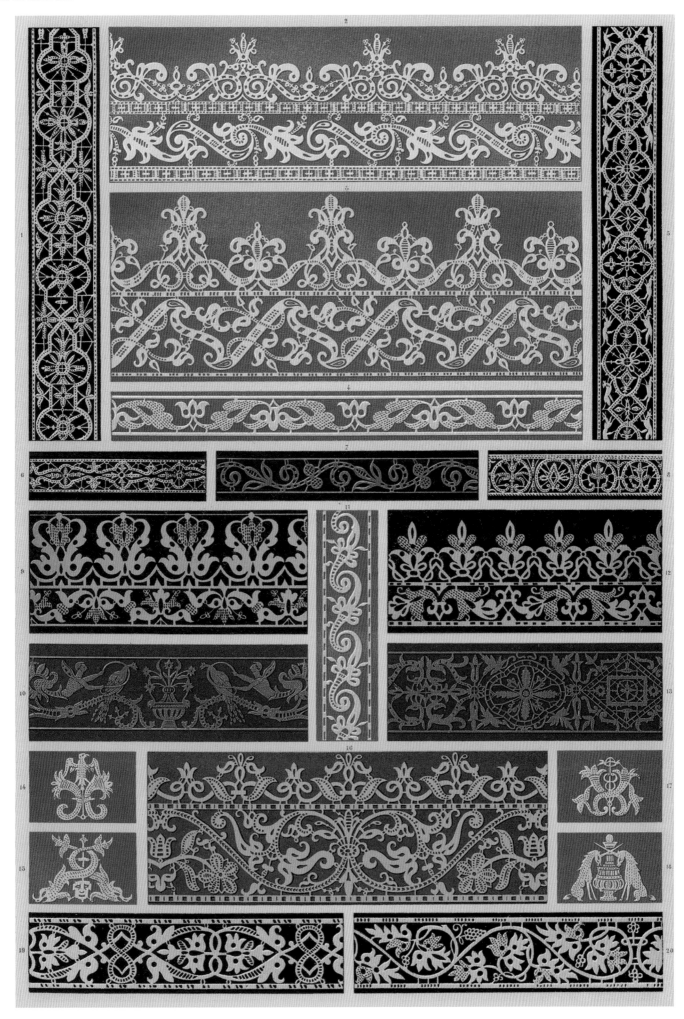

Jewellery

The jewellery shown in the plate dates mainly from the 16th century. It is supplemented by examples of the decoration of European jewellery from the 17th and 18th centuries, and this will give an idea of the evolution in style that, as a rule, followed developments in the fine arts of the period, up to the complete triumph of the diamond. Cutting revealed the diamond's magnificence and the play of light, and thanks to this it managed to take the principal place in personal jewellery. At the same time, because of constant changes in fashion, the gold or silver setting became less and less noticeable until it eventually lost any independent artistic value.

Most of the examples shown are decorated with enamelling, niello or semi-precious stones. The jewellers of the time viewed the decoration of costume jewellery differently from the way that we do today. In their hands each gem had a unique appearance so that there is not even a hint of mass-production. Our forefathers valued above all a jewel that was imbued with a rich play of colour and seemed to have its own life so that it looked striking against a background of velvet, satin, lace or a bare arm. A gem could shine magically with the rainbow-like colours of

a beetle or exhale the freshness of some delicate flower, of some short-lived miracle to which the jeweller had given the chance of eternal life.

Despite what one might expect, although they are durable by nature and were produced in countless numbers, jewellery articles have not come down to us for a large number of reasons that we will not go into. Jewellery work of the 16th century is represented by only a handful of genuine articles in the museums of France and in a few private collections. The finest jewellery objects are known above all from engravings: these are an inexhaustible source of knowledge about the subject. The only pity is that monochrome engravings cannot provide any information about the range of colours that added to the magnificence of old jewellery. Of all the genres of decorative and applied arts, jewellery that was intended for personal decoration would seem to require the highest level of analytical knowledge. Be that as it may, it embodied the skill of the finest craftsmen to the full.

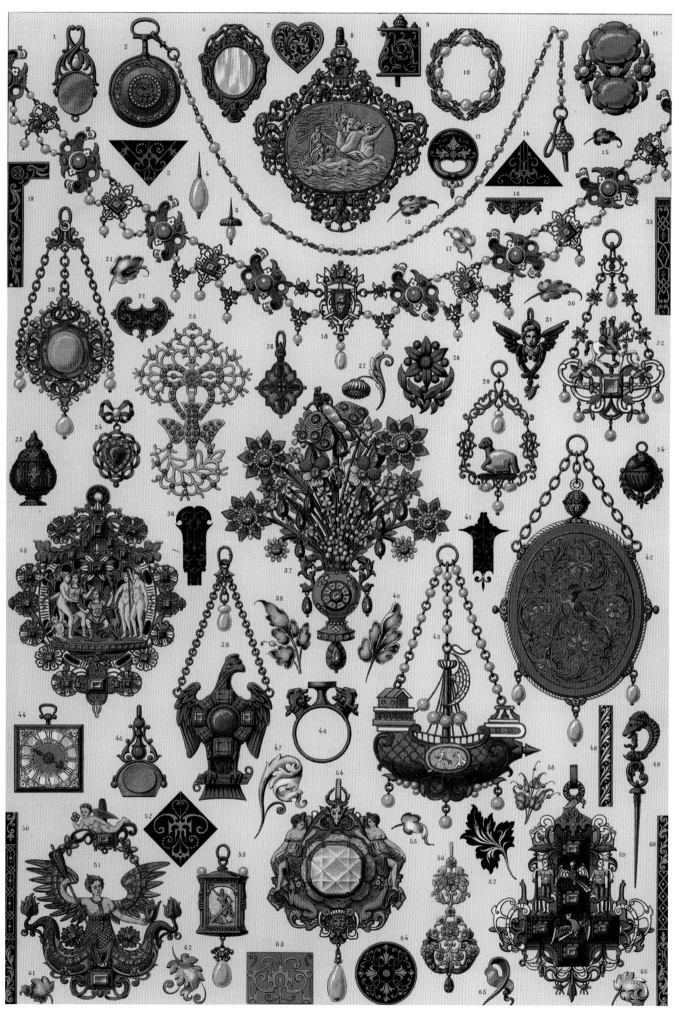

Friezes with cartouches and continuous
friezes

Reproductions of 44 ornamental motifs.

The motif on a green background with the
monograms of Henri II and Catherine de'
Medici (in the lower part of the plate) dates
back to the paintings in Catherine de' Medici's
chapel in the château of Chenonceau. Below
it is a vertical ornament on a yellow background,
and at the very bottom in the centre there is
a fresco from the chapel in Chenonceau.

The remaining 42 subjects come from the
historical portrait gallery of André Thévet's *True
Portraits and Lives of Illustrious Men, Greek, Latin
and Heathen, made from their Portrayals, Books
and Medals, Ancient and Modern* (Paris, 1584).
This extensive collection of full-length portraits,
which were engraved on copper at the end of the
16th century, is astonishingly rich for its unique
architectural ornamentation whose elements
change from page to page. In a way Thévet's
great work exhausts the possibilities of the genre.
The illustrations were painted at the same time.

Cartouches

It is interesting to trace the evolution of the cartouche throughout the history of French art. The examples shown here belong to the second half of the16th and the first half of the 17th centuries.

Cartouches 1-4, which decorate a manuscript in the Arsenal Library in Paris, are attributed to Jean Cousin. Others (mainly of Flemish origin) come from various sources. Usually cartouches decorated geographical maps, but their use was not limited to this, especially as wood and leather were used in the decorative details.

175   16TH–17TH CENTURIES

Decorative portières with appliqué work.

The following motifs are shown:

Above and to the right are two fragments from Genoa with wool appliqués on the same material and trimmed with silk.

On the left there is a fragment of a portiere (door hanging) from Milan. The background is purple silk brocade (Lyon style) and the edges are trimmed with yellow satin.

Striking in their precision and relief work that is suggestive of decorative wood carving, these patterns are worthy of the most skilled craftsmen of the time.

Painting, open-work and embossing

The fragments shown here belong to one period and represent what is called the

'Louis XIII style', as is definitely indicated by motif 7.

1 Wooden panel inlaid with pieces of ivory and mother-of-pearl (reproduced in full size), 1508. This elegant and complex work was probably created to gain the title of master in a craft guild;

2, 3 Open-work engraved silver frames (reproduced full-size), 17th century;

4 Frieze in the Queen Mother's Pavilion at Fontainebleau, Louis XIII;

5 Monogram of Louis XIII and Anne of Austria (from the same source);

6 The upper part of the left-hand leaf of a gilded wooden door in the palace of Fontainebleau (before restoration);

7 Small casket in the rococo style which belonged to Anne of Austria. It is decorated with gold embossed overlay on a velvet background.

PLATE 176

Coloured leather panel with border
Louis XIII style

This plate presents a magnificent example of the leather articles with embossed gilded and silvered designs that were made in the 16th–17th centuries, the heyday of the industry in France. The name *Cordovan* (Cordoba coloured leather), which is often applied to such products, presupposes a Spanish origin, but they do not have anything to do with Spain. The luxurious leather panels originated in Venice, England, Holland and Flanders (with the centre in Mechelen) and leather working factories also existed in Lyon. Similar panels were made from calf, goat or sheep skin, adorned with embossed patterns; at first they were decorated with silver and then with gold; gilding was done with a lacquer that imitated gold paint. Soft, resistant to moisture and corrosive chemicals, these leather goods were considered luxuries and were in huge demand.

Frescoes, miniatures, enamels and niello.

1 Wall panel in the Queen Mother's pavilion, Fontainebleau;

2 Décor of a painted *plafond* in the apartments of Anne of Austria in the Louvre;

3 Wall panels in the Luxembourg Palace (Paris);

4, 5 Floral designs from a manuscript made for Anne of Austria;

6-12 The frescoes in the Church of St Eustache in Paris;

13, 14 Fragments of gold articles, decorated with enamel and niello.

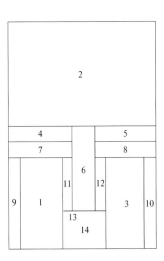

Large-scale decoration.
Decorative arras

Legend has it that this wall tapestry is one of a cycle given to Louis XIV, King of France, by King James II of England. In all likelihood the tapestries were woven at Mortlake shortly after the Restoration (1660), although it is quite possible that work began on them at the time when Charles I (then still Prince of Wales) established the tapestry works in Mortlake, where the weavers worked from their own cartoons on replicating Raphael's *Acts of the Apostles* (Brussels weavers led by Peter van der Alstom reproduced Raphael's cartoons as tapestries for Pope Leo X; they are kept in the Vatican). These arras, which were woven using silk, wool, gold and silver threads on a vertical loom, were large and their different shapes are due to the arrangement of the cartoon scenes which were reproduced with the utmost precision. The Raphael scene from the New Testament, *The Miracle on the Sea of Galilee*, is horizontal, while the arras reproduced in the plate is nearly square. Judging by the nature of the border of the entire cycle, it has retained the features of the prototype and stylistically belongs to the reign of Louis XIII.

The ornamentalist has made every border into something resembling a commentary on the main scene. He has managed to achieve great scenic beauty: the palette includes light pink colours, silvery highlights and fresh, glowing shades. The arras are reproduced in their entirety, since it is impossible to appreciate the border without the central scene. It should be noted that the cartoons that were so important in the history of decorative art were reproduced by the masters in a very arbitrary manner. Colouration was outlined only in general terms, thus providing the weaver with the freedom and initiative for creativity.

Cartouches

Cartouches 1–4, which date from the first
half of the 17th century, decorate a painted
panel and a double arch in the Hinisdal Chapel
of the Carmelite order. Cartouches with
heart-shaped empty spaces are often found in
the ornamentation of maps. Many of them
are dated, with the latest one being from 1645.
They were engraved by Flemish masters and
then painted by hand.

Motifs 5 and 6 are made from drawings by
Bernardo Castello. The *mascarons* and stylised
plant motifs which fill some of the cartouches
are also of Flemish origin and date back to
the same period; they are based on sketches by
Johann Christoph Feinlein.

PLATE 180

Drapery, embroidery and tooling.

The subjects come from various sources and the appliqué work is executed in a single manner.

1 Leather hangings from the Château of Cheverny near Blois. 1635;

2 Wooden frame with tin inlay from Touraine (of the same period);

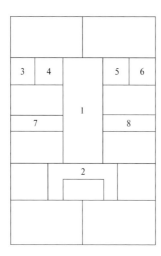

3-8 Tooling in the Flemish style based on sketches by Johann Christoph Feinlein.

Other ornamental motifs in German embroidery are so similar to the embroidery patterns published by Raidel (Ulm, 1613) that there is no doubt about their origin. Due to the necessary reduction of these interesting motifs, it is impossible to reproduce the intensely coloured backgrounds to which they were often attached. The relief designs look very impressive against white silk or red, purple or dark green velvet.

Plate 181

Decorative panels
Borders of arras

The three painted wooden panels are examples of large-scale décor (the height of each original is 2.1m) and form part of a very large architectonic composition. The paintings on a white background and the gilded relief surround display the joy and lightness that were still considered to be indispensable in the decoration of royal chambers in the 18th century. Given the lack of more precise information, they are attributed to the Parisian painter Simon Vouet (1590-1649). After spending fifteen years in Italy, he returned to France in 1627 during the reign of Louis XIII. His work was influenced by the energetic manner of Caravaggio and the more restrained although more colourful manner of Guido Reni. After being appointed the 'first royal painter' and being given an apartment in the Louvre, Vouet became a virtual dictator of the arts of the period, a role that after him passed even more absolutely to Charles Le Brun, the director of the Gobelins manufactory. Artists of such a rank conceived and carried out their work themselves, and Simon Vouet, whose imagination was truly inexhaustible, created a large number of sketches for the tapestries of the royal court, as well as carrying out important design work for the royal residences in the Louvre, the Luxembourg Palace, the Castle of Saint-Germain and the palaces of Versailles and Fontainebleau.

In the panels shown in the plate, heavy and clumsy elements are combined with forms of exceptional elegance: the artist creates compositions by means of his imagination, using a variety of decorative motifs. Here, there is no other logic but the artist's imagination. Marble sculptures, gilded or painted wood that has been worked by every known method, the human form in all its nobility, mythical monsters, quadrupeds, birds, butterflies, the classical acanthus, naturalistically executed flowers, *mascarons* and vases with flowers, and finally grisaille and metal work with enamel decoration: these were the depictive range of ornamentalists of the school which developed under the influence of the Italian Renaissance.

Arras adorned with two large corner motifs (1, 3). The central motif (2) is reminiscent of a carved wooden decoration, and is borrowed from a vignette surround in the wonderful collection of *Royal Medal* prints dating from the second half of the 17th century.

Large-scale decoration
Corners and borders of arras

6   Between 1570 and 1600 a tapestry factory
known as the Paris Royal Manufactory
was operating in Paris and was at one
time directed by the Fleming Marc
Comans. The factory, where tapestries
were woven on vertical looms, was known
as the Royal Factory. It was founded by
Henri IV in 1610 in the Place Royale
district but around 1630 it was moved to
the Gobelins district. It was different from
the first factory for pile carpets, known
as the Savonnerie, which was founded
by Henri IV in 1627 and located in the
Louvre Gallery. In 1662, under Colbert's
instructions, a factory known historically
as the Royal Gobelins Manufactory
(or the Royal Furnishing Manufactory)
was opened which produced arras,
furniture, silverware and embroidery. Its
first director was the painter and decorator
Charles Le Brun.

Paris Royal Manufactory.
Border of the first tapestry of the six-part series
The Story of Artemisia (wool and silk. 3.83 x
5.20m). The cartoons for these tapestries were
modified several times, and our example is
probably from the end of the 16th century;

2   Tapestry factory in Mortlake (England).
Border of the second tapestry of the
five-part series *Venus and Vulcan* (wool,
silk, gold and silver threads, 4.30 x 5.80m).
The border includes the monogram of
Francis Crane (d. 1568), the first director
of the factory which was founded by
the Prince of Wales (the future Charles I)
in 1625;

3   Royal Factory.
The corner and part of the border of the
tapestry *The Hunt of Meleager*, woven with
silk and wool threads.
The monogram *CC* is woven into the
border;

4   Gobelins Manufactory.
The outer border is in the style of Jean
Le Pautre;

1, 5   The additional elements of the surrounds
(a collection of medals struck in honour
of Louis XIV) represent small-scale
decorations of a mixed character which can
be dated to the end of the 17th century.

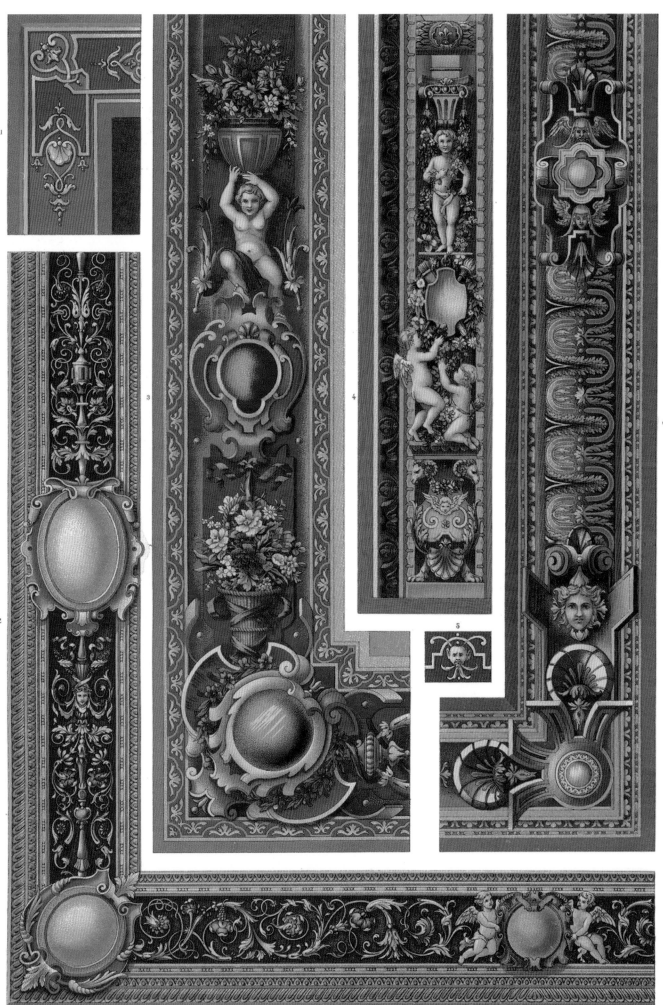

Main ornamental composition.
Carved and painted decoration of the
abutments of a vault

The abutment of a vault is a slab that is placed
between the base of the vault and the top of
the wall with its columns. The décor rises and
unfolds along architectural lines, forming a
logical structure with symmetrically positioned
cartouches of various shapes and sizes. This
decorative composition, consisting of moulded
high reliefs and real (or false) bas-reliefs, is just
a 'frame' for the multi-coloured murals enclosed
within it; the restrained colouring of the décor
sets off the painting very effectively. In fact, the
cartouches represent windows with illusionistic
compositions that seem to float in the air on
traditionally dense clouds.

Part of the *plafond* of the Apollo Gallery in the
Louvre is reproduced here. Louis XIV ordered
the décor from Le Brun in 1661 following the
fire which destroyed the first gallery begun
under Charles IX and completed under Henri IV.
Neither the spirit nor the nature of our décor is
in any way reminiscent of the loud immoderate
eulogising of the rule of a great king that
provided the theme for the ceiling painting in
the Great Gallery of Versailles.

Lebrun's skill comes through in every part of
its décor, in the selection of scenes, of curved
shapes, and of the harmony of ornamental

motifs and symbolic images. Remember that the
'Sun King' chose Apollo, the god of light and art,
as his symbol and his device was the sun shining
over the entire world with the inscription:
Nec pluribus impar (Inferior to none). The image
of the sun is placed in one of the two angles of
the octagon at the left edge of the plate.

The second angle of the octagon contains
Apollo's lyre. Each motif is complemented
by a cornucopia. Le Brun divided the vault
into eleven main cartouches. In the central
one he intended to depict Apollo in his
chariot surrounded by the attributes of the
sun. The *Four Seasons* were to be placed in
the four cartouches closest to the centre,
with *Morning* and *Evening* in two medallions
and *Night* and *Dawn* in two octagons further
away. *The Awakening of Water* and *The
Awakening of Land* in the first rays of the sun
were to be placed in the half domes at the
opposite ends of the vault. However, in 1662
Le Brun was appointed director of the Gobelins
Manufactory, and the ceiling of the Apollo
Gallery remained unfinished until the beginning
of the 19th century.

Large-scale decoration.
Carpets and arras

These two fragments, part of a carpet and the corner of the border of an arras, illustrate the most striking period in the field of decorative arts under Louis XIV. The carpet (8.90 x 3.90m) forms part of group of thirteen carpets intended for the Apollo Gallery in the Louvre.

Woven from wool yarns, they are products of the Savonnerie factory. The merits of this wonderful carpet speak for themselves: the boldness of the central motif, the skilful execution, clear division into parts, rich colour with contrasting backgrounds and, finally, all the fullness and variety of its ornamental composition. Suffice it to say that the boldness of composition and the intense colours of the background correspond particularly well to the use of a material such as wool which, when lit horizontally, combines all the nuances of colour into one harmonious whole.

We have already noted in plate 184 the scale and integrity of Le Brun's large-scale and decorative schemes. In 1661 Le Brun presented Louis XIV with a complete décor for the Apollo Gallery and there is no doubt that the patterns of the future floor covering played a key role.

The section of a border (at the bottom of the plate) belongs to a very beautiful cycle of arras woven in the Gobelins Manufactory. All fourteen scenes that present *The History of Louis XIV* (Le Brun was the author of the cartoons) are framed by a similar border which can be seen in full in the engraving by Sébastien Leclerc the Elder. The colouring of the part reproduced here is typical for the colour range of the whole cycle. This luxurious arras is woven using wool and silk, as well as gold and silver threads.

Mosaics and painting.

1 Fragment of a *plafond* in Versailles painted by Mignard (has not survived.)

2 Fragment of the décor of the main staircase in Versailles from a sketch by Le Brun (has not survived);

3 Décor of the Main Gallery at Versailles from a sketch by Le Brun;

4 Sketch for the decoration of a marble table top attributed to Robert de Cotte;

The four painted *plafonds* (right and left bottom) in a house in the rue de Beaune in Paris and in the reception room of the former Hôtel de Mailly-Nesle on the corner of the quai Voltaire and the rue de Beaune have been attributed to Daniel Marot (see plate 192).

Metal inlay.
Palace furniture.

Metal inlay work as the main decorative element only appeared in the second half of 17th century. During the reign of Louis XIV furniture was decorated with inlaid pieces of tortoise shell and shining metal, so as to fit in with the surrounding splendour of the royal apartments. In the hands of the great innovator André Charles Boulle representational palace furniture took on a beauty and grace that was previously unknown, and which was not surpassed by anyone at the time.

This plate shows a secretaire desk in the Apollo Gallery in the Louvre, made in the Royal Furniture Manufactory under the direction of Le Brun. The noble architectonic form is emphasised by straight lines, and the overall composition and ornamental details are a manifestation of the revival of Roman antiquity promoted by Poussin. While stylistically belonging to the first period of Gobelins Manufactory production, our sample does not show any signs of the decline characteristic of later periods. Boulle's magnificent ornamental system was used for almost thirty years and produced perfect examples of palace furniture, after which the fashion spread to furniture used by the urban population.

André Charles Boulle, the 'first royal cabinet maker' was also an architect, sculptor and engraver, as his work proves. The design work displays his architectural skill, and the engraved gilt bronze is transformed into a first-class sculpture. Finally, in order to portray the veins of a plant 'lattice', engraving is used: the lines made by a cutting tool are reminiscent of niello work.

Metal inlay became an excellent replacement for the inlaid woodwork (marquetry) that was going out of fashion. The metal plates lie close to each other like the pieces of coloured wood in inlaid work, although they were attached with mastic instead of glue. Ornamental motifs using pieces of tortoise shell were made in the same way. They were either in their natural colour or stained on the inside. Metal inlay became so popular in the second half of the 17th and beginning of the 18th centuries, that wardrobes, chests of drawers, bookcases, writing desks, secretaires, pedestal tables and chiffoniers were adorned with the same decorative system, using the same technique.

At the bottom of the plate:

2-5 Engraving on precious metals by
      Louis Cossin;

7, 9 Boxes by Daniel Marot;

  6 Snuff box with gold and silver inlay;

  8 Lid of a box.

Furniture with embossed bronze overlay
and metal inlay.
Palace furniture.

André-Charles Boulle's creations were so diverse that only numerous examples can reveal the features of their stylistic unity. The types of plastic expressiveness originated primarily in the purpose of the item of furniture, but we cannot ignore the immense capabilities of this extraordinary master who was sculptor, engraver and inlayer. Wardrobes like the one shown in this plate represent a strict architectural form. The general décor has the same significance as the small decorative details, and from compositions that are just as subtly conceived, such as the decoration of this wardrobe or the decoration of the secretaire (see plate 187), where Louis XIV shines radiantly in the magnificent armour of Mars, or in the ornamentation of the extremely decorative console table (plate 189), we can understand how the ornamentalist resolved the problem of the overall use of the object. The Dauphin's Apartments in the Palace of Versailles, which were demolished on the orders of Louis XIV in 1747 to allow for a new design, had, as a contemporary noted in his diary, such lavish décor, luxurious furniture and spectacular wooden panels made by Boulle, that Louis XIV showed them to his most august guest James II on 18 February 1689, as one of the wonders of Versailles.

These magnificent wooden panels with their truly architectural proportions have not survived. This seems almost incredible; even if we were to assume that Boulle's work appeared to be an excessively expensive whim for the 18th century, the master's personal contribution still continued to be valued very highly. The panels, however, disappeared without a trace, and as far as the furniture is concerned, it was dispersed among the other apartments in Versailles and other royal palaces. Who could complain that the furniture which is now in the Apollo Gallery in the Louvre once stood in the apartments of the Dauphin? It is, of course, fully worthy of its new sanctuary. Boulle's tables and chests of drawers with their beautiful marble slabs were intended to display priceless collections of art objects, foreign marvels, bronzes, porcelain and crystal.

Marquetry.
Engraved and embossed motifs.

A console table completes this series of examples of Boulle's furniture from the Apollo Gallery in the Louvre. Its bronze engraved plates are less effective than those on other objects, as here inlay plays the main decorative role. Boulle developed his own version of furniture intarsia (or marquetry), reducing it to a positive or negative drawing that was formed by a combination of metal and tortoise shell. In the first case (see the plate), pieces of tortoise shell serve as the background for ornamental motifs executed in copper, and in the second, ornaments made of tortoise shell are arranged against a copper background. The master made extensive use of natural materials like tortoise shell, ivory, horn, ebony and mother-of-pearl as well as metals, including copper, tin, silver and gold. Curved pieces of tortoise shell (either translucent gold or dark brown or black) could be softened in hot water or over a flame, pressed down and cut into flat layers of the desired thickness; the underside was stained with scarlet, green, blue or charcoal-black paint,

then a sheet of paper was placed directly on the surface so as to seal the paint. Red copper or brass (an alloy of two-thirds of copper and one third zinc oxide) were used. Adding red copper to silver and gold gave them the flexibility and malleability needed for inlaying. Gold goes very well with mother-of-pearl and tortoise shell. To achieve more subtle nuances of colour, different shades of gold were used: white, yellow, red or green. The desired hardness of tin was achieved by adding red copper.

Striking materials and graceful compositions were sometimes highlighted by engraving not just the metal parts, but also the pieces of tortoise shell which had drawings cut into their surface. To make the image clearer, a mixture of black mastic and molten tree resin was rubbed into the groove with a spatula; finally, the areas unaffected by the engraving were polished.

Boulle inlays.

Boulle-style inlays, one of France's significant achievements in the field of decorative inlay work on wood, are now regaining the deserved popularity which they enjoyed at the end of the 17th and beginning of the 18th centuries.

André Charles Boulle, who worked in the Louis XIV style, was born in 1642 and lived to be ninety. He brought the talent of a true artist to the art of creating palace furniture. As the first cabinet maker at the court of Louis XIV, and 'architect, mosaicist, engraver and bronze caster', with apartments and studios in the Louvre, he gathered a huge collection of sketches, prints and works of art, some of which unfortunately went up in smoke along with the workshops and property during a fire in 1720; the rest were sold to satisfy creditors. To a certain extent, the abundance of precious materials available to Boulle before this disaster helps us to understand the perfection of the original works of this unsurpassed master.

Two people who continued Boulle's work were the bronze caster Caffieri and Cressent, the creator of rococo furniture and a cabinet maker and sculptor; the type of marquetry ornamentation to which Boulle gave his name is still being successfully reproduced today. The Boulle inlay is not only distinguished by its beauty and the variety of its designs, but first and foremost by the harmonious combination of exotic wood types with metals which form a most important part of the polychrome ornament.

1-5   Case of a desk clock with multi-coloured inlay of tortoise shell, brass and tin. The surface of the case looks like silver thanks to a special varnish applied on the metal background, giving it a silvery pearl-like tint;

6-10   Decorated chests with tortoise-shell inlay in conjunction with engraved gilt plates;

11-14   Overall appearance and details of the decoration on pieces of furniture in the Louis XIV style. The inlay is ebony with gilded ornamental plates. The main subject is *Hercules Defeats the Lernaean Hydra*;

15-17   Boulle inlay motifs.

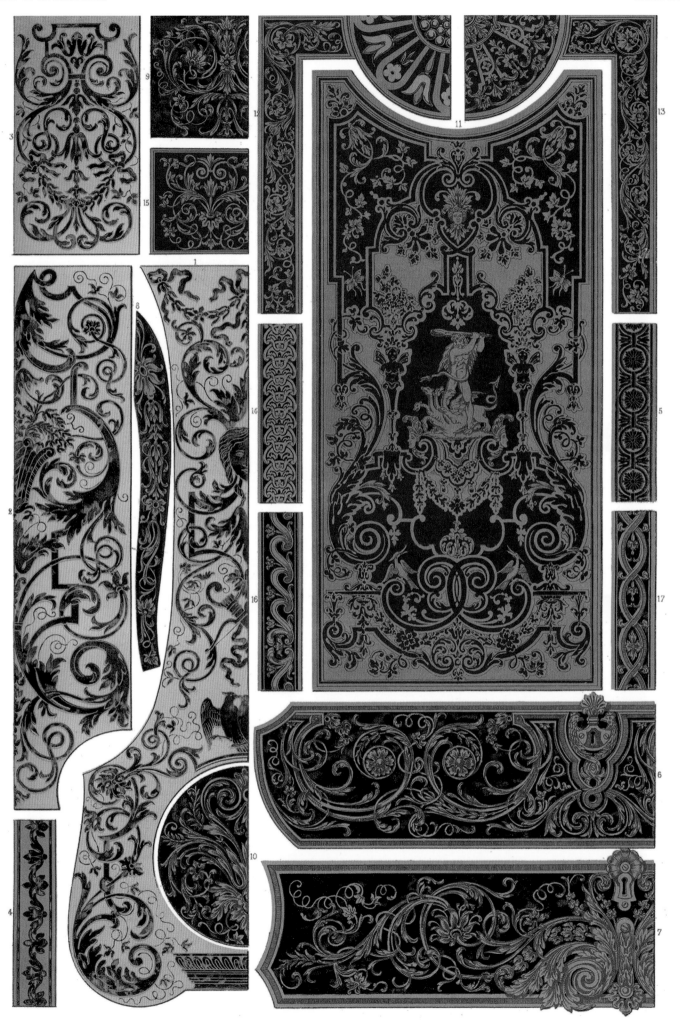

Decorative frescoes.
Main and side panels from the Apollo
Gallery in the Louvre.

The two main subjects shown in the plate were part of the decorative design for the *Window of Charles IX*.

Jean Berain, 'designer and decorator for the King of France', whose designs were used for the grotesque ornaments painted on the walls of the Vatican Loggia, made sketches of ornamentation for furniture and tapestries, as well as for wall or ceiling paintings. Having studied Raphael's murals, which were based on ancient models, Berain took from his style the things which in his opinion produced the greatest effect. His inexhaustible imagination transformed the legacy of Raphael in his own way, according to French taste, and Berain achieved such perfection that foreign artists often borrowed his ornamental style and his decorative compositions; they became extremely popular in the second half of the 17th century and were known as *Berainades*.

PLATE 191

Painted *plafond*.

Part of the gilded *plafond* of the former
Hôtel de Mailly-Nesle on the corner of the
quai Voltaire and the rue de Beaune in Paris
is reproduced in this plate in a reduced size.
Decorated in the luxurious and elegant style of
the late 17th century, this exceptional ceiling
is worthy of the brush of Berain or Marot, the
most talented artists and decorators of the time.
It is fair to assume the author to be Marot or
his school because of its striking similarity to
an engraved sketch for a painting on another
plafond by Marot.

Decorative painting and book miniatures.

These horizontal and vertical fragments of friezes were designed as moulded architectural ornamentation. The large-scale initials and the cartouche are derived from the decoration of a Bible. Executed by the master himself, the *Deer Hunt* (top) and *The Triumph of Neptune* (centre) are borrowed from the book *Architectural Works* by Jean Le Pautre, Architect of the Royal Buildings, a volume containing engravings of unfulfilled plans for urban and out-of-town homes that show the artist's wonderful imagination and fantasy. The first of the engravings shown is part of the series *Friezes and Floral and other Italianate Ornaments* (circa 1660), and the second is part of a series of *Classical Vertical Ornaments* (1659). Both engravings are characteristic of the rich and luxurious decorative legacy of Le Pautre.

Jean Le Pautre the Elder was one of the most diligent of Le Brun's collaborators at the Gobelins Manufactory from its founding in 1662. The dates of the engravings prove that by that time he was already a fully accomplished master. Apparently Le Brun had to restrain his colleague's creative enthusiasm since there is no sign of Le Pautre's hand in their joint work, and it is most likely that his personality could only be revealed in engravings. Thus these prints, which were coloured by Le Pautre himself or under his direction, seem to us the most interesting: these are the compositions which allowed the artist to give expression to his temperament.

The horizontal frieze and the vertical ornamental strip demonstrate different degrees of the artist's inspiration. The triumphal nature of the ornamental strip requires more serenity and a deeper, more saturated colour. To be able to evaluate their merits as they deserve, it is enough to picture the motifs in the context of the elaborate architecture of the time: it was only against such a background that their ornamental properties could achieve their unique effect.

3, 7 Border motifs from a tapestry of the same period. When compared to the magnificent ornamentation, the other motifs look more modest. The four initials and the cartouche were made by Le Brun from originals in the four-volume *Antiphons* from the Church of Saint-Vincent in Paris; the collection was recopied and illuminated between 1705 and 1729, but the originals still retain their freshness.

Tapestries with borders

The main subject (on the left) and its border (1, 3) come from a magnificent tapestry from the castle of Grignan. Judging by the style of execution and the costumes worn by the characters, the two figurative motifs (2, 4) can be attributed to the end of the 17th century. One of them, with two shepherdesses (bottom right), is executed in the style of the traditional ornamentation of the time. It may belong to the *Months of the Year* series of tapestries and symbolises June (as indicated by sheep being sheared and the zodiac sign of Cancer in the cartouche; it is so tiny in the original that it cannot be reproduced). It is interesting to note the differences in the manner of execution between these figurative subjects and the ornaments of the Grignan tapestry. In the latter the colour elements are devoid of any outlines, while the contours of the figurative motifs are emphasised by a bright drawing on a dark background or a dark drawing on a bright background. The second form is widespread in the ornamentation of Indian and Persian textiles.

Silk fabrics and bindings.

Two pieces of pale silk date from the late 17th century. The delicate tracery of the cloth at the top shows an Eastern influence that was widespread in France due to familiarity with Persian ornamentation. The positioning of the vertical ornamental bands is highly expressive; essentially this elegant design with its subtle and simple monochrome colouring stands in pleasant contrast to the mannered decorative trends of the period.

At the bottom of the plate is a fly-leaf that is pasted over with printed silk. Under Louis XIII, it was usual to cover the inside of a binding with patterned cloth. The ornamentation recalls the paintings of Berain, Marot and other painter-decorators. A continuous motif is formed by volutes with a double outline and acanthus leaves that include an elegant bunch of grapes.

Ceramics: French factories.

Decorative motifs on French ceramics:

1-14 Rouen manufacturies. The first faience factories did not appear in Rouen until the middle of the 17th century, and they turned the city into one of the largest

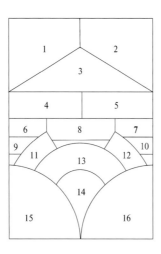

centres for making faience in France. Inspired by Colbert, the king gave them numerous commissions, and the masters painted the tableware from sketches by the most famous painters of the time. The motifs shown here of lambrequins and other stylised ornamentation represent the heyday of the Rouen faience factory.

15 Dish with the mark of the Lille ceramist Feburier Borne, 1716;

16 Faience from the Moustiers factories.

Leather goods with gold tooling.

The origin and production of coloured leather goods with gold embossed patterns have already been mentioned above (see plate 177). Although a very wide range of colours is used, special preference is given to lighter and more delicate shades, rather than to the colour palette of the period of Louis XIII. This is characteristic of the more refined, yet always more deliberate, system of the ornamentation, rather than of the one which came to take its place at the beginning of the 18th century. The beauty of the décor will not seem surprising if we remember that sketches for the decoration of such luxury goods were usually ordered from the finest artists and designers of the era, such as Meissonier, Oppenord and others.

Borders of tapestry

The fragment of a border (at the top) is a cartouche with the name of the main subject of this cycle of tapestries called *The Story of Jason*, which was woven from sketches by Jean-François de Troyes. The border imitates a gilded wooden frame in the rococo style. The tapestry was woven on a vertical loom using wool and silk threads, and is signed by Gerard Audran and dated 1751 (Gobelins Manufactory).

Fragment 2 is the border of a tapestry called *The History of Emperor Constantine the Great* from a sketch attributed either to Giulio Clovio or Rubens, woven from wool and silk with the inclusion of gold and silver threads (Royal Manufactory circa 1610).

Motif 3 fills the border of an eighteen-part cycle of tapestries entitled *The Story of Esther* from a sketch by de Troyes; it was made of wool and silk at the Gobelins Manufactory by a weaver called Monmerque and is based on cartoons by Pierre-François Cozette (1738-1752).

Motif 4 adorns the border of a tapestry from a nine-part *History of Alexander the Great* from sketches by Charles Le Brun. The ornamentation of the borders is varied. It interweaves large acanthus leaves with a flower garland to frame such figurative subjects of the cycle as *Alexander and the Family of Darius*, battles and other scenes. The tapestry material was woven on a vertical loom and consists of silk, wool and gold and silver threads (Gobelins Manufactory).

Finally, the ornament on the fringe of the clothes (5) can be found in the second part of the cycle of tapestries *The Story of Artemisia*, from sketches by Antoine Caron. This tapestry was woven from wool and silk threads in the Paris Royal Manufactory.

Plate 198

Decorative painting

This two-colour painting, which was executed
in the first quarter of the 18th century, adorns
the *plafond* of the former bathroom in the
apartments at Versailles of Princess de Conti, the
daughter of Louis XIV and Louise de La Vallière,
and includes her monogram. This remarkable
work is a masterpiece of French decorative arts,
and the graceful ornamental motifs confirm that
it is from the hand of a master.

Tapestries and book decoration

The tapestry (7), which measures 3.75 x 2.50m, represents a type of carpet weaving that was widespread at the end of the 17th and beginning of the 18th centuries. At that time tapestries tended to form part of the furnishings and decoration of residences in winter, and were replaced by silk draperies in summer. In the magnificent royal palaces they served as portières. Woven portières with scenes from *The Seasons* hung on the four doors of the bedrooms in Louis XIV's apartments at Versailles. In this almost architectonic figurative composition, the artist's imagination, which had hitherto been constrained by the laws of symmetry, finally broke free. It was sufficient to master the architectural principles which at that time were familiar to every professional artist, but in his hands they become like a game. It is quite obvious that the artist and designer was guided by his personal taste when he created these purely conventional designs which include classical forms, cameos, the faces of medals and floral motifs.

The elegant structural features look like the carved wooden frame around an arras; this was a type that the French ornamentalist Jerain Berain the Elder was very fond of. However, in this tapestry, like all Berain designs, they are treated with a delicate grace that is reminiscent of the school of Claude Gillot, who taught Watteau.

Gillot's hand can be felt in the types of figures and in a freer treatment of decor that is not so typical of tapestries based on designs by Berain. This can be judged by the beautiful, stable group in the central field, contrasting with the rippling framing; at the same time, the boldly executed background places the work of this artist and decorator in a class above the work of Berain. Luxurious tapestries such as these were woven from wool and silk and incorporated gold and silver threads. The name of Gerard Audran appears among the names of the masters.

The large fragment (6) appears on a handwritten page, and is part of a border ornament which imitates a wood carving. This and other motifs derive from a French collection of *Antiphons*, five motifs of which are shown in plate 193.

The initial *O* (4) is traced out in gold against a blue monochrome landscape (monochrome landscapes were usually executed in a dark blue, reddish-purple or greenish tone, or in burnt sienna).

The centre of the small circular cartouche (8) is filled with a coat of arms with episcopal emblems.

Carpet in the style of Louis XIV

The pattern of this carpet was based on sketches
by Robert de Cotte. De Cotte, the pupil and
son-in-law of the famous architect Mansard,
was a well-known architect and designer
during the reign of Louis XIV. His main works
include completing the construction of the
chapel at Versailles, the Ionic colonnade at the
Trianon, the fountain in the place Palais-Royal
(demolished in 1848), the gallery of the Hôtel
de La Vrillière (now the building of the Bank
of France), as well as drawings of the place
Bellecour in Lyon, the Abbey of Saint-Denis and
the portal of the Church of Saint-Roch in Paris

Tapestries

Six designs can be found among the sketches
by Robert de Cotte. It is doubtful whether the
four motifs located at the bottom of the plate
are the work of de Cotte, the person who created
the ones at the top (he was also the creator of
the carpet in plate 201). With this reservation,
they can be attributed to the same school which
was characterised by architectonic composition
and the magnificent luxury of the décor.

Tapestries

Nothing could better exemplify the French artistic style than these beautiful tapestries. There is no doubt that Gillot, Watteau's teacher, created them, as he frequently turned his unique talent to producing sketches for the décor of tapestries.

The central subject (5) decorates the tapestry back of a chair, and would seem to form part of a series illustrating the fables of La Fontaine, namely *The Oak and the Reed*. In the other fragments the symbolic representations merge with masterfully conceived strange semi-realistic, semi-grotesque figures of enormous size that are consistent with contemporary ideas about barbarians, Asians, etc. They recall the magnificent heroic and comic theatrical performances at Versailles and Sceaux.

Motifs 1–3 form a single border. It is interesting to note the isolation of the lower border (1); this was characteristic of tapestry décor when a relief foreground covered with floral arras was used.

Ornamental pelmets in the upper border (4) give the same effect.

PLATE 203

Decorative painting

The repeated motifs shown in the plate constitute the external décor of an immense harp dating back to the first half of the 18th century. Currently this great instrument is located in the Cluny Museum in Paris. The paintings are executed on a gilded wooden surface. The spirit of elegant improbability inherent in the composition was a favorite decorative device of painters such as Gillot, Watteau and others.

The two pieces of décor (top) appear to flow into one another: the left-hand side of the upper fragment continues the right-hand side of the lower. Flanking each motif, the inverted elements together with various figures and flower garlands complete the frieze; a trellised arbour makes up the centre. A decorated part of the harp is at the bottom of the plate.

PLATE 204

Tapestries, bindings and panel edging

The two large motifs (top) belong to tapestries woven at the Beauvais Manufactory. The framing to stories based on the fables of La Fontaine combines ideally with the gilded wood carvings of couches whose seats and backs are covered in tapestry fabric. The central field, coloured in so-called 'royal red', is enclosed in a carved wooden frame which creates a link between the gilding and the figurative subject. The magnificent décor dates back to the beginning of 18th century. Antoine Michel Padeloup, a skilled bookbinder at the time of Louis XIV, created the ornamental motifs embossed in gold on a green background on a leather binding. The two corner motifs are based on sketches by the painter Pierre d'Ulin a member of the Royal Academy of Painting and Sculpture, and by Perrault. The moulded consoles belong to the same period. The heraldic royal lilies placed in a classical ornamentation of continuous volutes (centre) is particularly characteristic for the decorative system of the time.

Decorative panel
Tapestries: borders and corner sections

The pastoral composition *The Triumph of Pomona* (the sketch was by Boucher and the engraving by Charles-Nicolas Cochin) is a large-scale engraving, half a metre high, that has preserved its improvisatory nature. This is apparent from the dissimilar decorations in the upper corners, and is dictated by the need to leave more space for the curved ornamental element which seems to hang in the air above the figurative composition. Cochin, who was born in 1715, was the son of an engraver. Despite his professional training, he only produced this, the first and most mature of his works, in 1735 when Boucher was already at the zenith of his fame. (He had just turned twenty when he won the first prize at the French Academy in 1724).

It is possible that Boucher did this sketch long before 1735: the composition shows that to achieve his favourite decorative effects, the artist exclusively used motifs that he borrowed from other artists. Of course it could be said that such was Boucher's nature, but in the sketch shown here we cannot see even the slightest inclination to merge these motifs into a unified whole: he just includes them in the composition, without worrying about harmony.

Boucher was working on this sketch during the period when the Louis XVI style was being established, and while still a novice ornamentalist he became one of its most brilliant exponents. The borders of 18th-century tapestries mainly imitated carved gilt frames. In essence, the motifs that filled the corner sections of borders made it possible to get rid of straight lines, and their asymmetrical curves have the appearance of breaking through into the central field.

Another type of frame (5), with a scalloped inner edge, allows the ornamental motif to merge with the composition of the central part. This scheme is particularly suited to vertical tapestries (for example portières over doors).

Motif 2 confirms this effect; it is both lavish and elegant at the same time.

PLATE 206

Tapestry and corner ornamentation
of borders

One of the four parts of the cycle *The Fables of
La Fontaine* woven at the Gobelins Manufactory
and based on cartoons by François Boucher
(figures) and Charles Tessier (décor). The
composition dates from 1757 and each section
is 4.25m high.

All four tapestries imitate large-scale moulded
panels in the rococo style. The central medallion
with the picturesque subject of *Aurora and
Cephalus* in an oval frame of carved gilded wood
is suspended by ribbons against a background of
pink silk upholstery fabric with a floral pattern.
This pink silk is in turn placed in an elegant
woven frame against the backdrop of yet another
border of dark red patterned silk. Finally, all
this splendour is enclosed in a richly ornamented
rectangular frame, but this time a genuine
one made of carved wood with gilding. Under
the central medallion, a Sèvres vase on a stand
emerges from the décor of the outer border.
Garlands of flowers woven in relief with birds

fluttering or sitting on branches and two
amusing animal figures (a monkey with a
shotgun and a porcupine stealing up to a bird)
give the décor brilliance and vividness and cast
a shadow over the pink silk background; when
combined with the genuine oval frame in the
central field they successfully create the effect
of an illusion.

The two corner motifs from borders (bottom)
belong to tapestries woven in Beauvais. The
border, which imitates a gilded wooden frame
with carved oak leaves, includes grotesque
ornaments in the spirit of Berain, and this makes
it possible to date this tapestry to the beginning
of the 18th century.

The second border with the heraldic lily in
the corner cartouche dates from the reign of
Louis XV.

Decorative panels, gilt wood carving, relief decorations and 'trophies'

The motifs shown here come from the décor of the so-called Small Apartments of Louis XV at Versailles. According to legend, the king was tired of the immense ceremonial suites of his great-grandfather and ordered changes to be made to the layout of the palace so as to create a 'comfortable bourgeois residence' for himself where he could shake off the burden of courtly etiquette. A completely new style of architectural and decorative furnishing came to replace the old style that was associated with the names of Mansard, Lepautre, Marot and Berain. The new type of decor used mostly wood painted white and with gilding, and this combination gave a very impressive decorative effect. The new technique corresponded to the new forms that were now introduced in the ceremonial royal apartments, and these were decorated with unrestrained splendor.

The salon of Adélaïde, Louis' daughter, can serve as an excellent example, and it is from there that some of the motifs shown here originate (1–4, 6); this is the most luxuriant of the Small Apartments and it wallows in moulded decoration and carved wood thickly covered with gold (circa 1750).

The period that we are describing left behind a rich legacy of prints and engravings, and the motifs shown here provide examples of the 'trophies' of this series. Each 'trophy' is sharply individualistic: there are musical instruments (1, 3) fishing tackle (2), garden tools and moulding on the base of a pilaster from the same room (6).

Another fragment of decoration on the base of a pilaster (7) is from the Clock Room, a very beautiful salon in the Small Apartments; it was decorated in 1748.

Two 'trophies' (5, 8) decorate panels that are flanked by bookcases. Unlike the the others, they herald the emergence of the Louis XVI style, with its hitherto unprecedented splendour. The *trompe l'oeil* painting imitates gilded wood carving. One of the 'trophies' is dedicated to music, lyric poetry and dance (5), and the other is linked to the art of oratory, comedy, the burlesque, and satiric and epic poetry.

Durin. lith.

Imp. Firmin Didot & Cie. Paris

Cartouches

With this plate we are concluding the series on the history of the cartouche, a decorative element about which we have already spoken.

1 Cartouche in a prayer book from the Church of Saint-Gervais in Paris, with three monochrome medallions in a pale blue colour;

2, 3 Motifs with monochrome medallions by Bernard Picard. The first three cartouches, like 12 and 13, are in the artistic style of the late 17th century;

4-7 Cartouches of the 18th century in an ambiguous style that is characterised by the sinusoids and flourishes which for some time almost eliminated straight lines in ornamentation;

8 Faience stand with underglaze painting;

9 Bookplate in the rococo style, made in 1752 by the miniaturist Elias Nilsson, the head of the Augsburg Academy;

10, 11 Cartouche with emblems based on sketches by de la Joue; the four *mascarons* are based on sketches by Abraham Bosse. 17th century;

2, 3, 8 Medallions with gold inlay. 1720s–1730s.

Jewellery

Some of these chatelaines (chains worn on
a belt to keep keys, charms, etc, or decorations
made of two brooches connected by a chain)
in the form of scrolls were made by the master
goldsmith Pierre-Edmé Babel in the style that
was dominant between 1719 and 1746 and
which came into vogue thanks to Oppenord
and Meissonnier. The remaining chatelaines
are later in origin. At that time, art jewellery
and its techniques, especially inlaying, reached
an extremely high level. The French school of
decorative arts, which had fully mastered the
freedom of form that typified the new Italianate
style, managed to adopt it with astonishing
subtlety, charm and intelligence.

1-8, 10, 11 Chatelaines made by Gilles Légaré
in the style of Berain and Marot
(17th century) enjoyed tremendous
success at the end of the 17th and
beginning of the 18th centuries;

9 Seal by Gilles Légaré;

12-19 These ornaments make up an almost
complete set of women's jewellery in
the Louis XIV style: a chatelaine with
a watch and signet, clasps, pins and
aigrettes of various sizes for clothing and
hairstyles. Each of the other large chains
forms part of a set of men's or women's
jewellery that consisted of similar items.

PLATE 210

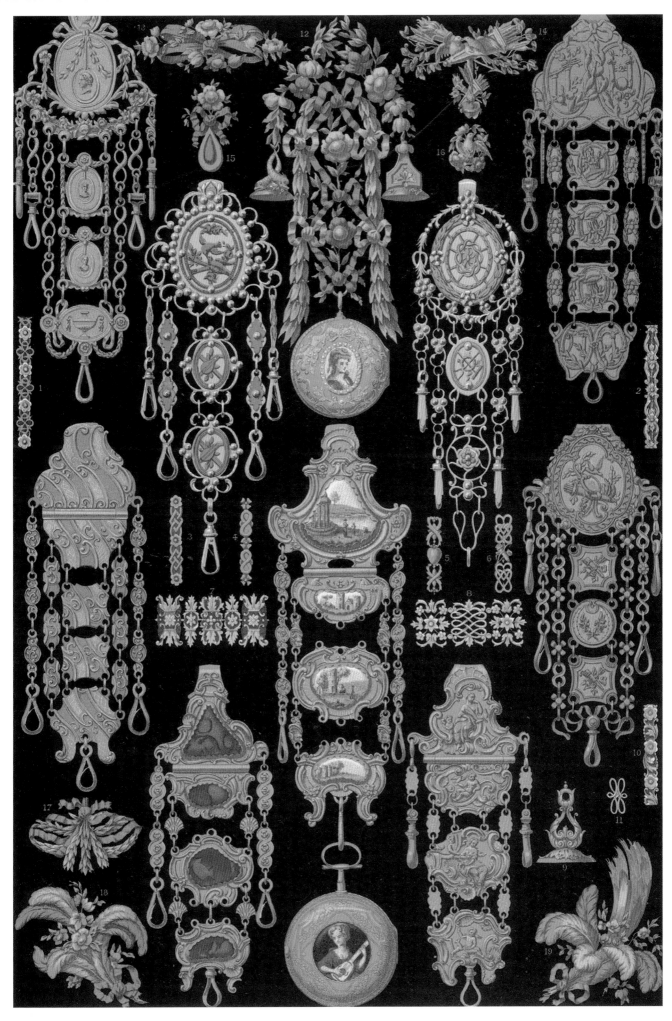

Panels, furniture upholstery, drapery and
clothing
Woven from originals

Authentic silk fabrics were made in French
manufactories which received the full support
of Colbert during the reign of Louis XVI.
The twelve fragments shown here are divided
into four groups as follows:

  1–6 Upholstery and portières; skirts from
        court dress;

  7–9 The same (two-coloured fabrics; Louis
        XVI style);

10,11 Lightweight silk (Louis XVI style);

  12   Border of a dress (Louis XVI style).

Motifs 1–4 show the influence of Persian
ornamentation. Particular attention should be
paid to the system of ornamentation in motifs
3 and 4, where the shimmering background
transmits to the simplest patterns a luxury
and freedom which would otherwise have been
impossible. Finally, in regard to the technical
side of production, motifs 2–4 and 10 and 11
adorn silk fabrics by incorporating gold and
silver threads, thus giving the fabrics a localised
colouring.

Plate 211

Decorative tapestries, relief weaving and
ornamental meanders

The larger motif is presented in full (top) and
the other as a fragment (bottom centre). We
will turn to the first to explore the decorative
principles of the time. Its bright, natural and
purely decorative appearance is very different
from previous types of ornamental tapestry,
including those made in the first half of
the 18th century. During the 18th century
ornamental motifs underwent changes that
began with the proliferation of elegant and
magnificent carved and shaped woodworking,
a typical feature of the interior decoration
of the time. Painters and decorators finally
understood that tapestry that is inserted into a
genuine wooden frame with relief carving which
also has a border that imitates an identical frame
was just too much! The illusionistic border
frame becomes unnecessary and gradually
disappears, thus opening up wide vistas for the
artist and decorator. From being an integral
component of interiors, tapestry becomes a
decoration, and nothing else. The main motif
of the upper tapestry is the 'noble pastoral'.
Its subject is an undying 18th-century allegory

which gives meaning to the image. In the left-
hand medallion we see a bare, bleak landscape:
the land is barren because it is not being tilled.
In the right-hand medallion there is a lush
garden with flowers, thus asserting the benefits
of civilisation.

Mannered and unpretentious, but thanks to
this fact appealingly attractive, tapestries
are among the best works of the Beauvais
Manufactory. Their material is wool and silk
(wool yarns for the shadows and half-tones,
and silk for the light and bright parts of the
composition). The Beauvais weavers liked this
kind of décor so much that in 1783 they clashed
with the management of the manufactory when
they were given instructions to switch to other
subjects that, in their opinion, were not as
sublime (and perhaps they were right!). We can
trace the trend in mastering the classical heritage
from the continuous bas-relief motifs that
imitated carved friezes in the Louis XVI style.

Embossing, enamel and painting

1 Fan. 1750s–1760s. This fan is particularly remarkable for the delicacy of its work. Almost transparent pieces of ivory and mother-of-pearl are superimposed on one another so that when open the decoration of the fan is revealed in all its richness and elegance. The composition is made in the elegant style of the engraver Babel, and there is reason to believe that if the fan was not made by him, it was certainly from his studio;

2-4 Snuff box (outside of lid, bottom, sides). 1769. Made of beaten gold, with a red enamel background, the snuff box was made by Auguste Laterre, a famous jeweller of the time;

5-7 Snuff box (outside of lid, bottom, side). 1780. It is believed that the embossed decoration is the work of Mathis de Beaulieu, a goldsmith at the court of Louis XVI; embossed ornaments frame a charming pictorial miniature, a portrait of Marshal Turenne painted by Jean Petitot;

8-10 Snuff boxes. 1780s-1790s. Gold snuffbox with monochrome figurative ornaments in painted enamel;

11-14 Ornamental borders based on sketches by Jean-François de Neufforge.

Tapestries

1–8 Motifs dating to the first half of the
18th century, ie, the time of Mariette's
publication.

9 Motifs of the same period. Woven from
motifs by Bernard Picard;

10 Part of a panel from the second half of
the 18th century;

11, 12 Continuous ornament on a woven
edging from the end of the 18th century.

One cannot help but note the contrast between
the pretentious ornamentation of the rococo
style and the simplicity and elegant décor
that prevailed in French art from the 1760s; it
resulted from the excavations in Herculaneum
and Pompeii which marked the development
of the classical style (the style of Louis XVI).

PLATE 214

Painting on porcelain

After a series of setbacks, in 1769 the chemist
Macquer from Sèvres reported the invention
of hard porcelain to the French Academy and
demonstrated his excellent designs. In 1800
Brongniart, the then director of the Sèvres
porcelain factory, changed the factory over
exclusively to the production of hard porcelain.
This technology makes transparent painting
possible and this resulted in huge production
volumes. However, although hard porcelain
was much more practical, people still preferred
products made of soft paste porcelain.

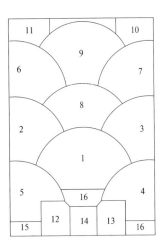

1   Dish from the service of *The Birds
    of Buffon* which the famous French
    naturalist called his 'Sèvres edition'.
    The service consisted of at least a
    hundred items, painted with images
    of birds mentioned in Buffon's work.

2–5   Plates.
      The plate numbered 5 bears the
      monogram of Madame du Barry;

6–9   Plates from various porcelain services;

10, 11   Inner corners of pastry dishes;

12, 13   Undersides of plates;

14–16   Open-work sides of pastry dishes.

Decorative motifs: 'trophies' and bunches
of lowers

The three motifs on a gold background (bottom)
are pastoral 'trophies', painted in oils and
varnished in the fashion of the first half of the
18th century. A contemporary author wrote:
'By emulating Chinese and Japanese lacquers,
the famous royal varnisher Martin caused a real
sensation with his vases and snuff boxes made of
papier-mâché which were hugely successful from
1745. However, since the varnishing technique
proved not to be very difficult, for the next
six years Paris was inundated by varnishers who,
wishing to beat the competition, were selling
their snuff boxes literally for pennies. Only
Martin and his brothers were able to preserve
the integrity of the true art by resurrecting the
technique of the ancient art of Oriental lacquer-
work, and their talent far exceeded the ability to
varnish carriages or create "pearly" snuffboxes'

(Watin, *L'art du peintre doreur et vernisseur*.
Paris, 1776). Martin's lacquer-works have
become a rarity and are highly prized to this day.

One of the motifs shown (bottom centre) bears
the monogram of Queen Marie-Antoinette.
The four grisaille motifs on wall panels form the
composition *The Seasons*, which is painted in a
free pictorial manner by the confident hand of a
master. The vase with the bouquet of flowers that
emerges from symmetrically arranged acanthus
leaves is signed 'Carlle' and is executed in a
modified ornamental style that is typical of the
period when the neoclassical style that emerged
following the excavations of Herculaneum and
Pompeii was developingi.

Painting under glass
Louis XVI period

In front of us are two panels from a cabinet for valuables that was given to Marie-Antoinette by the citizens of Paris in 1787. This masterpiece by French furniture makers is made of mahogany and mounted on an eight-legged stand. The cabinet is divided into three sections and the four flanking caryatids symbolise the seasons. The right and left sections as well as the sides are decorated with glass medallions with figurative compositions in gilded mother-of-pearl frames with a row of small pearls along the edge. The panel with the circular central medallion is the side panel and the other is the front. The pictorial images in the medallions are applied simply using oil paint on paper that is pressed down by the glass (this can be seen in one inset with broken glass: the cabinet was in the Tuileries and was slightly damaged during the Revolution of 1830). By firmly adhering to the glass, the carved frame of the medallion creates the illusion that the painting is directly on the transparent surface. As a result, this work has gained such a restrained opulence that no painting on glass can bear comparison with it.

The style of painting reflects the main artistic trend of the time, a classical renaissance brought about by the influence of the excavations in Pompeii. The laws of symmetry are observed with unsurpassed elegance. There is a clear rhythmic link between the male and female figures growing out of the acanthus leaves and balancing against a yellow background and the overall ornamental structure of the painting.

Decorative painting

This remarkable painting is from the brush of
Gerard van Spaendonck, a famous Dutch painter
who had settled in France. He owes his fame
to his decorative compositions that include a
realistically treated flowering tree; his palette
is delicate, bright and transparent, and full of
freshness and harmony. This panel illustrates
these qualities perfectly.

Continuous plant motifs, wallpaper and fabrics

For all the variety of fabrics and wallpapers, their image is always located in the central field or against the main background. Without going into details about the quality of design or execution, we can state that the more perfect the principle of chromatic relations, the more spectacular are the results it produces. It can be said that harmony is the result of diversity in unity. According to the law of contrast, colour achieves its maximum intensity when it is next to its complementary colour. The law of complementary colours allows us to mute or enhance any colour without turning it into a murky one; it is possible to reinforce a colour, without actually touching it, by changing the adjacent colours. These additional colours constitute an intermediary between the main ones, and they moderate the effect of each individual colour for the benefit of the whole. We have before us five examples of variations in the colour range in which the law of quantitative relations between their shape and their colour has been carefully studied. The plate includes designs of authentic fabrics which show the hand and experience of a true master. A similar process can be applied to the production of patterned wallpaper and in general to any large-scale decoration. This process is achieved by imposing local colours, which are then 'achromatised' with additional colours which, if required, provide it with the illusion of a visual mixture, according to the skill applied. The original painting does not require any mixing of paint on the palette. 'Achromatisation' requires the reciprocal interpenetration of all the colours and shades in their pure form.

Ornamentation of printed fabrics
Integral field with flower motifs

Continuation of the previous plate.

These motifs on French muslin, which are reproduced from the original, confirm these to be the creations of truly talented fabric printers. They should be considered in the context of a specific manufactory for which they were created. French muslin is a fabric that does not require special treatment for it to achieve flowing tones. Its soft matt surface absorbs some of the colour values, and the sharpest contrasts are not without a certain harmony which gradually softens their sharpness. The pattern may, however, display values of a maximum intensity which, as fabric artists know, subsequently lose their sharpness. The text to plate 219 mentioned the rule of chromatic relations, according to which the dominant hue binds together the various colours used in such a décor. One need only add that the 19th century was more familiar with the flora of our gardens and fields than preceding centuries, and we can but admire the simple and elegant compositions of anemones, daisies, bindweed, sweet peas and roses in all their diversity. Never have such motifs been employed so openly and with such an unprecedented effect as in the 19th century.